Tourism, Hospitality & Event Management

More information about this series at http://www.springer.com/series/15444

Andrés Artal-Tur · Metin Kozak ·
Nazmi Kozak

Editors

Trends in Tourist Behavior

New Products and Experiences from Europe

 Springer

Editors
Andrés Artal-Tur
Department of Economics
Technical University of Cartagena
Cartagena, Spain

Metin Kozak
School of Tourism
Dokuz Eylül University
İzmir, Turkey

Nazmi Kozak
Faculty of Tourism
Anadolu University
Eskişehir, Turkey

ISSN 2510-4993   ISSN 2510-5000   (electronic)
Tourism, Hospitality & Event Management
ISBN 978-3-030-11159-5   ISBN 978-3-030-11160-1   (eBook)
https://doi.org/10.1007/978-3-030-11160-1

Library of Congress Control Number: 2018966844

This Springer imprint is published by the registered company Springer Nature Switzerland AG
The registered company address is: Gewerbestrasse 11, 6330 Cham, Switzerland

Preface[1]

Compiling and editing a volume like this is always a teamwork. In this case, the present volume on *Trends in Tourist Behavior: New Products and Experiences from Europe* starts in June 2017, with the *9th Conference for Graduate Research in Tourism, Hospitality and Leisure*, together with the *5th Interdisciplinary Tourism Research Conference* taking place in Cartagena, Spain, at Business Faculty of the Universidad Politécnica de Cartagena (UPCT). Those two conferences moved for the first time out of Turkey, where Profs. Nazmi and Metin Kozak, chairs of the events, where inviting a number of colleagues and experts in tourism and hospitality along the last decade. The presence of more than 150 experts and academic researchers for the 5 days of the conference allowed to gather very interesting papers and contributions, whose findings should be disseminated across the industry and academia. One of these dissemination efforts is the present book by Springer. We want to acknowledge the Springer Publisher Company here to be always ready to cooperate with us on improving and spreading the knowledge on tourism and economics that we have been generating.

The present volume gathers and compiles 14 chapters focusing on the analysis of tourist behaviour and experiential tourism. The volume also allows to present different cases of study along the European space. The book presents two main blocks or parts. The first part is devoted to the analysis of "New Tourism Products and Consumer Behaviour". Tourism has become a global industry with more than 1.3 billion international travellers worldwide in 2018. New destinations emerging all around the world seek to participate in the benefits of this highly growing industry. New products are also developed in order to attract and satisfy new visitors and international travellers. According to the characteristics of these new products, new behaviours also arise at destinations. In this first part, authors analyse such new personal behaviours linked to new products. It is important to understand

---

[1]Prof. Andrés Artal-Tur acknowledges financial support by Groups of Excellence of the Region of Murcia, Fundación Séneca, Science and Technology Agency, project 19884/GERM/15, and FEMISE Association (Project ENPI/2014/354-494) Research Projects FEM 41-04 and FEM 41-13.

and explain consumer behaviour in these new segments appearing at destinations. A better understanding of the new personal behaviours would result without a doubt in a higher capacity of destination managers to successfully anticipate and planning the near future. Sports' events, surf, wine and equestrian tourism, city trip activities or the youth tourism market are some of the fields of study in this first part of the book.

The second part mainly focuses on analysing the role of experiential tourism in today's tourism market. New tourists looking for experiential trips where mixing with the local residents, learning about the environment or discovering new experiences at traditional destinations are becoming significant in the first decades of the twenty-first century. Accordingly, the second part of the book deals with relevant questions of the tourism research, such as the factors that lead tourists to revisit and engage with destinations, how the outstanding vacation experiences could lead to promotional campaigns by the consumers themselves through social networks, for example, or the importance of the tourism experience in conforming the motivations of consumers regarding the trip.

In sum, the present volume on *Trends in Tourist Behavior: New Products and Experiences from Europe* compiles a selected number of chapters aiming to provide a basis for the interested reader on how the tourist behaviour is shaped by the new tourist products and segments appearing in the market, and learning how the tourist experience could influence the post-trip evaluation of the destination and tourism activities. The rigorous analysis in the book leads to very practical recommendations for Destination Management Organizations (DMOs) on how to improve the performance of destinations and particular businesses. Moreover, the volume is written by outstanding researchers in the tourism academy and industry, providing relevant material for graduate students and professionals in terms of methodology of research and dissemination of research findings.

Finally, we don't want to finish this introductory section without thanking all people that have made this book possible, with special regard to *Maria Cristina Acocella*, Associate Editor for Business & Economics from Springer, who has guided us all along the editing process of the volume.

Cartagena, Spain   Andrés Artal-Tur
İzmir, Turkey   Metin Kozak
Eskişehir, Turkey   Nazmi Kozak

Contents

Part I
New Tourism Products and Consumer Behaviour

Chapter 1
A Diagnose of Equestrian Tourism: The Case of France and Romania

Sorina Cernaianu and Claude Sobry

1.1 Introduction

The equestrian tourism is a fast growing sector considered as a form of active recreation, of adventure tourism, ecotourism or nature-based tourism.

Equestrian activities are diversified, as horseback riding, hiking with a donkey, travelling the countryside with a caravan in the step of a horse discovering the fauna and flora, several days or just a few hours, but also site visits, sports events, museums, shows, etc. Besides the staff specialized in the breeding and the horses it is also necessary to feed them and to look after them, to maintain the material, to plan the home sites of the tourists and their frame, to maintain ways, etc., which represents a means to develop some economic elements.

The aim of this research is to analyze the equestrian tourism in France and Romania, highlighting the potential of each country, in order to see how the experience of a country could be used by another one, how this kind of tourism contributes to sustainable development and how could be an ecotourism alternative.

S. Cernaianu (✉)
University of Craiova, Craiova, Romania
e-mail: s_cernaianu@yahoo.com

C. Sobry
University of Lille, Lille, France
e-mail: claude.sobry@univ-lille.fr

S. Cernaianu · C. Sobry
URePSSS (EA 7369), IRNIST, Lille, France

© Springer Nature Switzerland AG 2019
A. Artal-Tur et al. (eds.), *Trends in Tourist Behavior*,
Tourism, Hospitality & Event Management,
https://doi.org/10.1007/978-3-030-11160-1_1

1.2 Literature Review

Equestrian tourism has begun to develop in Europe, North America and Australia since 1950s–1960s (Konyves & Suta, 2009; Delambre, 2011; Cochrane & Daspher, 2014; cited by Pickel-Chevalier, 2015).

According to Delambre (2011), the first definition of equestrian tourism consists of a tourism activity for pleasure, on the back of a horse of over 24 h.

Equestrian tourism is defined as "all equestrian activities undertaken by tourists outside their normal place of residence, i.e. training courses, improvement courses and other aspects or diverse types of vacation principally revolving around the horse" (International Federation of Equestrian Tourism, 2012). Le Borgne and Kouchner (2002) added a temporal dimension to this definition: "all forms of leisure related to equines (horse, pony, donkey) practiced by a person travelling outside his/her usual residence for a period of at least 24 h and not more than 4 months".

According to Atout France (2011) the equestrian tourism offer consists of:

- *activities with the horse*, divided into: activities on horseback (sports stays, discovery stays, multi activity stays, leisure and travel) and not on horseback (harness, trailer, hiking donkey);
- *activities related to the horse*, placing the horse as a main center of interest (site visits, exhibitions, sport events, museums) or as a secondary one (shows, traditional festivals).

Leaning on the typology of the activities defining the sports tourism, including, among others, a travel to practice sport or to attend a sports event (Gibson, 1998; Pigeassou, 2002), the definition of the equestrian tourism includes all the aspects of travels with and/or for horses, as well a trail as travelling to attend an equestrian event. In parallel with the opportunity sport tourism, the equestrian activities during holidays are undertaken in the definition. This way, the market is wider and wider but it is not surprise. During the last twenty years the outdoor activities are the fastest growing segment of sport tourism. Equestrian tourism follows this trend.

The International Federation of Equestrian Tourism (FITE—Fédération Internationale du Tourisme Équestre), created in 1975 at the initiative of French National Committee of Equestrian Tourism (CNTE—Comité Nationale du Tourisme Équestre) and greatly influenced by the French federation through economic support (Delambre, 2011) "groups together the organizations who are in charge in their national territory of the organization of equestrian tourism, and horse riding as leisure activity in all its forms…" (FITE, 2016). Currently, FITE counts 21 national equestrian tourism organizations, Romania being part of it.

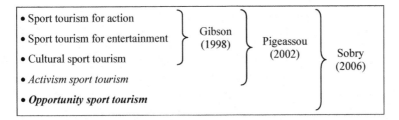

Fig. 1.1 Sport tourism typology

1.2.1   From Equestrian Tourism to Sustainable Sport Tourism

When speaking about sport tourism and sustainable sport tourism, the most difficult is to define the terms and concepts to obtain the widest possible consensus (Sobry, Liu, & Li, 2016).

Concerning sport tourism and since Weed and Bull (2004) show it is a field of research in itself the definitions flourished. Starting from the definitions of the pioneers, we keep the definitions of Pigeassou (2002) and Gibson (1998) but rejecting the Pigeassou's idea according to which it is the motivation which determine if a travel is sport tourism or not. We add to the four elements of his typology, three being common with Gibson's, the *opportunity sport tourism* (Fig. 1.1), what Leiper (1990) calls *tertiary attraction*, and Gammon and Robinson (2003) *tourism sport*: "The holiday or visit, rather than the sport, is the prime travel motivation". Many small and very small-scale companies subsist on this kind of practice of opportunity, as the activity they offer comes in addition to a site that is the main tourist attraction (Bouchet & Bouhaouala, 2009; Bouhaouala & Sobry, 2017).

Equestrian tourism enters perfectly in this definition. Examples can be found at every level and, as said earlier, the opportunity equestrian sport tourism is well developed with the holiday cards and all the riders out of any structure.

Can this specific form of sport tourism participate in the sustainable local development of a territory? How to confine the notion of sustainable tourism and how does it apply to sport tourism?

We hold the notion of sustainability such as expressed by the Brundtland[1] report: a development that meets the needs of the present without compromising the ability of future generations to meet their own needs' (WCED, 1987, p. 43). The three pillars of sustainable development are a combined and, if possible, simultaneous development of the components: economy, social and environmental.

The World Tourism Organization (UNWTO) defines the sustainable tourism as *"Tourism that takes full account of its current and future economic, social and environmental impacts, addressing the needs of visitors, the industry, the environment*

---

[1] In 1987 a report entitled «Our Common Future» was written by United Nations, World Commission on Environment and Development (WCED), chaired by Norwegian Prime Minister Gro Harlem Brundtland.

and host communities". In other words, the three keys for sustainable tourism are: "meeting the needs of the host population in terms of improved living standards both in the short and long term; satisfying the demands of a growing number of tourists; and safeguarding the natural environment in order to achieve both of the preceding aims" (Cater, 1993; cited by Liu, 2003, p. 460).

On its side, the United Nations Organization works on the notion of sustainable development thanks to sport, resting on the International Labour Office. The object of this work is to set up the conditions to attract international tourists by valuing the local natural and human resources and to develop the material and human conditions of welcome at the local level to create a synergy appropriate to an economic development which is in line with the sustainable development concept.

According to these approaches, the *bucket*[2] *theory*[3] explains metaphorically that, in the complex systems, when we consider the vital subsets of the system (as the vital organs of a body), they are any important. It is of no use to have an excellent level on one of the pillars or the element of sustainability (the economy for instance) if another element (social or environment) is degraded, because the quality or performance level of the set is controlled by the lowest board of the bucket.

In the case of sport tourism, it is of no use to be very successful in one (the economic) or two domains if the third one is totally neglected. In both cases the system will dysfunction, maybe not in short-term but in medium or long-term.

Leaning on a work of Atout France (2011), Pickel-Chevalier (2015) wonders if equestrian tourism can be a tool for local sustainable development. She focuses on three case studies where the tourism development of local protected areas (Natural Regional Parks) is associated, through deep historical or/and geographical links, with horses and equestrian tourism:

• the Natural Regional Park of the Camargue (Camargue horse)—south of France;
• the Natural Park of the Marquenterre (Henson horse)—north of France;
• the Natural Regional Park of the Cevennes (Przewalski horse)—center of France.

If the three cases generally meet the sustainable criteria (local economic development by increasing the number of tourists; social cohesion by involving the host population; intercultural meetings by bringing a positive experience for local people and tourists; environmental awareness and environmental protection policy), they cannot meet all of them at the same level.

Then she studies the practices and motivations of the equestrian tourists. The results of her cross analyze of different surveys are clear: their common centers of interest concentrate on comfort, safety and conviviality. "They are not insensitive to the quality of the landscape or the presence of tourism, cultural or natural sites, but these attractions only come after the more practical criteria which ensure the comfort and safety of the excursion". She adds "Regard for economic and social issues (local development, social cohesion) does not seem to characterize the riders'

---

[2]Here, it is a bucket made of wooden small boards, as in the past.
[3]Lamiot, http://wikipedia.org/wiki/developpement_durable.

collective consciousness. They are looking more for friendly relationships with other enthusiasts".

She concludes, this characteristic leads to the fact that whereas equestrian tourism can be an agent for sustainable development, lack of interest or misinformation often lead to conflicts of interests, especially in protected areas such as public forests. The French Equestrian Federation (FFE) tries to raise riders' awareness through riding schools. In 2010 the FFE got together with the Ministry of Ecology, Energy, Sustainable Development and the Sea and encouraged clubs to organize events during Sustainable Development Week, in particular for children. However, only 40 clubs took part out of more than 8000 riding schools throughout France. Professionals have not yet understood the advantages for them and their club members of such associations and do not automatically register their activities within the tenets of sustainable development.

1.3 Methodology

In the first phase of the research we explore the potential of each country concerning the development of equestrian tourism, starting with infrastructure (accommodation, tracks and trails, lodges and stopovers) and continue with equestrian tourism products. In the second phase we analyzed if equestrian tourism complies with ecotourism and sustainable development.

For the purposes of this study we collected secondary data provided from different sources like: websites of different associations, federations and national bodies, books, articles, laws, national strategies, reports etc. We tried to highlight more clearly the equestrian activities in the two countries and the transfer of good examples to Romania.

1.4 The Development of Equestrian Tourism in France

The world's first tourist destination with 82.6 million international visitors in 2016 (UNWTO), France is also the first destination of equestrian tourism.

Equestrian tourism started and grown in France during the 1950s–1960s, in the same time than in other countries in Europe, North America, and Australia (Equipe MIT & Knafou, 2005). It followed the expansion of other leisure activities (Sobry, 2003).

Created in 1921 (under the name of French Federation of Equestrian Sports), the French Equestrian Federation is the 3rd French Olympic Federation in number of license-holder (after football and tennis) and the first one in number of women. Under its umbrella is National Committee for Equestrian Tourism, the Regional Committee for Equestrian Tourism (CRTE—for each French region) and depart-

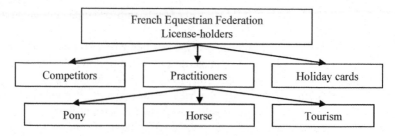

Fig. 1.2 The categories of license-holders in France

mental committees. They have to maintain the marked trails and organize events, training and competitions.

In 1963 was created the National Association for Equestrian Tourism (Association Nationale pour le Tourisme Équestre). It became the National Confederation for Equestrian Tourism (Délégation Nationale au Tourisme Équestre) in 1987 then the National Committee for Equestrian Tourism in 2000.

France has 60,000 km of equestrian trails, of which 20,000 are marked (Delambre, 2011).

In France, the FFE license-holders are divided into three categories: competitors, practitioners, and holiday cards. Occasional riders can choose a holiday card, valid only for one month and includes the same insurance as the other licenses. This card could be purchased from a club, an association or owners of a stable affiliated to the FFE.

License-holders are segmented in three kinds of practitioners: horse, pony and tourism (Fig. 1.2).

With 813,452 license-holders in 2017, 59.11% more than in 2001 (FFE, 2018b), the FFE is the 3rd of the French Olympic Federations in number of license-holder (after football and tennis) and the first one in number of women (82.93%).

Concerning the holiday cards, 6853 tourists purchased in 2017, of which 74.97% were women. An important increase was recorded from 2001 to 2008, from 5501 to 7762 license-holders (41.1%). We observe that the number of these license-holders actually began to slightly decrease since 2013 (Table 1.1).

The share of holiday cards licenses in the total number of license-holders during the last 17 years was registered a maximum in 2007 (1.12%), with 1.48% for the males and 1.02% for the females (Fig. 1.3).

The share of tourism licenses in the total number of license-holders had a maximum in 2006 (10.56%), with the majority being males. The maximum was reached by males in 2012 (13.96%), while females registered the best share in 2006 (9.59%) (Fig. 1.4).

In 2011 the French riding tradition was listed by UNESCO as an example of the Intangible Cultural Heritage of Humanity. It is probably why, according to several inquiries 24% of the French people that have never ridden declare they would like

Table 1.1 Evolution of the FFE holiday cards and tourism license-holders in France (data processed from FFE, 2018b)

Year	HC Female	HC %	HC Male	HC %	HC Total	T Female	T %	T Male	T %	T Total
2001	3768	68.50	1733	31.50	5501	29,385	64.44	16,216	35.56	45,601
2002	3633	66.71	1813	33.29	5446	32,635	65.67	17,063	34.33	49,698
2003	3834	68.01	1803	31.99	5637	36,249	66.65	18,138	33.35	54,387
2004	4058	68.77	1843	31.23	5901	40,751	67.66	19,481	32.34	60,232
2005	4005	70.14	1705	29.86	5710	44,896	68.97	20,199	31.03	65,095
2006	4740	68.97	2133	31.03	6873	47,091	69.93	20,247	30.07	67,338
2007	5384	71.01	2198	28.99	7582	50,612	71.02	20,653	28.98	71,265
2008	5658	72.89	2104	27.11	**7762**	54,546	71.98	21,238	28.02	75,784
2009	5478	73.07	2019	26.93	7497	58,762	73.31	21,390	26.69	80,152
2010	5218	73.57	1875	26.43	7093	63,127	74.17	21,984	25.83	85,111
2011	5209	75.17	1721	24.83	6930	65,882	75.18	21,745	24.82	87,627
2012	5355	75.21	1765	24.79	7120	67,005	75.59	21,637	24.41	88,642
2013	5588	74.90	1873	25.10	7461	66,606	76.04	20,984	23.96	87,590
2014	5393	74.38	1858	25.62	7251	66,829	76.46	20,580	23.54	87,409
2015	5526	74.92	1850	25.08	7376	64,657	76.76	19,573	23.24	84,230
2016	5575	75.00	1858	25.00	7433	63,781	77.13	18,913	22.87	82,694
2017	5138	74.97	1715	25.03	6853	60,374	77.06	17,970	22.94	78,344

HC Holiday cards licenses; *T* Tourism licenses

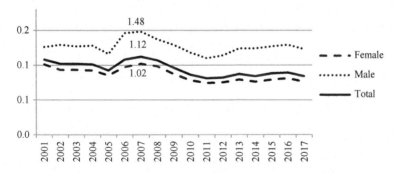

Fig. 1.3 Share of holiday cards licenses in the total number of license-holders

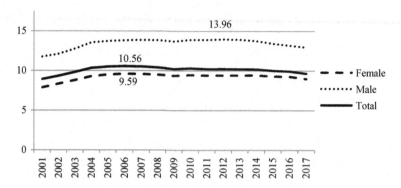

Fig. 1.4 Share of tourism license holders in total number of license-holders

to do it (Sociovision Cofremca, 2006) and that 53% would like equestrian holidays (FFE, 2011).

It is noticeable that the profile of outdoor riders is different from the riders in clubs. Female riders are the majority too but with only 70% (vs. 82.93%). The average age is 36 years, when the average age for horse riders in general is 62% under 17, mostly because of pony riding and the change of sport activities after 15. This client base comes from the middle and upper classes, with a generally modest level of horsemanship (Pickel-Chevalier, 2016).

The increase of riders' number induces a change in the demand of the riders (Tourre-Malen, 2009; Grefe & Pickel-Chevalier, 2015; Pickel-Chevalier & Grefe, 2015), expectations (Pickel-Chevalier, 2016) and expected services (Sigurðardóttir, 2015; Sigurðardóttir & Helgadóttir, 2015; Eslan, 2018). The FFE being mostly turned toward competition seems to meet problems to answer to these new ways of looking at the horses and riding. This induces an increasing self-organization of the equestrian activity. A study shows that more and more of equine owners having between 33 and 90% of the equines are not linked with the federation (Vial, Aubert, & Perrier-Cornet, 2011).

Among the touristic activities we can observe a decrease of the several days tours but an increase of one or two hours ballades, especially when there are thematic ballades for instance with a chief cook who propose gastronomic meals or these looking back on ancestral practices as on the transhumance. Or even just to discover the territory on a horse back listening to the guide comments.

If the equestrian tourism began to grow in France during the '50s–60s, it really launched during the '70s with the development of pony clubs (Tourre-Malen, 2009) which were officially recognized only in 1971. Less expensive and less impressive, pony riding made riding more accessible to more socially diverse population groups.

Very few equestrian structures in France are specialized in stabling and/or equestrian tourism, only 20% of the 8,000. It is mostly because club members specialized in outdoor tourism are not numerous: 78,344 out of a total of 644,800 (12.15% of the riders) (FFE 2018c). It is probably because these outdoor riders often owned their horse and don't need to be club members, plus, as said earlier, the gap between the demand of these riders and the offer of the FFE and its member clubs.

If we compare with golf for instance, we find a similar typical profile of outdoor/tourism riders: adult riders with average skill level and some purchasing power wishing to escape from the technical abilities taught in clubs with a performance objective. They enjoy free riding in the countryside and they require comfort, safety and ease of use. This profile fit with the one of the French people having an outdoor activity: essentially middle and upper classes most of the time during holidays, and for recreational and relaxation purposes (Ministère de la Jeunesse des Sports et de la Vie Associative and INSEP, 2005).

The development of equestrian tourism impulses a higher standard of professionalism. The equestrian tourism services in France are labelled with the *Equestrian Tourism Center* (Centre de Tourisme Equestre) for the establishments specialized in organization of different activities (horseback riding, trekking etc.). It covers around 3000 schools which link this activity to a high-quality welcome and choice of horses. Another label, the *Stopover Accommodation for Horses* (Cheval Etape), was created to identify and promote high quality accommodations which can accept horses and ponies during stopovers, of at least a night, particularly in the context of equestrian tourism (FFE, 2018a).

The French Horse and Riding Institute (IFCE), a state operator in terms of information about the equine sector, develops, among others, a set of institutional cooperation actions that favouring rapprochement between different countries of the world (IFCE).

1.5   Some Aspects of Equestrian Tourism in Romania

Every year, equestrian tourism becomes more and more popular in Romania. Although at the beginning, this kind of tourism tries to develop the local economy of the country. Horseback riding holidays in the Carpathian Mountains and rural areas become increasingly attractive for both domestic and foreign tourists.

An investigation of routes and equestrian accommodation were done by FITE, in different national committees organizations with the purpose "to realize an international group of routes – with maps - to move from one country to another without breaking off of continuity". Several indicators like: framework of equestrian routes, equestrian routes mark out, specific mark, list of accommodations, projects implemented etc. were taken in consideration.

The conducted inquiry shows that in Romania there is no framework of equestrian routes and no listed accommodations. Also, the maintenance and management of routes is not assured. The positive side of the answers was that exist equestrian routes marked out and specific mark in the national/natural parks and national reserves, thanks to the collaboration with the National Governance of Forests (ROMSILVA).

Concerning the projects implemented in Romania, the "On horse in the Carpathians" aims "to turn equestrian tourism into an eco-tourist alternative while contributing to the development of the communities living in the protected areas" (Piper & Pop, 2012).

According to the National Strategy for Ecotourism Development in Romania (2009), ecotourism activities may include, among others, equestrian tourism on pre-determined routes. The equestrian tourism activities in this country are available in 7 of 28 major natural protected areas (biosphere reserve, national parks and natural parks), the majority of them (57.14%) being in national parks. There are nine suitable equestrian activities in the protected areas (Table 1.2).

Romania is one of the first countries in Europe who developed a system for evaluating eco-destinations, based on the European Ecotourism Labelling Standard and recognized by the Global Sustainable Tourism Council (OECD, 2016). This certification system is provided by the National Authority for Tourism (ANT) and the Association of Ecotourism in Romania (AER), and concerns: ecotourism programs offered by tour operators or guides (maximum 15 participants) and boarding houses in rural and natural areas with an accommodations capacity of up to 25 rooms (AER).

According to the current Romanian legislation (Order no. 1832/856 of July 6, 2011) regarding the approval of the Classification of Occupations in Romania issued by Ministry of Labour, Family and Social Protection, the profession of equestrian tourist guide could be practiced by any person who has completed a professional specialization course for career development offered by an authorized training provider in tourism and the hospitality industry.

One important event which helped to promote the equestrian tourism was the first edition of the Equestrian Travel Forum of Romania, held in Bucharest, in 2016. This event gathered media representatives, travel agencies, accommodation providers with equestrian facilities, and equestrian tour guides. Some of the issues raised during this forum were related to non-collaboration between accommodation providers and travel agencies, to the low number of specialized equestrian guides (it exists only one training school in Romania), to the quality of services (unfortunately, of the 100 equestrian accommodation structures only 40 offer good quality services), to the classification of equestrian centres according to their facilities etc. Currently, Romania has only one tour operator agency specialized in promoting equestrian tourism and there are no statistical data concerning the number of equestrian tourists (InfoTravel Romania, 2016).

As S. Saveja (former general secretary of the Romanian Equestrian Federation) declared, Romania faced a boom in the last three years regarding the development of Romanian equestrianism. There are about 150 riding centers in Romania and the number of clubs affiliated to the federation is 51 (Romanian Equestrian Federation). There are also many private clubs owned or run by stuntmen or private individuals.

Table 1.2 Activities and attractions available (A) and suitable (S) in Romanian national/nature parks and nature reserves (adapted from ROMSILVA, cited by National Strategy for Eco-tourism Development in Romania, 2009)

	Biosphere reserve (1)				National parks (13)				Nature parks (14)				Total	
	A	%	S	%	A	%	S	%	A	%	S	%	A	S
Climbing	0	0	0	0	10	71.43	0	0	4	28.57	0	0	14	0
Cross-country skiing and skiing	0	0	0	0	3	75	3	42.86	1	25	4	57.14	4	7
Cultural attraction	1	5.26	0	0	6	31.58	1	100	12	63.16	0	0	19	1
Cycling	1	12.5	0	0	3	37.5	7	53.85	4	50	6	46.15	8	13
Equestrian tourism	**1**	**14.29**	**0**	**0**	**4**	**57.14**	**0**	**0**	**2**	**28.57**	**9**	**100**	**7**	**9**
Fishing	1	8.33	0	0	2	16.67	0	0	9	75	1	100	12	1
Nautical sports (canoe, kayaking, rafting)	1	25	0	0	1	25	2	22.22	2	50	7	77.78	4	9
Ornithology tourism	1	11.11	0	0	4	44.44	6	50	4	44.44	6	50	9	12
Scientific	1	4.35	0	0	13	56.52	0	0	9	39.13	4	100	23	4
Skiing	0	0	0	0	3	50	1	50	3	50	1	50	6	2
Speleology	0	0	0	0	5	50	2	100	5	50	0	0	10	2
Trails	1	4.76	0	0	13	61.9	0	0	7	33.33	1	100	21	1
Wildlife tourism	1	10	0	0	4	40	7	53.85	5	50	6	46.15	10	13
Total	9	–	0	–	71	–	29	–	67	–	45	–	147	74

1.6 Conclusion and Implications

With a high-quality tourism activity, France, represented by National Equestrian Tourism Committee and French Equestrian Federation, plays an important role in organizing, developing and promoting equestrian tourism at national and international level. Although at the beginning, Romania tries to develop this kind of tourism despite of an inadequate equestrian infrastructure. In this regard, the Romanian National Equestrian Tourism Committee needs to have the government support, and not only, to implement an equestrian tourism trail project, in link with protected areas, as an ecotourism solution.

The development of equestrian tourism needs several elements: a real equine sector plus a structured tourism sector plus an environmental politic, all the actors working together in the framework of a will, at the highest level of State, to develop an economic segment. This segment is already seriously developed in France, and Romania has all the assets to reach the aim to develop equestrian tourism. When comparing the two countries concerning this sector it is possible to bring to the fore the lacks in Romania but, more important, the possibilities of collaboration between the two countries for the benefit of both, thanks to the existing structures as the IFCE in France.

References

Association of Ecotourism in Romania (AER). *Certification system.* Retrieved January 10, 2017, from http://www.eco-romania.ro/reteaua-eco-romania/membrii-certificati.

Atout France. (2011). *Tourisme et cheval, une ressource au service des destinations.* Paris: ATOUT France.

Bouchet, P., & Bouhaouala, M. (2009). Tourisme sportif: un essai de définition socio-économique. *Teoros, 28*(2), 3–8. https://doi.org/10.7202/1024801ar.

Bouhaouala, M., & Sobry, C. (2017). Le tourisme sportif: opportunité socio-économique pour le développement des destinations touristiques. *Juristourisme, 198,* 19–22.

Cater, E. (1993). Ecotourism in the third world: Problems for sustainable tourism development. *Tourism Management, 14*(2), 85–90. https://doi.org/10.1016/0261-5177(93)90040-r.

Cochrane, J., & Daspher, K. (2014). Characteristics and needs of the leisure riding market in the UK. *Mondes du tourisme. Cheval, tourisme et sociétés,* 82–91.

Delambre, H. (2011). La destination France et ses territoires dans l'offre cheval: Interview avec le président de la FITE. In: Atout France (Ed.), *Tourisme et cheval, une ressource au service des destinations* (pp. 156–157). Paris: ATOUT France.

Equipe MIT, & Knafou, R. (Eds.) (2005). *Tourismes 2, Moments de lieux.* Paris: Belin.

Eslan, C., et al. (2018). *L'équitation: un décalage entre les représentations et la pratique.* Retrieved February 17, 2018, from http://mediatheque.ifce.fr/doc_num.php?explnum_id=22357.

French Equestrian Federation (FFE). (2011). Les Français, le sport et l'équitation. Retrieved February 10, 2017, from https://www.ffe.com/journaliste/content/download/11287/112462/version/1/file/Sondage–BVAFFE-2011.pdf.

French Equestrian Federation (FFE). (2018a). *Labels.* Retrieved January 10, 2017, from https://www.ffe.com/club/Labels

French Equestrian Federation (FFE). (2018b). *Statistics licenses*. Retrieved February 10, 2018, from https://www.telemat.org/FFE/sif/?milles=2017&dep=®=&cs=4.668bf9696507c334ee3f2 19597582f359a6e4a599cafcf38cee60c363d3bd071c5ae7bcd6f967ed30f1e3cc62ea377ade638b f51a0a9c6b883bbae8ba3e4d6a7274a07c8002318d123a5abc1e9abd34e785c.

French Equestrian Federation (FFE). (2018c). *Statistics licenses*. Retrieved February 10, 2018, from https://www.telemat.org/FFE/sif/?cs=4.72c29b2f3d481b081b6e5d663d5ffe243353b0c3a4 8432b05b1eee7b8de7a1c2ad6302e18278a9ec1f01b8aeeb6c6361a082.

French Horse and Riding Institute (IFCE). Retrieved January 10, 2017, from http://www.ifce.fr/.

Gammon, S., & Robinson, T. (2003). Sport and tourism: A conceptual framework. *Journal of Sport & Tourism, 8,* 21–26.

Gibson, H. J. (1998). Sport tourism: A critical analysis of research. *Sport Management Review, 1*(1), 45–76. https://doi.org/10.1016/s1441-3523(98)70099-3.

Grefe, G., & Pickel-Chevalier, S. (2015). De la transformation des établissements équestres en France lorsqu'ils intègrent la société des loisirs et de consommation. *Mondes du tourisme. Cheval, tourisme et sociétés*, 136–149.

International Federation of Equestrian Tourism (FITE). (2012). *Equestrian tourism*. Retrieved January 10, 2017, from http://en.fite-net.org/content/view/full/12260.

InfoTravel Romania (2016). Cum a fost la Forumul de Turism Ecvestru, editia I? Retrieved December 15, 2016, from http://www.infotravelromania.ro/blog/2016/10/cum-a-fost-la-forumul-de-turism-ecvestru-editia-i/.

International Federation of Equestrian Tourism (FITE). (2016). *Statutes of the FITE*. Retrieved December 15, 2016, from https://en.fite-net.org/content/view/full/12283.

Konyves, E., & Suta, E. (2009). The importance of equestrian tourism enterprises in tourism destination management in Hungary. *Applied Studies in Agribusiness and Commerce, 3,* 25–28.

Le Borgne, A., & Kouchner, F. (2002). *Créer et commercialiser des produits de tourisme équestre*. Paris: Atout France.

Leiper, N. (1990). Tourism attraction systems. *Annals of Tourism Research, 17*(3), 367–384.

Liu, Z. H. (2003). Sustainable tourism development: A critique. *Journal of Sustainable Tourism, 11*(6), 459–475. https://doi.org/10.1080/09669580308667216.

Ministere de la Jeunesse, des Sports et de la Vie associative/Insep/Insee. (2005). *La pratique des activités physiques et sportives en France*. Paris: l'Insep.

National Authority for Tourism (ANT). Retrieved November 22, 2016, from http://turism.gov.ro/.

National Governance of Forests (ROMSILVA). Retrieved December 15, 2016, from http://www.rosilva.ro/.

National Strategy for Ecotourism Development in Romania (2009). Retrieved December 15, 2016, from http://turism.gov.ro/wp-content/uploads/2016/02/Strategia-na%C5%A3ional%C4%83-de-dezvoltare-a-ecoturismului-%C3%AEn-Rom%C3%A2nia-Faza-I-2009.pdf.

OECD. (2016). "Romania". In *OECD Tourism Trends and Policies 2016*. Paris: OECD Publishing. Retrieved December 15, 2016, from http://dx.doi.org/10.1787/tour-2016-55-en.

Pickel-Chevalier, S. (2015). Can equestrian tourism be a solution for sustainable tourism development in France? *Loisir et Société/Society and Leisure, 38*(1), 110–134. https://doi.org/10.1080/09669580308667216.

Pickel-Chevalier, S. (2016). *L'équitation française et sa patrimonialisation dans la société des loisirs*. Retrieved November 10, 2016, from http://www.espacestemps.net/articles/lequitation-francaise-et-sapatrimonialisation-dans-la-societe-des-loisirs/.

Pickel-Chevalier, S., & Grefe, G. (2015). Le cheval réinventé par la société des loisirs en Occident: une mythologie révolutionnée? (XVIIè-XXIè siècle). *Mondes du tourisme. Cheval, tourisme et sociétés*, 26–49.

Pigeassou, C. (2002). Sport tourism as a growing sector: The French perspective. In S. Gammon and J. Kurtzman (eds) *Sport Tourism: Principles and Practice* (Vol. 76, pp. 129-140). Eastbourne, UK: Leisure Studies Association.

Piper, D., & Pop, M. (2012). A presentation of the national experiment and national projects and the activities of the Carpathian Crescent in Transylvania. In *Proceedings of the 1st European Congress of Equestrian Tourism Routes*, Paris.

Romanian Equestrian Federation (FRE). *Cluburi membre*. Retrieved December 15, 2016, from http://fer.org.ro/wp-content/uploads/lista_cluburi_20141.pdf.

Sigurðardóttir, I. (2015). Identifying the success criteria of the Icelandic horse based tourism businesses: Interviews with operators. *Mondes du tourisme. Cheval, tourisme et sociétés*, 150–160.

Sigurðardóttir, I., & Helgadóttir, G. (2015). Riding high: Quality and customer satisfaction in equestrian tourism in Iceland. *Scandinavian Journal of Hospitality and Tourism, 15*(1–2), 105–121.

Sobry, C. (2003). *Socioéconomie du sport. Structures sportives et libéralisme économique*. Louvain-la-Neuve: De Boeck.

Sobry, C., Liu, X., & Li, J. (2016). Sport tourism: Contribution to a definition and categorization. *Acta Turistica, 28*(1), 7–26.

Sociovision Cofremca. (2006). Le cheval et les loisirs des français, quelles sont les réelles opportunités de développement à l'horizon 2010. In *Internal Seminar of the Haras Nationaux*, November 16–17, Paris. Diaporama.

Tourre-Malen, C. (2009). Évolution des activités équestres et changement social en France à partir des années 1960. *Le Mouvement Social, 229*(4), 41–59. https://doi.org/10.3917/lms.229.0041.

Vial, C., Aubert, M., & Perrier-Cornet, P. (2011). Le développement de l'équitation de loisir dans les territoires ruraux: entre influences sectorielles et périurbanisation. *Revue d'économie régionale et urbaine, 3,* 549–573.

Weed, M., & Bull, C. (2004). *Sport tourism: Participants, policies and providers*. Oxford: Elsevier Butterworth-Heinemann.

World Commission on Environment and Development (WCED). (1987). *Our Common Future*. Oxford: Oxford University Press.

World Tourism Organization (UNWTO) (2016). *Tourism highlights*. Retrieved November 12, 2016, from https://www.e-unwto.org/doi/pdf/10.18111/9789284418145.

Chapter 2
Analysis and Segmentation of Sports Events' Participants: The Marathon Course in Palma de Mallorca

Margarita Alemany-Hormaeche, Francisco Rejón-Guardia and María Antonia García-Sastre

2.1 Introduction

The pace of modern life often leads individuals to seek forms of escapism in their leisure time, often looking for active holidays in which sport plays a significant part. This may explain the success, in recent years, of sporting events organised in mature destinations to complement the traditional tourism product (García-Sastre, Alemany-Hormaeche, & Trías-Villar, 2015). Many people are following the trend of participating in marathons, motivated by various reasons: competition, extrinsic achievement, socialising, camaraderie and athletic identity (Gillett & Kelly, 2006).

The increasing interest in participation in sporting events has been taken into account by the organizers of these events in mature destinations as an instrument for tourism, specifically: to attract visitors outside of peak season, thereby reducing seasonality; to extend demand to alternative geographic areas; to diversify and increase the attractiveness of the destination for existing or new markets; and to project a favourable image of the destination instead other alternatives (Connell, Page, & Meyer, 2015).

This study evaluates the tourists taking part in, and the economic impact of a sporting event as a tourism instrument in the Balearic Islands. As well as being an ideal environment for the practice of sports such as running, Palma de Mallorca offers all the resources a sports tourist could wish for. This cosmopolitan city is renowned for its gastronomy, offers a wide range of cultural activities, and commercial services, and

M. Alemany-Hormaeche · F. Rejón-Guardia · M. A. García-Sastre (✉)
Department of Business & Economics, University of the Balearic Islands, Mallorca, Spain
e-mail: garcia.sastre@uib.es

M. Alemany-Hormaeche
e-mail: marga.alemany@uib.es

F. Rejón-Guardia
e-mail: f.rejon@uib.es

© Springer Nature Switzerland AG 2019
A. Artal-Tur et al. (eds.), *Trends in Tourist Behavior*,
Tourism, Hospitality & Event Management,
https://doi.org/10.1007/978-3-030-11160-1_2

has good connectivity with the main European cities. The location of the city, which is open to the sea, and the design of the event routes, allow participants to enjoy the main tourist resources of the city with its abundant, Renaissance, Gothic and Modernist architectural legacy. The city of Palma has a long tradition of welcoming tourists, and currently has a total of 237 establishments with 43,633 tourist beds, plus apartments offering accommodation. This guarantees sufficient capacity to accommodate the athletes and spectators of sporting events that the city usually hosts.

In recent years, Palma has experienced a broad growth in the practice of athletics at the grassroots level. Events such as the "Cursa popular Ciutat de Palma el Corte Ingles", "Mitja Marató Ciutat de Palma", "10 Km Port de Palma, Cursa Popular Palmadona", "Palma de Mallorca Maraton", among others, are examples of the growing popularity of this type of event. Palma de Mallorca Marathon is a relatively new event, which has been held since 2015, taking over from the TUI Marathon after eleven successful years. It has the intention of growing in every respect, from the level of participation in the quality of the sport. In the most recent races, the event has had the average annual participation of 11,000 runners. Palma de Mallorca's Marathon course is entirely urban, taking competitors past the city's most important tourist attractions, showing runners the main monuments, and the most important, well-known streets and avenues along the 42,195 m of the route.

Following the literature review, this study is structured as follows: The first part focuses on the analysis of the levels of satisfaction experienced by the participants in the Palma de Mallorca Marathon, with the objective of identifying the main dimensions which explain satisfaction. The second part explores segmentation through cluster analysis, enabling the identification of different segments of marathon runners through variables of socio-demographics and consumer behaviour, such as loyalty and previous experience. Finally, the main conclusions and the implications for the management of the tourist destination are highlighted, as well as the limitations and future lines of research.

2.2   Literature Review

The most relevant research is described below as follows: First, the studies which evaluate sports events as tourism products are highlighted. Then, the importance of the analysis of levels of satisfaction to differentiate the profile of the sports tourist is explained. Finally, the review concludes by highlighting the usefulness of segmentation to support marketing strategy development and planning, and segmentation as a tool to identify key segments in order to better understand their needs and tourism motivations.

2.2.1 Sporting Events as Tourism Products

The sport has been described as one of the most important social phenomena in the world (Kurtzman & Zauhar, 2003), and the binomial of sport and tourism is becoming one of the most popular leisure and recreational experiences (Ritchie & Adair, 2004). The tourism industry, encouraged by this situation, has been promoting the development of sports tourism products, pursuing high specialization through high tech in sports equipment, and new technologies (Redmond, 1991).

There has been a recent boom in the organization of urban sporting events. The United States and Europe show clear examples of this trend and several factors explain this growth: the greater availability of consumer income for the consumption of recreational and leisure activities (Thwaites, 1999); a greater concern for health and well-being (Knop, 1987; Kurtzman & Zauhar, 1995); and the effort of cities to equip themselves with sports facilities and infrastructures as a boost for territorial development (Turner & Rosentraub, 2002). The interest of large cities in hosting major sporting events is clear, with the increasing number of agencies whose main objective is to attract sporting events to their respective communities, to coordinate the efforts of different administrations and seek the support of private sponsors (Jones, 2001).

The organization of these events occasions important benefits from both the economic and social perspectives and, of course, inherent burdens for the host cities. Among the former, the promotion and implementation of strategies for urban regeneration and tourism development should be highlighted (Benur & Bramwell, 2015; Biachini & Schengel, 1991; Loftman & Spirou, 1996), in addition to the relaunching of the image of the city linked to the success of the event (Roche, 2002), or the revitalization of the local economy through the expenditure made by visitors and participants in the events. Although sports tourism has become an important economic activity for many regions (Shonk & Chelladurai, 2008), it requires heavy investment by public administrations, whether from central or regional governments, which may not always be translated into economic benefits. There have been examples of negative experiences of cities that have hosted mega-events, where the infrastructures and equipment financed by public funds have been subsequently underutilized (Kidd, 1992; Whitson & Macintosh, 1993), or where negative effects have been detected in different segments of the host community (Hodges & Hall, 1996; Wearing & Wearing, 1996).

Mega-events, or hallmark tourism events, are important fairs, exhibitions, cultural or sporting events of an international nature, which are held regularly with a brief or limited duration, organized by a country or city, and which aim to attract an important number of participants and spectators, with international media coverage and high investment in infrastructure, logistics and security (Aguado, Osorio, Arbona, & Peña-Vinces, 2017). The scientific literature has devoted important efforts to the analysis of the economic impact generated by large-scale events (Añó Sanz, Calabuig Moreno, & Parra Camacho, 2012; Baade, Baumann, & Matheson, 2008; Domingues,

Junior, & Magalhães, 2011; Li, Blake, & Thomas, 2013; Parra-Camacho, Añó-Sanz, Calabuig-Moreno, & Ayora-Pérez, 2016; Saayman & Saayman, 2012).

Major sporting events have traditionally received attention in the literature, both internationally (Baade et al., 2008; Fernández & Martinez, 2003; Pillay & Bass, 2008; Soutar & McLeod, 1993; Sturgess & Brady, 2006; Waitt, 2003) and nationally (Añó Sanz et al. 2012; Barajas & Sanchez, 2011; Ramírez Hurtado, Ordaz Sanz, & Rueda Cantuche, 2007) which analyse the economic impact of major sporting events. Yet, small- and medium-sized sporting events have traditionally received little attention in the literature.

However, in recent years, sporting events have increasingly been considered as major economic driving forces, especially in medium-sized communities, with growing evidence that medium-sized events have more positive repercussions than large-scale events on host communities (Higham, 1999; Veltri, Miller, & Harris, 2009). Researchers' interest in events of small or medium dimensions has increased correspondingly (Agha & Taks, 2015; Matheson, 2012; Taks, 2013; Veltri et al., 2009). Some of the most important studies into the effects of small- or medium-sized events on host communities are those of: (Baade et al., 2008; Barajas & Sanchez, 2011; Pillay & Bass, 2008; Sturgess & Brady, 2006; Veltri et al., 2009)

2.2.2 Tourist Satisfaction with the Sports Event

Customer satisfaction is defined as a pleasurable fulfilment response to a good service benefit, or reward. Customer satisfaction has become a priority for organizations, especially for those firms that work with intangible and heterogeneous assets (Cronin Jr. & Taylor, 1992). Positive indices about the client's experience with the product or the brand stimulates the intention to repurchase in the future, as well as other advantages, such as positive word-of-mouth, cross-buying, improved profits, lowered marketing expenditure and customer loyalty (Anderson, Fornell, & Lehmann, 1994; Palmatier, Dant, Grewal, & Evans, 2006).

Considering the specific characteristics of services and, especially, the heterogeneity and variability of the same, customer satisfaction is understood in relation to service quality (Cronin Jr. & Taylor, 1992; Dabholkar, Shepherd, & Thorpe, 2000; Parasuraman, Zeithaml, & Berry, 1994). Mackay and Crompton (1988) define service quality as the difference between the expectations of the consumer about each of the dimensions of the service, and what it really perceives about it. Service quality has been linked to concepts such as: customer satisfaction (Ko & Pastore, 2004); customer loyalty (Kandampully, 1998; Zeithaml, Parasuraman, & Berry, 1990); value (Laroche, Ueltschy, Abe, Cleveland, & Yannopoulos, 2004); and repurchase intention (Fornell, 1992).

In the field of sports products, the quality of services and customer satisfaction has been addressed by authors such as: Howat, Absher, Crilley, and Milne (1996), Kim and Kim (1995), and McDonald, Sutton, and Milne (1995) following the model proposed to measure quality and satisfaction in other sectors (banking, insurance, hospitality, etc.) adapted to the characteristics of sports products.

It is usual in this context, to differentiate between two types of public for sports products. On the one hand, there are the participants directly involved in sports practice (Crompton & Mackay, 1989; Howat et al., 1996; Kim & Kim, 1995; Papadimitriou & Karteroliotis, 2000; Van der Graaf, 1994; Williams, 1998). Studies can be found on the quality of services provided in fitness centres (Alexandris, Zahariadis, Tsorbatzoudis, & Grouios, 2004); or at golf courses (Crilley, Murray, Howat, March, & Adamson, 2002). On the other hand, there are the spectators of sport (Greenwell, Fink, & Pastore, 2002; Kelley & Turley, 2001; McDonald et al., 1995; McDonald & Milne, 1998; Theodorakis, Kambitsis, & Laios, 2001; Wakefield, Blodgett, & Sloan, 1996).

Sports tourism, as a service provider, incorporates and measures quality in all its dimensions (Kouthouris & Alexandris, 2005), and the analysis of tourist satisfaction with events is a widely used analytical tool (Tkaczynski & Rundle-Thiele, 2011). There is evidence in the tourism literature of a positive correlation between tourist satisfaction and intention to return (Bigne, Sanchez, & Sanchez, 2001; Kozak, 2001; Yoon & Uysal, 2005). Green and Chalip (1998) underline the necessity for event organisers to control the expectations and experiences of participants, as these are key factors in the level of involvement, and the intention to repeat (Casper & Stellino, 2008).

2.2.3 Segmentation in Sports Tourism

Segmentation techniques are tools which allow the grouping of individuals who show similar characteristics and needs (Kotler, Bowen, Makens, Moreno, & Paz, 2004). Slabbert (2016) points out that segmentation studies analyze a matrix of consumer characteristics, which include geographical information, behaviour patterns, personality characteristics, spending, seasonality and motives. Of the different variables used in segmentation, the demographic variable is the most general, is relatively inexpensive to perform, and helps identify the profile characteristics associated with the consumer in each segment.

One of the most widely used demographic variables in the market segmentation literature is the age variable. The age of a person has been used frequently, due to the belief that it is a low-cost proxy (Sowell & Mounts Jr., 2005), and it provides the necessary information to select different age groups (Bennett, Henson, & Zhang, 2003).

In the sports literature, segmentation is used to identify more homogeneous groups of athletes showing similar needs, desires and demographic profiles (Mullin, Hardy, & Sutton, 2000). Of the demographic variables, age has been applied as a segmentation factor, since it has been shown to influence different aspects such as performance, the behaviour of the athlete, and their commitment and attitudes (Myburgh, Kruger, & Saayman, 2014). In a sporting context, age as a variable of demographic segmentation implies classifying participants who belong to the same age groups and who tend to have similar interests and experience. This will influence their behaviour and patterns of participation.

Over the years, segmentation in the field of the sports tourism has used a wide range of instruments that have furthered knowledge about participants in certain sports. In the field of diving, for example, Rice (1987) classified the practitioners of this modality into three levels: hard core, tourist and potential. Nogawa, Yamaguchi, and Hagi (1996), proposed two categories for cross-country skiing and walking: sports tourist and sports excursionist. The geographical and family life cycle variables have been used by (Bojanic & Warnick, 1996) in ski resorts; demand models based on the characteristics of skiers and the attributes of ski resorts (Johnston & Elsner, 1972); psychographic profiles to identify potential skiers (Mills, Couturier, & Snepenger, 1986) or the motivations for understanding the segment of skiers (Klenosky, Gengler, & Mulvey, 1993; Richards, 1996). Hall (1992) presents two groups of sports tourists: the active participants and the hobbyist. Stebbins (1992) created the concept of "work on serious leisure" to understand the different types of sports tourist.

Previous experience or frequency of participation, are relevant behavioural variables (Kruger, Botha, & Saayman, 2012), which identify first-timers as the new market, and repeaters as the core market of a sporting event. The use of different tactics and programmes specific to each group based on this distinction may be interesting to practitioners (Filo, Funk, & O'Brien, 2008; Kaplanidou & Gibson, 2012; Um, Chon, & Ro, 2006).

It is evident that every sporting event, and the type of participants they attract, is unique, and for this reason, the organizers of sporting events must identify the different clusters that will allow them to develop specific programmes for each segment of the market (Myburgh et al. 2014). The organization of an event such as the Palma de Mallorca Marathon requires extensive knowledge of the profile of the participants in the different types of races, in order not to consider them as a homogeneous group (Kruger et al. 2012).

2.3   Methods

2.3.1   Context and Sampling

The study was undertaken in the context of the annual Palma de Mallorca Marathon (previously named the TUI Marathon) held on Sunday 15th October 2016. A questionnaire was created, with four main sections, composed of 36 mainly closed-ended questions, addressing various aspects of the experience. The first section assessed behaviourally-oriented variables such as: choice of marathon race, purpose of visit, number of accompanying persons, length of stay, and amount of expenditure. The second section measured motivation for choosing the sports destination using 12 items developed for this study. The third section evaluated previous experience and levels of satisfaction. The final section examined the demographic characteristics of respondents. The questionnaire was provided in Spanish, English, and German and delivered by e-mail from October to November 2016. Respondents were selected opportunistically from the 7,871 competitors in the marathon. In total 1,661 runners responded to the questionnaire (response rate 21.1%).

2.4 Results

Palma de Mallorca Marathon is one of the most important sports events to be held in the city of Palma. In the 2016 event, of the 7,871 participants, 6,352 were non-local runners and 1,519 were local runners. The fact that this race had the highest number of participants of any event held in the city, led to a need to know the socio-demographic characteristics of the participants, and their levels of satisfaction with the event, in order to improve the future management of the event. In addition, the economic impact of the marathon was evaluated for the host city of Palma. The runners could register in three types of races: the 10 km race (32.76% of the participants), a half-marathon (48.60%) or the marathon (17.39%). The frequency of repetition of the participants, showed that 54.75% were attending for the first time; 17.08% for the second time; 7.69% had participated between three and five times; and 5.21% had participated 6 or more times. Of the total number of participants, 62% were men and 38% were women. By age, it was observed that 12.3% were under 35 years old, 17.1% between 35 and 39 years old, 9.3% from 40 to 44 years old, 19.2% from 45 to 49 years old, and 20.6% between 50 and 54 years old. The remaining 21.4% were 55 or older. As for the level of education of the runners, there were three large groups: 24% with primary and secondary education, 50% with a university education, and the remaining 26% declared having other types of studies.

By nationalities, the majority of the participants were German (54.9%); the second largest number were runners from the United Kingdom (20.4%); the remaining nationalities had a lower representation (6.8% Swedish, 3.4% Austrian, 3% Estonian, 1.6% Dutch, 1.6% Norwegian, 1.5% Swiss, 1.2% Italian). One of the most important questions for the organizers of the event is to know how the participants became aware of it. 31.3% declared learning about the event through their friends; 24.6% had learned about it through other runners; and 10.3% through their club. Other minority channels were: advertising in magazines (7.6%); Facebook (7.4%); relatives (5.8%); the race calendar (4.6%); or through other sources (7.6%). Regarding the sources of information used to stay informed about the event, 78% of the runners used the vent webpage, 18% used Facebook, only 3% used the newsletter, and 1% used Twitter (see Table 2.1).

To evaluate the advantages that an event such as this may imply for the host city, a section of questions related to aspects of the trip and tourist expenditure were included in the questionnaire (see Table 2.2). The main results reveal that 97% of the runners arrived on the island by plane, and that 77.13% stayed in hotels; 14.03% stayed in

Table 2.1 Socio-demographic information

Variable	Categories	%
Distance	10 km	32.76
	21.1 km (Half Marathon)	48.60
	42.195 km (Marathon)	17.39
Frequency of participation	Once	54.75
	Twice	17.08
	3, 4 or 5 times	7.69
	More than 5 times	5.21
Gender	Male	62
	Female	38
Age	From 25 to 29	4.7
	30–34	5.8
	35–39	17.1
	40–44	9.3
	45–49	19.2
	50–54	20.6
	55–59	10.2
	60–64	6.8
	65–69	2.9
	70–74	1.2
	More than 75	0.3
Level of education	High School/College	24
	University	50
	Other	26
Country of origin	Germany	54.9
	UK	20.4
	Sweden	6.8
	Austria	3.4
	Estonia	3.0
	Netherlands	1.6
	Norway	1.6
	Switzerland	1.5
	Italy	1.2
	Denmark	1.1
	France	0.9
	Other	3.7

(continued)

Table 2.1 (continued)

Variable	Categories	%
Awareness of the event	Friends	31.3
	Other athletes	24.6
	Club	10.3
	Advertisement in magazine	7.6
	Facebook	7.4
	Family	5.8
	AIMS Race calendar	5.5
	Expo at other events	4.6
	Poster/flyer	3.0
Information about the event	Event website	78
	Facebook	18
	Newsletter	3
	Twitter	1

Source Own elaboration

rented houses or apartments; 4.76% in the homes of family or friends; 2.47% in an agritourism; and the remaining 1.62%, in other types of accommodation.

An additional but fundamental question, when analysing the economic impact of a sporting event, is to quantify not only the expenditure of the participants in the event, but also that of their accompanying party. Only 5.38% of the runners came to the event unaccompanied; the vast majority (94.62%) were accompanied to the event. Specifically, 22.05% were accompanied by one person; 11.28% by 2 persons; 13.93% by three persons; 5.21% by four persons, 7.35% by 5 persons and the remainder were accompanied by six persons or more. It should be noted that 20.51% of the runners were accompanied by a group of more than 10 people.

With regard to the length of stay, the average was 5.94 days. Only 0.5% of the participants spent one night in the city; 4.88% spent two nights. Most runners who came to the event spent several days in Palma: 19.43% three nights; 19.85% four nights; 14.63% five nights; 6.98% six nights; 17.75% seven nights; and the remaining 11.01% stayed over seven nights. In addition to participating in the Palma de Mallorca Marathon during their stay, the runners, took part in other activities such as: enjoying the sun and beach (60.99%); discovering the local cuisine (51.90%); shopping (46.30%); cultural visits (30.28%); water sports (29.68%); nightlife (27.09%); and other activities (6.56%). The overall expenditure per stay of the participants amounted to 999.78 euros, which, with an average length of stay of 5.94 days meant a daily expenditure of 168.18 euros, well above the average daily expenditure of tourists in Mallorca during the same dates (119.43 euros). A breakdown of average expenditure by runners during their stay is distributed between the following items: accommodation (361.28 euros); plane/boat (251.52 euros); food and drink (195.08

Table 2.2 Tourism behavioral variables

Variable	Categories	%
Transport	Plane	97
	Car	2
	Other	1
	Boat and car	0
Accommodation	Hotel	77.13
	Rented houses or apartments	14.03
	Staying with friends or family	4.76
	Finca/Agroturismo	247
	Other	1.62
Number of accompanying persons	None	5.38
	1	22.05
	2	11.28
	3	13.93
	4	5.21
	5	7.35
	6	2.39
	7	5.38
	8	2.65
	9	2.39
	10	1.45
	More than 10	20.51
Length of stay	1 night	0.50
	2	4.88
	3	19.43
	4	19.85
	5	14.63
	6	6.98
	7	17.75
	8	3.78
	9	2.78
	10	3.87
	More than 10 nights	0.67

Source Own elaboration

euros); shopping (149.69 euros); various concepts (35 euros); nightlife (120 euros); car rental (67 euros); and cultural activities (70 euros).

Finally, taking into account the expenditure of the total number of participants and their accompanying parties, the economic impact amounted to approximately 11,421,463 euros, a considerable figure for the host city, considering that Palma de Mallorca Marathon is a medium-sized event taking place on a single day, in the low-mid season of the destination.

2.4.1 Analysis of the General Satisfaction of the Sample

With a view to evaluating the satisfaction of the competitors in the sporting event, a total of 14 items were measured using a 5-point Likert scale (1—not satisfied, 2—less satisfied, 3—neutral, 4—satisfied, 5—very satisfied). An exploratory factor analysis was carried out using a Varimax rotation, to obtain the main dimensions which would group the satisfaction of the runners in the race. The results of the adequacy of the factorial analysis show values of the Kaiser-Meyer-Olkin Test of sampling adequacy KMO = 0.858 (Bartlett's Test of Sphericity − X2 (91) = 4344,876, p < 0.000), indicating the presence of three dimensions. Table 2.3 shows that the main dimension of "satisfaction with the event" correlated with the "characteristics of the event location" (mean value = 4.21), which included the weather (4.57), hospitality of residents (4.38), restaurants (4.31), transport to the island by plane and boat (3.96), and additional services (3.86). The second factor of satisfaction was "race conditions" (race signage, road closures, road surface, road signage). The lowest scoring category of satisfaction was the "service and cost" factor (public transport, travel costs, other hotel services (Wi-Fi), special offers for athletes in hotels, and service costs).

2.4.2 Cluster Analysis of Event Participants

An exploratory analysis was carried out by means of a cluster in two stages, with the intention of discovering natural groupings within a set of data which would not otherwise be apparent. The results of the cluster analysis indicate that a four-cluster solution appeared to appropriate. The results of the analysis show the existence of four groups differentiated in terms of the level of sports activity and loyalty. To this end, they were segmented using the level of sports activity as criteria, in line with the classification proposed by many authors who divide the activities between gentle/moderate or hard/intense.

Among the *hard-loyal* runners, it should be noted that the vast majority have attended the event once or twice and are mainly males aged 41–50. The non-loyal hard runners have participated in the marathon between three and six, or more than six times. The *soft* runners who are loyal to the event, are those who were running

Table 2.3 Results of factor analysis of runners' satisfaction. Total variance explained by the factor analysis and rotated component matrix

Motivation factors and items	Factor loading	Variance (%)	α	Mean
F1: Services and cost		3.803	0.793	3.51
Service costs	0.812			3.30
Other hotel services (ej: wifi)	0.775			3.45
Special offers for athletes in hotels	0.750			3.31
Public transport	0.576			3.76
Travel costs	0.568			3.75
F2: Characteristics of event location		13.678	0.811	4.21
Restaurants	0.819			4.31
Hospitality of local residents	0.773			4.38
Transport to the island: plane, boat	0.667			3.96
Additional services	0.628			3.86
Weather	0.608			4.57
F3: Race conditions		9.358	0.759	3.76
Road closures	0.800			3.79
Race signage	0.767			3.82
Pavement of route	0.719			3.76
Road signage	0.656			3.67
Total variance extracted (%)		58.839		

Source Own elaboration

for the first or second time, and stand out for including a wider age range, and as the group spending least overall and per item at the destination. However, the group formed of the non-loyal soft runners seemed to have been loyal at some point, as the majority declared having participated in the marathon on between three to six previous occasions. This group spent significantly more overall at the destination per person, on aspects such as hotel accommodation and other items.

2.5   Conclusion and Implications

This study has analysed a marathon as a sports event of small-medium size, by examining the participating tourists and their tourism behaviour, as well as the economic impact of the race. The strong point of this research lies in having applied the vast majority of variables widely recommended by previous studies, that is, socio-demographic, geographical (place of residence), psychographic (satisfaction) and behavioural variables (experience, expenditure, etc.) in the tourist analysis (Tkaczyn-ski & Rundle-Thiele, 2011).

The main objective of the study was to determine the socio-demographic profile of the participants. Among the main findings it was observed that these sports tourists were mainly men of 50–54, with university education, and of German nationality. They learned about the event through friends and the event website, which was also their main source of information for following the event. The participants generally used the plane as a means of transport to the destination, they stayed in hotels near the route of the race, were accompanied, and stayed for an average of four nights in the city. The estimated economic impact generated by the event amounted to 11,421,463 euros.

Once the study sample was described, a factorial analysis of satisfaction with different aspects of the sporting event was carried out, with the intention of identifying the main factors that gather aspects of satisfaction with the race (Tkaczynski & Rundle-Thiele, 2011). The main conclusions of the study indicate that the satisfaction of the runners with the Palma de Mallorca Marathon is due to diverse factors which can be grouped into three categories: characteristics of the event location (date of the event being the most important); race conditions (highlighting the race signage); and services (mainly public transport) and cost (general travel cost as the most important), in a similar way to those conclusions reached in studies of satisfaction carried out by Shonk and Chelladurai (2008).

Competitors in the Palma de Mallorca marathon were segmented according to their level of activity as runners (Getz & McConnell, 2014; Pomfret, 2006). In addition, other variables were considered, such as future loyalty to the event and destination, tourism behaviour such as expenditure and length of stay at the destination, and socio-demographic variables. The results of the segmentation and the cluster analysis show the presence of four differentiated groups (named *hard loyal runners, non-loyal hard runners, soft runners and non-loyal soft runners*). The most significant findings are that runners who will attend in the future and will also run other races, were the newcomers whose tourism behaviour in terms of expenditure was found to be close to the average. Another finding of interest is that those runners who are no longer loyal and who will not run another race during the year, are those who spend significantly more on all items of expenditure. However, they are runners who have participated on previous occasions and do not intend to repeat, which may suggest a certain exhaustion of the product for these participants. In terms of expenditure, a direct correlation is observed with previous experience. Thus it is more profitable for the destination to attract older athletes who have participated previously.

The main recommendation to the management of the event points towards the need to captivate the most experienced runners once again and intensify efforts with newcomers. In relation to satisfaction, services linked to items such as public transport and travel costs should be improved, in addition to underlining the specific value of the climate, the hospitality of local residents, as well as road closures and route signage. Finally, events organized in the destination deserve greater attention, particularly in light of the continuing globalization of event tourism and heightened competition for event tourists.

Among the future lines of investigation, there is the evaluation during the time of the tourist that attends sporting events of running, as well as to see its evolution in terms of spending. A comparison with other sports events in the destination would allow the examination of the similarities or differences in the tourist participating in different events, as well as providing strategic information to the managers of the destination in order to attract one segment or another. An accurate estimate of the new money associated with a sporting event is pivotal in assessing its economic impact. Likewise, the resident's vision could be studied, for example, by evaluating negative environmental consequences, increased crime, crowding, administrative problems, security and over-commercialization, all of which can negatively influence the local community.

References

Agha, N., & Taks, M. (2015). A theoretical comparison of the economic impact of large and small events. *International of Sport Finance, 10*(3), 199–217.

Aguado, L. F., Osorio, A. M., Arbona, A., & Peña-Vinces, J. C. (2017). Efectos de la realización de un megaevento deportivo sobre una economía loc8al. El caso de los Juegos Mundiales 2013 Cali. *Journal of Economics, Finance and Administrative Science, 22*(43), 131–153.

Alexandris, K., Zahariadis, P., Tsorbatzoudis, C., & Grouios, G. (2004). An empirical investigation of the relationships among service quality, customer satisfaction and psychological commitment in a health club context. *European Sport Management Quarterly, 4*(1), 36–52.

Anderson, E. W., Fornell, C., & Lehmann, D. R. (1994). Customer satisfaction, market share, and profitability: Findings from Sweden. *The Journal of Marketing, 58*(3), 53–66.

Añó Sanz, V., Calabuig Moreno, F., & Parra Camacho, D. (2012). Impacto social de un gran evento deportivo: el Gran Premio de Europa de Fórmula 1. *Cultura, Ciencia y Deporte, 7*(19).

Baade, R. A., Baumann, R., & Matheson, V. A. (2008). Selling the game: Estimating the economic impact of professional sports through taxable sales. *Southern Economic Journal, 74*(3), 794–810.

Barajas, A., & Sanchez, P. (2011). Aplicación del análisis coste-beneficio (ACB) al Campeonato de España de Natación Master 2011. *I Gijón Workshop de Economía del Deporte: El Impacto Económico en el Deporte, Gijón, Universidad de Oviedo.*

Bennett, G., Henson, R. K., & Zhang, J. (2003). Generation Y's perceptions of the action sports industry segment. *Journal of sport management, 17*(2), 95–115.

Benur, A. M., & Bramwell, B. (2015). Tourism product development and product diversification in destinations. *Tourism Management, 50,* 213–224.

Biachini, F. & Schengel, H. (1991). Re-imaging the city. In J. Corner & S. Harvey (Eds.), *Enterprise and heritage: Crosscurrents of national culture* (pp. 214–234). Routledge, London.

Bigne, J. E., Sanchez, M. I., & Sanchez, J. (2001). Tourism image, evaluation variables and after purchase behaviour: Inter-relationship. *Tourism Management, 22*(6), 607–616.

Bojanic, D. C., & Warnick, R. B. (1996). Segmenting the market for winter vacations. *Journal of Travel & Tourism Marketing, 4*(4), 85–95.

Casper, J. M., & Stellino, M. B. (2008). Demographic predictors of recreational tennis participants' sport commitment. *Journal of Park & Recreation Administration, 26*(3).

Connell, J., Page, S. J., & Meyer, D. (2015). Visitor attractions and events: Responding to seasonality. *Tourism Management, 46*(C), 283–298.

Crilley, G., Murray, D., Howat, G., March, H., & Adamson, D. (2002). Measuring performance in operational management and customer service quality: A survey of financial and non-financial metrics from the Australian golf industry. *Journal of Retail & Leisure Property, 2*(4), 369–380.

Crompton, J. L., & Mackay, K. J. (1989). Users' perceptions of the relative importance of service quality dimensions in selected public recreation programs. *Leisure Sciences, 11*(4), 367–375.

Cronin Jr., J. J., & Taylor, S. A. (1992). Measuring service quality: A reexamination and extension. *The Journal of Marketing,* 55–68.

Dabholkar, P. A., Shepherd, C. D., & Thorpe, D. I. (2000). A comprehensive framework for service quality: An investigation of critical conceptual and measurement issues through a longitudinal study. *Journal of Retailing, 76*(2), 139–173.

Domingues, E. P., Junior, A. A. B., & Magalhães, A. S. (2011). Quanto vale o show?: Impactos econômicos dos investimentos da Copa do Mundo 2014 no Brasil. *Estudos Econômicos (São Paulo), 41*(2), 409–439.

Fernández, I., & Martinez, A. (2003). *El impacto económico de la Copa del América.* Instituto de Economía Internacional, Universidad de Valencia.

Filo, K. R., Funk, D. C., & O'Brien, D. (2008). It's really not about the bike: Exploring attraction and attachment to the events of the Lance Armstrong Foundation. *Journal of Sport Management, 22*(5), 501–525.

Fornell, C. (1992). A national customer satisfaction barometer: The Swedish experience. *The Journal of Marketing, 56*(1), 6–21.

García-Sastre, M. A., Alemany-Hormaeche, M., & Trías-Villar, M. (2015). Are regional political decisions the key element in reducing seasonal variation in tourism? The case of the Balearic Islands. *Tourism Economics: The Business and Finance of Tourism and Recreation, 21*(6), 1207–1219.

Getz, D., & McConnell, A. (2014). Comparing trail runners and mountain bikers: Motivation, involvement, portfolios, and event-tourist careers. *Journal of Convention & Event Tourism, 15,* 69–100.

Gillett, P., & Kelly, S. (2006). 'Non-local' masters games participants: An investigation of competitive active sport tourist motives. *Journal of Sport Tourism, 11*(3–4), 239–257.

Green, B. C., & Chalip, L. (1998). Sport tourism as the celebration of subculture. *Pergamon Annals of Tourirm Research, 25*(2), 275–291.

Greenwell, T. C., Fink, J. S., & Pastore, D. L. (2002). Assessing the influence of the physical sports facility on customer satisfaction within the context of the service experience. *Sport Management Review, 5*(2), 129–148.

Hall, C. M. (1992). *Adventure, sport and health tourism* (pp. 141–158).

Higham, J. (1999). Commentary-sport as an avenue of tourism development: An analysis of the positive and negative impacts of sport tourism. *Current issues in Tourism, 2*(1), 82–90.

Hodges, J., & Hall, C. (1996). The housing and social impacts of mega events: Lessons for the Sydney 2000 Olympics. In *Tourism down under II; towards a more sustainable tourism* (pp. 152–166).

Howat, G., Absher, J., Crilley, G., & Milne, I. (1996). Measuring customer service quality in sports and leisure centres. *Managing leisure, 1*(2), 77–89.

Johnston, W. E., & Elsner, G. H. (1972). Variability in use among ski areas: A statistical study of the California market region. *Journal of Leisure Research, 4*(1), 43.

Jones, C. (2001). Mega-events and host-region impacts: Determining the true worth of the 1999 Rugby World Cup. *International Journal of Tourism Research, 3*(3), 241–251.

Kandampully, J. (1998). Service quality to service loyalty: A relationship which goes beyond customer services. *Total Quality Management, 9*(6), 431–443.

Kaplanidou, K., & Gibson, H. (2012). Differences between first time and repeat spectator tourists of a youth soccer event: Intentions and image approaches. *Current Issues in Tourism, 15*(5), 477–487.

Kelley, S. W., & Turley, L. W. (2001). Consumer perceptions of service quality attributes at sporting events. *Journal of Business Research, 54*(2), 161–166.

Kidd, B. (1992). The Toronto Olympic commitment: Towards a social contract for the Olympic Games. *Olympika: The International Journal of Olympic Studies, 1*(1), 154–167.

Kim, D., & Kim, S. Y. (1995). QUESC: An instrument for assessing the service quality of sport centers in Korea. *Journal of sport management, 9*(2), 208–220.

Klenosky, D. B., Gengler, C. E., & Mulvey, M. S. (1993). Understanding the factors influencing ski destination choice: A means-end analytic approach. *Journal of leisure research, 25*(4), 362–379.

de Knop, P. (1987). Some thoughts on the influence of sport on tourism. In *International seminar and workshop on outdoor education, recreation and sport tourism. Proceedings of an international seminar* (pp. 38–45). Wingate Institute for Physical Education and Sport.

Ko, Y. J., & Pastore, D. L. (2004). Current issues and conceptualizations of service quality in the recreation sport industry. *Sport marketing quarterly, 13*(3), 158–166.

Kotler, P., Bowen, J., Makens, J., Moreno, R. R., & Paz, M. D. R. (2004). *Marketing para turismo.* Pearson Pr.

Kouthouris, C., & Alexandris, K. (2005). Can service quality predict customer satisfaction and behavioral intentions in the sport tourism industry? An application of the SERVQUAL model in an outdoors setting. *Journal of Sport & Tourism, 10*(2), 101–111.

Kozak, M. (2001). Repeaters' behavior at two distinct destinations. *Annals of tourism research, 28*(3), 784–807.

Kruger, M., Botha, K., & Saayman, M. (2012). The relationship between visitor spending and repeat visits: An analysis of spectators at the Old Mutual Two Oceans Marathon. *Acta Commercii.*

Kurtzman, J., & Zauhar, J. (1995). Tourism sport international council. *Annals of tourism Research, 22*(3), 707–708.

Kurtzman, J., & Zauhar, J. (2003). A wave in time-The sports tourism phenomena. *Journal of Sport Tourism, 8*(1), 35–47.

Laroche, M., Ueltschy, L. C., Abe, S., Cleveland, M., & Yannopoulos, P. P. (2004). Service quality perceptions and customer satisfaction: Evaluating the role of culture. *Journal of International Marketing, 12*(3), 58–85.

Li, S., Blake, A., & Thomas, R. (2013). Modelling the economic impact of sports events: The case of the Beijing Olympics. *Economic Modelling, 30,* 235–244.

Loftman, P., & Spirou, C. (1996). Sports stadiums and urban regeneration: the British and US experience. In *Tourism and Culture Conference.* University of Northumbria Sept.

Mackay, K. J., & Crompton, J. L. (1988). A conceptual model of consumer evaluation of recreation service quality. *Leisure Studies, 7*(1), 40–49.

Matheson, V. (2012). Assessing the infrastructure impact of mega-events in emerging economies.

McDonald, M. A., Sutton, W. A., & Milne, G. R. (1995). TEAMQUAL: Measuring service quality in professional team sports. *Sport Marketing Quarterly, 4*(2), 9–15.

McDonald, M., & Milne, G. (1998). Measuring service quality in professional sport. In *Proceedings of the 6th Congress of the European Association of Sport Management.*

Mills, A. S., Couturier, H., & Snepenger, D. J. (1986). Segmenting Texas snow skiers. *Journal of Travel Research, 25*(2), 19–23.

Mullin, B. J., Hardy, S., & Sutton, W. A. (2000). *Sport marketing* (2nd ed.). Champaign, IL: Human Kinetics.

Myburgh, E., Kruger, M., & Saayman, M. (2014). A motivation-based typology of triathletes. *South African Journal for Research in Sport, Physical Education and Recreation, 36*(3), 117–134.

Nogawa, H., Yamaguchi, Y., & Hagi, Y. (1996). An empirical research study on Japanese sport tourism in sport-for-all events: Case studies of a single-night event and a multiple-night event. *Journal of Travel Research, 35*(2), 46–54.

Palmatier, R. W., Dant, R. P., Grewal, D., & Evans, K. R. (2006). Factors influencing the effectiveness of relationship marketing: A meta-analysis. *Journal of marketing, 70*(4), 136–153.

Papadimitriou, D. A., & Karteroliotis, K. (2000). The service quality expectations in private sport and fitness centers: A reexamination of the factor structure. *Sport Marketing Quarterly, 9*(3), 157–164.

Parasuraman, A., Zeithaml, V. A., & Berry, L. L. (1994). Reassessment of expectations as a comparison standard in measuring service quality: Implications for further research. *The Journal of Marketing,* 111–124.

Parra-Camacho, D., Añó-Sanz, V., Calabuig-Moreno, F., & Ayora-Pérez, D. (2016). Percepción de los residentes sobre el legado de la America's Cup. *Cuadernos de Psicología del Deporte, 16*(1), 325–338.

Pillay, U., & Bass, O. (2008). Mega-events as a response to poverty reduction: The 2010 FIFA World Cup and its urban development implications. *Urban Forum.*

Pomfret, G. (2006). Mountaineering adventure tourists: A conceptual framework for research. *Tourism Management, 27*(1), 113–123.

Ramírez Hurtado, J. M., Ordaz Sanz, J. A., & Rueda Cantuche, J. M. (2007). Evaluación del impacto económico y social de la celebración de grandes eventos deportivos a nivel local: el caso del Campeonato de Tenis femenino de la ITF en Sevilla en 2006. *Revista de Métodos Cuantitativos para la Economía y la Empresa, 3.*

Redmond, G. (1991). *Changing styles of sports tourism: industry/consumer interactions in Canada, the USA and Europe* (pp. 107–120).

Rice, K. (1987). Special report: SCUBA diving: Dive market requires specialized skill and information. *Tour and Travel News, 9,* 7–24.

Richards, G. (1996). Production and consumption of European cultural tourism. *Annals of tourism research, 23*(2), 261–283.

Ritchie, B. W., & Adair, D. (2004). *Sport tourism: Interrelationships, impacts and issues* (Vol. 14). Channel View Publications.

Roche, M. (2002). *Megaevents and modernity: Olympics and expos in the growth of global culture.* Routledge.

Saayman, M., & Saayman, A. (2012). Determinants of spending: An evaluation of three major sporting events. *International Journal of Tourism Research, 14*(2), 124–138.

Shonk, D. J., & Chelladurai, P. (2008). Service quality, satisfaction, and intent to return in event sport tourism. *Journal of sport management, 22*(5), 587–602.

Slabbert, L. M. (2016). The impact of an accreditation system for trails on growth in hiking tourism.

Soutar, G., & McLeod, P. (1993). Residents' perceptions on impact of the America's Cup. *Annals of Tourism Research, 20*(3), 571–582.

Sowell, C. B., & Mounts Jr., W. S. (2005). Ability, age, and performance: Conclusions from the Ironman Triathlon World Championship. *Journal of Sports Economics, 6*(1), 78–97.

Stebbins, R. (1992). *Amateurs, professionals and serious leisure.* London: McGill.

Sturgess, B., & Brady, C. (2006). Hosting the FIFA World Cup. *World Economics.*

Taks, M. (2013). Social sustainability of non-mega sport events in a global world. *EJSS. European Journal for Sport and Society, 10,* 121–141.

Theodorakis, N., Kambitsis, C., & Laios, A. (2001). Relationship between measures of service quality and satisfaction of spectators in professional sports. *Managing Service Quality: An International Journal, 11*(6), 431–438.

Thwaites, D. (1999). Closing the gaps: Service quality in sport tourism. *Journal of Services Marketing, 13*(6), 500–516.

Tkaczynski, A., & Rundle-Thiele, S. R. (2011). Event segmentation: A review and research agenda. *Tourism Management, 32*(2), 426–434.

Turner, R. S., & Rosentraub, M. S. (2002). Tourism, sports and the centrality of cities. *Journal of Urban Affairs, 24*(5), 487–492.

Um, S., Chon, K., & Ro, Y. (2006). Antecedents of revisit intention. *Annals of Tourism Research.*

Van der Graaf, A. J. (1994). Service quality and sport centers. *European Journal of Sport Management, 1*(1), 42–57.

Veltri, F. R., Miller, J. J., & Harris, A. (2009). Club sport national tournament: Economic impact of a small event on a mid-size community. *Recreational Sports Journal, 33*(2), 119–128.

Waitt, G. (2003). Social impacts of the Sydney Olympics. *Annals of Tourism Research, 30*(1), 194–215.

Wakefield, K. L., Blodgett, J. G., & Sloan, H. J. (1996). Measurement and management of the sportscape. *Journal of Sport Management, 10*(1), 15–31.

Wearing, B., & Wearing, S. (1996). Refocussing the tourist experience: The flaneur and the choraster. *Leisure studies, 15*(4), 229–243.

Whitson, D., & Macintosh, D. (1993). Becoming a world-class city: Hallmark events and sport franchises in the growth strategies of Western Canadian cities. *Sociology of Sport Journal, 10*(3), 221–240.

Williams, M. H. (1998). *The ergogenics edge: Pushing the limits of sports performance*. Human Kinetics Publishers.

Yoon, Y., & Uysal, M. (2005). An examination of the effects of motivation and satisfaction on destination loyalty: A structural model. *Tourism Management, 26*(1), 45–56.

Zeithaml, V. A., Parasuraman, A., & Berry, L. L. (1990). *Delivering quality service: Balancing customer perceptions and expectations*. Simon and Schuster.

Chapter 3
Sailboat Race Events: Exploring the Effects of a Regatta in the Balearic Islands

Francisco Rejón-Guardia, María Antonia García-Sastre and Margarita Alemany-Hormaeche

3.1 Introduction

The economic model of the Balearic Islands is based on the tourism industry. The figures from Exceltur in 2014 state that tourism accounted for 44.8% of the total GDP of the Balearic Islands, 32% of total employment in the Balearic Islands was attributed to employment in the tourism industry, and tourism activity accounted for 40.4% of the tax revenue levied in the Balearic Islands in 2014.

In 2016, the Balearic Islands welcomed more than 14 million visitors. However, before reaching this figure, the tourism activity has passed through the various stages, of Butler's theory of the development and evolution of a tourist destination Butler (1980). This theory perceives the tourist destination as a product which passes through six phases: exploration, involvement, development, consolidation, stagnation and decline. Each stage presents a series of characteristic features regarding demand, supply, commercialisation and competition. Butler's theory of the Tourist Area Life Cycle (TALC) (1980) is the most commonly used paradigm because it is the most complete model. It explains the development of tourist destinations, not only by the changes in the space, and the attitudes of both tourists and residents, but it also includes the history and composition of the visitors; the involvement of local stakeholders; the accessibility of the destination, and the competition. Despite the fact that Butler's model and the concept of the tourist area life cycle, are widely considered to be the most influential approach to the analysis of local tourism development,

F. Rejón-Guardia (✉) · M. A. García-Sastre · M. Alemany-Hormaeche
Department of Business & Economics, University of the Balearic Islands, Mallorca, Spain
e-mail: f.rejon@uib.es

M. A. García-Sastre
e-mail: garcia.sastre@uib.es

M. Alemany-Hormaeche
e-mail: marga.alemany@uib.es

© Springer Nature Switzerland AG 2019
A. Artal-Tur et al. (eds.), *Trends in Tourist Behavior*,
Tourism, Hospitality & Event Management,
https://doi.org/10.1007/978-3-030-11160-1_3

the model has not been exempt from criticism, adaptation and revision since its publication. The contributions made by Agarwal (1994, 2006) have provoked more profound reflexion. He observed that there is no evidence of the irreversible state of decline that Butler's model suggests, and confirms that measures have been taken by both private and public local initiative in order to strengthen the competitiveness of the mature destination, that is, to rejuvenate the destination in order to adapt it to market changes, and therefore proposes an intermediate phase of "reorientation".

The Balearic Islands as other mature destinations need to reposition themselves on the market with new products adapted to the new consumer demands of the XXI century. As a destination with the hegemonic status of sun and beach, the Balearic Islands require the promotion of a series of measures to ensure their dominant position in the international tourism context. Therefore, to this end, the public administration, together with the tourism industry, has implemented a series of tourism policies: urban redevelopment strategies for improving urban quality; product diversification strategies for singularization of the same destination offers for specific market segments closely related to sports, golf and cycling tourism; sustainability strategies aimed at expanding protected areas, and promotional strategies oriented towards generating markets which move more in accordance with the new image of reality.

One of the most important international events in the Balearic sports events calendar is the annual S.A.R. Princess Sofia Trophy sailing regatta. It has a long tradition, and in its 47th year in 2016, attracted almost one thousand sailing boats and 1,500 sailors to the Bay of Palma for the Trophy race. The S.A.R. Princess Sofia is among the seven best regattas in the world and has been part of the ISAF Sailing World Cup circuit since 2009.

This paper studies the profiles of the participants in the 47th annual S.A.R. Princess Sofía regatta, covering aspects such as socio-demographic variables, the description of the primary motivations to attend the event, the level of satisfaction of the sailors, and different segments of sportsmen and women participating in the race, with a view to developing marketing programmes adapted to the needs of the different groups taking part in the regatta. The study is organised in the following way: firstly, the topic is introduced, followed by a review of the literature on the subject of sports events, specifically regattas, and the use of motivations for market segmentation. It continues with a description of the method used. The findings are then analysed, and the principal theoretical conclusions are reached, along with their potential application within the framework of tourism in the Balearic Islands. Finally, limitations and future lines of research are presented.

3.2   Literature Review

The literature review focuses on the recommendations to manage mature and seasonal destinations; sports products as a tool to deseasonalize mature destinations; the usefulness of segmentation; and the analysis of motivations which characterize tourists.

3.2.1   Mature and Seasonal Destinations

The Balearic Islands are currently a combination of two circumstances: mature destination and seasonality. The recommendations set out in the literature on the evolutionary theory of TALC (Butler 1980), along with the contributions of Agarwal, would suggest that the Balearic Islands adopt measures in a reorientation phase to prevent the dreaded decline, and obtain a new competitive advantage which would allow the tourist area to reposition.

Agawarl's theory of productive restructuring (2006) points out the need to introduce corrective measures to avoid the effects of decline, which include both internal aspects related to the decrease in the competitiveness of the destination, and the external environment linked to the appearance of intense competition both nationally and internationally, in order to reorient resources and products towards current demand.

This new approach to coastal destinations has been analysed in different studies such as Antón Clavé (2004), Ávila and Gandara (2007), or Priestley and Mundet (1998), examining different tourism policies promoted in different territories. This paradigm of the management of tourist destinations requires the addition of sustainability to the desired competitiveness (Ritchie & Crouch, 2003), which is receiving attention, both from public administrations and numerous studies (Vera-Rebollo, 2001; Vera-Rebollo & Ivars-Baidal, 2003) internationally (Ko, 2005; Miller & Twining-Ward, 2005) and locally (Salom, Mas, Montaner, & Mateu, 2002; Sancho, Garcia, & Rozo, 2007) whose main objective is to make tourism use compatible with the preservation of the natural environment.

The Balearic Islands tourist destination has worked in recent years to curb its decline and reduce seasonality through its tourism policies. Among the strategies developed from the 1980s until the present day, activities geared towards the deseasonalisation of tourism activity through strategies of product diversification and differentiation have acquired particular importance. These measures encompass a range of areas of activity: strategies of urban restructuring; strategies of product restructuring and differentiation; strategies of sustainability and promotion of the destination.

According to the proposals in the latest Integral Plan for Tourism in the Balearic Islands (IPTBI), there is a commitment for the years 2016–2020 to the design of new tourism products to offer a broader range of products to lessen dependence on the well-known monoculture of sun and beach. Tourism proposals which do not depend on the weather; products targeted to very specific market segments related to sport, golf and cycling tourism; products related to recreational, nautical, and cruise tourism; segments involved with nature and local values, such as rural tourism, farmhouse tourism, inland tourism; and products related to professional activities such as congresses, meetings and incentive tourism. Sports products as seasonally-adjusted measures.

Strategies developed in mature tourist destinations since the eighties, especially coastal ones, have introduced the recreational aspect in order to diversify and differentiate the tourist offer (Antón Clavé, 2004). This recreational component is considered a catalyst for restructuring actions and singularization strategies, which are intended to maintain and retain demand, attract new segments, and increase tourist spending at the destination (Vera-Rebollo & Baños-Castiñeira, 2010).

The link between tourism and recreation is becoming one of the fundamental pillars of the tourism policy of the Balearic Islands for achieving deseasonalisation and extending the tourist season. The Balearic Islands enjoy a mild climate throughout the year, a privileged natural environment and strategic geolocation only two hours away from many major European cities. It is for these reasons that in the latest IPTBI, great attention has been paid to sports products for tourism, fundamentally: golf, nautical tourism, cycling tourism, hiking, athletics and track sports amongst others (Rejón-Guardia, García-Sastre, & Alemany-Hormaeche, 2017, 2018). Special mention must be made of golf, nautical, and cycling tourism products, as their contribution to the most recent tourist seasons has been extremely positive for the Balearic economy and the image of the destination, as will be seen below.

Golf as a tourism product is already strong and is becoming stronger. At present, the Balearic Islands have a total of 26 top class clubs, 49 hotels catering specifically for golfers, and international tournaments throughout the year. As an established product, golf generates an annual income of more than 160 million euros in the Balearic Islands. Nevertheless, it continues to be promoted widely, for example, in the Reheingolf fair in Düsseldorf, one of the most important fairs specialising in golf in the German and Dutch markets. This kind of tourism has two underlying characteristics of interest: an above average daily expenditure per tourist of €171.14 (Newman, 2011), above the average of €107.9 (IET, 2012); and that 74.5% of golfers prefer to play outside of the summer season (Garau-Vadell, 2008).

In the Balearic Islands, the sport of cycling, be it amateur or professional, is becoming very popular with many British and German tourists. With more than 1,400 km of routes with standardised road signage, a velodrome and 60 hotels catering specifically for cyclists; both amateur and professional competitions held annually, (Challenge Mallorca, Challenge Menorca, Vuelta Tour BTT Formentera, Cinturón Ciclista Vuelta Ciclista a Mallorca, Vuelta Cicloturista Internacional, Marcha Internacional Marcha Cicloturista Mallorca 312 Playa de Muro), the Balearic Islands have become an ideal place for the preseasons of both amateur and professional teams. Given the economic impact that 150,000 cycling tourists generate in destination, with one million overnight stays and almost 150 million euros per annum for the economy of the Balearic Islands, it is a product with great potential for deseasonalisation, since its activity is concentrated essentially from January to March and October to November: the low and mid-seasons in the Balearic Islands.

Another of the pillars upon which the new Tourism Policy of the Balearic Islands is supported is nature tourism. Citizens of large and medium metropolitan areas are increasingly demanding the opportunity to enjoy contact with the natural environment in a free, hedonistic and pleasurable way, and the Balearic Islands offer a multitude of natural resources: trails, mountains, mountain torrents, gorges, cliffs and coastline, suitable for all ages and permitting activity all year round. To facilitate these activities, the Balearic Islands have 432 hotels catering specifically for around 120,000 hikers (Ceballos, 2010).

Nautical tourism in the Balearic Islands is another example of an established product which is highly valued by tourists. The archipelago boasts excellent conditions and infrastructures for sailing: more than 1,400 km of coast, 69 marinas, 20,000 berths/moorings and six naval stations. It is host to international events and competitions such as: the S.A.R. Princess Sofía Trophy, the Copa del Rey and the Trofeo Almirante Conde de Barcelona in Mallorca; the Trofeo Nacional Almirante Ferragut de Snipes in Menorca; la Ruta de la Sal, and the International Sailing Week in Ibiza, to name but a few. Added to this sporting activity is the consolidation of the Balearic Islands as a port for the repair and maintenance of luxury recreational vessels from all over the world. The high purchasing power of nautical tourists and the high level of satisfaction of the nautical tourist in the Balearic Islands indicate that it is a very attractive type of tourism for improving competitiveness due to its average daily expenditure. For example, a yacht charter tourist spends an average of 170 euros, which is well above the average of 105 euros for tourists in the Balearic Islands (Alcover et al., 2011). In 2008, the recreational boating industry generated over 537 million euros, and the number of recreational boaters to the Islands was 324,522 (CITTIB, 2009). Moreover, in 2013, more than 2 million tourists arrived in the archipelago with the purpose of doing sport, representing around 15% of the total tourism. In low and mid-season, sports activity could reach more than 80% of tourists visiting the Islands, while in high season this is reduced to 10% due to the high temperatures.

3.2.2 Economic and Social Impact of Sporting Events

The celebration of sporting events is becoming a key instrument in the repositioning of the Balearic Islands tourist destination, due to its unquestionable ability to attract visitors outside the peak season and to curb the effects of seasonality.

Sporting events can be studied from a dual perspective: as physical activity, and as a revitalising stimulus for the economy of the host community. From the first perspective, the sports event is viewed as individual physical activity, generating considerable, well-known benefits related to the physical and mental health of participants (Herzog, Black, Fountaine, & Knotts, 1997; Maas, Verheij, & Groenewegen, 2006). The second perspective considers sports events as activities which produce considerable social and economic benefits for host communities. Studies show that sports events provide social and economic benefits, increased community and host community pride and spirit (Crompton & McKay, 1994; Thrane, 2002), and distribute spending among various sectors such as catering, transportation, lodging, entertainment and other support services (Crompton & McKay, 1994).

Most research on the impact of events on host communities has focused on mega-events or major sporting events (Añó-Sanz, Calabuig-Moreno, & Parra-Camacho, 2012; Parra-Camacho, Añó-Sanz, Calabuig-Moreno, & Ayora-Pérez 2016). Small- or medium-sized sporting events have traditionally received little attention in the literature, either internationally (Baade, Baumann, & Matheson, 2008; Pillay & Bass,

2008; Pulido-Fernández & Sánchez-Rivero, 2010; Sturgess & Brady, 2006; Waitt, 2003), or nationally (Año-Sanz et al., 2012; Barajas & Sanchez, 2011; Ramírez-Hurtado, Ordaz-Sanz, & Rueda-Cantuche, 2007). These studies analyse the economic impact of major sporting events.

However, in recent years sporting events have been considered as major economic driving forces, especially in medium-sized communities, which increasingly face the competition of communities bidding to host sporting events (Agha & Taks, 2015; Matheson, 2012; Taks, 2013; Veltri, Miller, & Harris, 2009). Some of the most important studies into the effects of small- or medium-sized events on host communities are those of (Baade et al., 2008; Barajas & Sanchez, 2011; Pillay & Bass, 2008; Sturgess & Brady, 2006; Veltri et al., 2009). Other contributions in this line of medium-scale events have been carried out by Ntloko and Swart (2008), Parra-Camacho, Calabuig-Moreno, Añó-Sanz, Ayora-Pérez, and Núñez Pomar (2014).

Marine tourism is a burgeoning sector of the tourism industry and is comprised of many sports. Of the many types of marine tourism, those of most strategic interest to the Balearic Islands are the regattas or sailboat races, because of their potential to reduce seasonality, and their positive economic impact on the regional economy. However, there has been little research into the impact of marine tourism on regional economies, with the exception of the study of Alcover et al. (2011), on the economic impact of charter boat activity, or studies on the impact of sports events such as the American Cup.

The present study analyses the profile of the participants, and the economic impact generated by the 47th S.A.R. Princess Sofia Trophy. This regatta is characterized as a small-scale event with a long tradition and high international impact. For the last 46 years, almost one thousand boats and some 1,500 athletes, including the top ten of each class, and European and Olympic champions representing up to 53 nations have gathered in the Bay of Palma, to participate in the race. For many of the competitors, this annual competition held in Mallorca is a qualifying event for the World Cup Series, and selective for the formation of their Olympic teams. The S.A.R. Princess Sofia Trophy has become a brand with its entity, and an emblem for Spanish and world sailing. It is considered among the best seven regattas in the world according to the ISAF Sailing World.

3.2.3 Segmentation

In addition to determining the profile of the sailors, the study undertakes a cluster analysis of the participants in the 47th annual S.A.R. Princess Sofia. Literature is examined regarding sports events, and the use of segmentation to identify more homogenous groups of sportsmen and women showing similar needs, desires and demographic profiles (Mullin, Hardy, & Sutton, 2000). For segmentation, demographic variables such as age are commonly used, however, behavioural variables such as previous experience are also used, dividing participants into first-timers or repeaters. Kruger, Botha, and Saayman (2012) indicate that it is beneficial to use frequency of participation as a variable of market segmentation. The categorisation that this segmentation allows, identifies two clearly distinct groups: first-timers are considered to be the new market, and repeaters the core market of the sporting event, necessitating and justifying the application of marketing tactics and specific programmes to each group (Filo, Funk, & O'Brien, 2008; Kaplanidou & Gibson, 2012; Um, Chon, & Ro, 2006; Wood, Snelgrove, & Danylchuk, 2010).

Motivation in the field of tourism has been approached from multiple perspectives. In general terms, Hodgetts and Altman (1991) understand motivation as a dynamic process linked to the impulse of action and subsequent execution. Motivations, understood as forces, usually manifest themselves as a result of an unmet need, thus generating an action (Cassar & Dias, 2005; Fodness, 1994; Mowen, 2000). Cassar and Dias (2005) point out the existence of generic motivations, which affect all tourists equally, such as an escape from daily routine, a reward for work done, a way of liberation from convention and a contribution to the development of spiritual values.

The traditional theory of motivations in tourism differentiate between push and pull motivations (Dann, 1977). Push motivations are considered to be intrinsic to the individual and pull motivations related to positive attitudes towards specific attributes of the destination. Push would explain the desire to travel, and pull would explain the selection of the destination (Crompton, 1979). The push factors are related to intangible and inherent issues to the traveller, such as the desire to escape, rest, have adventures or prestige; whereas pull motivations are related to tangible or intangible attractions offered by a destination (Uysal & Hagan, 1993).

The scientific literature shows that some motivations for sports tourism are common to general tourist motivations, such as recovery, escape from routine and self-determination (Suárez-Acosta, Zoghbi Manrique de Lara, & Aguiar-Quintana, 2013). To these, other specific motivations for sports tourist must be added, such as the need to compete, the desire to win and the opportunity to develop better levels of skill and dexterity (Weed & Bull, 2012).

3.3   Methodology

An online, self-administered questionnaire was the instrument used for primary data collection. After a preliminary review of the literature, the questionnaire was developed and refined following a pilot study held in January 2016. The questionnaire consisted of four major sections, composed of 48 mainly closed-ended questions addressing various aspects of the regatta. The first section assessed behaviourally-oriented variables, such as the choice of the sailing boat race, the purpose of the visit, the number of accompanying persons, length of stay and amount of expenditure. The second section of the questionnaire measured motivation for choosing the sports destination using twelve items developed for the study. The third section evaluated previous experience and levels of satisfaction. The final section examined the demographic characteristics of respondents. The questionnaire was provided in

Spanish and English and delivered by e-mail from March to April 2016. Respondents were selected opportunistically from the 1,010 participants in the 47th annual S.A.R. Princess Sofia Trophy held in Mallorca, from 25th March to 2nd April 2016. A total of 144 participants responded (response rate 14.26%).

The results of the study combine different methodologies. A descriptive analysis was used for the socio-demographic description of the sample, and for the analysis of the results of motivation and satisfaction of the participants, which were obtained from questions with a Likert-5 scale response. For the estimation of the economic impact, a basic model of five factors was used. Finally, to determine the profile of the sailors, a cluster analysis of the participants in the 47th annual S.A.R. Princess Sofia was conducted.

3.4 Results

3.4.1 Socio-demographic Description

The study sample was composed of 66.7% males and 31.9% females. Half of the sample consisted of individuals under 24 years of age (50.7%), followed by 25–30 years (15.5%), 31–40 years (14.1%) and 43 years or more (19.7%). Their place of residence was predominantly Southern Europe (27.8%), Western Europe (25.7%), and Northern Europe (16.7%). Other Countries (16%) and Eastern Countries (12.5%) were less represented. Most of the sample were highly educated, with 66% having college or university education, 28% high school education, with 1% having only completed elementary school; 3% with vocational training, and 2% other studies. The most used means of transport to reach the destination was boat and car (49.3%), followed by plane (45.1%). 53.2% of the sample were accommodated in a rented house or apartment, 39.7% in a hotel or aparthotel, and only 2.8% percent at home or a friend´s home. Among the parallel activities carried out by the participants in the regatta and their guests, the majority (39.6%) did other sports activities (golf, hiking, biking), discovered the local cuisine and gastronomy (19.4%), enjoyed the sun and beach (13.2%), nightlife (8.3%) or cultural activities (4.2%). 22.52% of tourists declared it to be their first time participating in the race, 12.61% their second time, 18.92% had participated three or four times, and the remaining participants had done so five times or more (17.12%).

The average length of stay was 18.22 days. Only 4.6% stayed for less than a week, 44% stayed between one and two weeks, 28.4% for two to three weeks and 4.6% for three to four weeks. The rest (18.3%) remained on the island between one and two months to train and prepare for the competition (Table 3.1).

Table 3.1 Demographic profile of respondent (n = 144)

Variable	Categories	%
Gender	Male	66.7
	Female	31.9
	N/A	1.4
Age	<24	50.7
	25–30	15.5
	31–40	14.1
	>43	19.7
Region of origin	Southern Europe	27.8
	Western Europe	25.7
	Northern Europe	16.7
	Other countries	16
	Eastern countries	12.5
	N/A	1.3
Level of education	Elementary school, vocational training	6.3
	High school	25.7
	University	66.7
	N/A	1.3
Means of transport	Boat and car	49.3
	Plane	45.1
	N/A	5.6
Accommodation	Hotel	39.7
	Rented house/apartment	53.2
	Home/friend's home	2.8
	N/A	4.3
Parallel or leisure activities	Sports activities	39.6
	Local cuisine and gastronomy	19.4
	Sun and beach	13.2
	Nightlife	8.3
	Cultural activities	4.2
First-time versus repetition	First time	22.52
	Second time	12.61
	Third time	18.92
	Fourth time	17.12
	Fifth time or more	28.83

(continued)

Table 3.1 (continued)

Variable	Categories	%
Length of stay	Less than 1 week	4.6
	From 1 to 2 weeks	44
	From 2 to 3 weeks	28.4
	From 3 to 4 weeks	4.6
	From 1 to 2 months	18.3

Source Own elaboration

3.4.2 Motivation Analysis

In order to ascertain the levels of motivation, questions were asked about the level of importance of various items when choosing the 47th annual S.A.R. Princess Sofia, using the Likert five-point scale. It should be noted that the dates chosen by the organization to hold the race were rated 3.77 out of 5 points, and the quality of the services offered scored 3.65 points. These were followed by the cost of the trip (3.55), good connections with the destination (Mallorca) (3.35), meteorology (3.29), and the recommendations of experts and journals (2.2).

3.4.3 Satisfaction Analysis

A fundamental objective of any study of tourism products is to ascertain the level of satisfaction of the tourist with their stay, and of different aspects of the same. In this case, the level of satisfaction was analysed from two perspectives: that of the destination, and that of the organization of the sporting event. Of the aspects relating to the destination, the highest scores were: quality of beaches and water (3.74), attractiveness of the coast (3.70), hospitality of residents (3.66), navigation conditions (3.64), meteorology (3.60), quality of restaurants and supermarkets (3.60), entertainment and leisure (3.58), good connections with Mallorca (3.56), and quality of the hotel (3.50). The lowest scores were given to private transportation (3.40), and the price level (3.26). Regarding the base port, aspects related to the welcome and reception (3.65), infrastructure and facilities (3.51), navigation information (3.40), organized complementary activities (3.23), repair and maintenance (3.15) and additional services (2.92) were highlighted.

3.4.4   General Economic Impact

Events can contribute to the tourist development of a city and benefit its inhabitants and companies. However, in order to design events correctly, it is necessary to understand which characteristics determine their economic impact. This research aims to contribute to this understanding by estimating the expenditure made by the participants and their accompanying party to estimate the economic impact. A basic model of five factors was adopted: (1) number of participants (sailors and coaches), (2) average cost per participant, (3) average stay per participant, (4) average expenditure on equipment, (5) expense incurred through the visits received by the participants in the race.

The exact number of sailors, coaches and teams of participants were provided through the collaboration of the organization of the 47th annual S.A.R. Princess Sofia. Secondly, the amounts and items of expenditure of the sailors, coaches and teams were obtained through a survey, as was the data related to the accommodation used and the length of stay. The average expenditure per team was obtained from the information provided by the coaches. Finally, the average expenditure made by the tourists (both sailors and accompanying parties) during the month of the race was estimated.

Taking into account the above considerations, the overall economic impact was estimated at 8,612,996 euros, generated by: the sailors (3,236,666 euros), the visits of friends and family received by the sailors (2,653,862 euros), the coaches (1,459,086 euros), the visits of family and friends received by the coaches (294,248 euros) and the expenditure incurred by the coaches on behalf of their teams (1,1014,133 euros).

3.4.5   Participants Cluster Analysis

A cluster analysis was employed to classify subjects into mutually exclusive groups by the Ward method using the K-means clustering procedure. The results of the cluster analysis indicate that a three-cluster solution appeared to be appropriate. More specifically, multivariate statistics indicate that statistically significant differences existed between the three clusters at $p < 0.001$. To create the clusters, the categorical variables of experience of the regatta, age, total expenditure, and time spent at the destination in weeks were used. Table 3.2 shows Cluster 1, ($n_3 = 57$; 41.3%), *moderately experienced*: a group having participated in the regatta on two to five occasions (100%), mainly under 24-year-olds (75.4%), spending less than 1,500 euros (35.1%), and spending two weeks at the destination (42.1%). Cluster 2, ($n_2 = 41$; 29.7%), *less experienced*: group participating for the first time (63.4%), mainly under 24-year-olds (63.4%), spending less than 1,500 euros (43.9%), and spending two weeks at the destination (43.9%). Cluster 3, ($n_1 = 40$; 29%) *more experienced*: group having participated in the regatta six times or more (72.5%), composed mainly of 46-year-olds or over (47.5%), spending more than 4,001 euros (47.5%), and mostly spending two weeks at the destination (37.5%).

Table 3.2 K-means cluster analysis

Variables	Cluster 1 Moderately experienced ($n_3 = 57; 41.3\%$)	Cluster 2 Less experienced ($n_2 = 41; 29.7\%$)	Cluster 3 More experienced ($n_1 = 40; 29\%$)
Experience of the regatta	Participated on 2–5 occasions (100%)	Participating for the first time (63.4%)	Participated six times or more (72.5%)
Age	Young people under 24 (75.4%)	Young people under 24 (63.4%),	People aged 46 and over (47.5%)
Total expenditure	Less than 1,500 euros (35.1%)	Less than 1,500 euros (43.9%)	More than 4,001 euros (47.5%)
Length of stay (in weeks)	2 weeks at destination (42.1%)	2 weeks at destination (43.9%)	2 weeks at destination (37.5%)

Source Own elaboration

3.4.6 Participant Differences: The Role of Previous Experience of the Event and Total Expenditure

The effect of experience of the event, number of participations in recent years, and their influence on the total expenditure at the destination were evaluated. Significant differences were observed between those attending the event for the first time, as opposed to those with more experience who had attended more than seven times ($F(1) = 5,445; p < 0.05$). Expenditure was considerably higher for the more experienced ($n_{first\ time} = 28; n_{first\ time} = 2750.14\ € < n_{+7\ times} = 29; n_{+7\ times} = 4598.38\ €$) (post hoc Fisher's least significant difference $LSD_{(J–I)} = 1848,245; s.e = 804,132; p = 0.023$). The analysis revealed the existence of significant differences between those who had attended the event between 2 and 4 times, and those who had attended more than 7 times ($n_{2–4\ times} = 60; _{2–4\ times} = 3197,59 < n_{+7\ times} = 29; _{+7\ times} = 4598.38$) (post hoc LSD mean difference$_{(J–I)} = 1400,795; s.e = 686,417; p = 0.043$). Consequently, it can be stated that the experience of participating in the event increased the total expenditure at the destination. This result could have significant implications for the management of sailing events.

3.5 Conclusion and Implications

In order to mitigate the adverse effects of seasonality, one of the leading lines of investigation by the autonomous community of the Balearic Islands has been, and continues to be, into the development of a wide range of tourism products, whether complementary or alternative to the traditional sun and beach tourism. The tourism and sports binomial are proving to be a good incentive for the off-season for the Baleares. The use of sporting events is becoming a key instrument to reposition the Balearics as a tourist destination, attracting visitors outside of high season, and reducing the effects of seasonality.

The Balearic Islands have long been considered a popular destination for sailing, and a world-renowned centre for repair and maintenance of luxury recreational sailboats. The high purchasing power, coupled with the high level of satisfaction of nautical tourists, indicate that it is an attractive type of tourism to improve competitiveness, as well as the average income generated per tourist.

The review of the literature highlights how sports events revitalize the economy of the locality hosting the event, as well as the social benefits for the host communities. Given that the literature has shown more significant interest in large events, generally overlooking the impact of small- or medium-sized events, the present study has focused on the evaluation of an event of small size, but with an international projection.

The present study has analyzed the profile of the participants in, and the economic impact generated by the 47th annual S.A.R. Princess Sofia Trophy, characterized as a small-scale event but which has a high international impact. The research aims to contribute by estimating the expenditure of the participants in the regatta and their accompanying parties, in order to estimate the economic impact of the event. The 47th annual S.A.R. Princess Sofia Trophy, held during the month of March–April 2016 represented a significant global economic impact of 8,612,996 euros for the city of Palma.

From the analysis of the sample of participants at the nautical event, two large groups stand out: mostly men, under 24 or 43 and over; coming from the south and west of Europe, with a university education, staying in a rented house or apartment, or hotel or aparthotel; the majority of whom took part in other sports activities besides sailing. Most tourists reported having participated for the second time or more than three times. The average length of stay was more than eighteen days; most respondents declared spending between one and two weeks at the destination. The main motivations for participation in the event were, in order of declared importance: the dates of completion of the event, the quality of the services offered, the cost of the trip and the good transport connections with Mallorca. The analysis of levels of satisfaction represents a useful tool for management of tourism destinations, as it allows for control over the measures taken and the gathering of feedback to establish future lines of action. The satisfaction analysis revealed the highest scoring aspects to be: beaches and water quality, attractiveness of the coast, hospitality of residents, navigation conditions, and meteorology. Regarding the base port, aspects related to the welcome and reception, infrastructure and facilities, navigation information, organized complementary activities, repair and maintenance were highlighted, with additional services in last position.

One of the objectives of the study was to determine whether there are differences between sailboat racing participants regarding socio-demographic variables, aspects of the trip, and expenditure. The main conclusions of the study indicate that socio-demographic and behavioural variables reveal three major segments: moderately experienced, less experienced, and more experienced. Those who spend more at the destination correspond to those who have participated more often in the regatta and who are older, as opposed to those who spend the least at the destination, comprised of individuals participating in the event for the first time.

A cluster analysis was employed, the results of which indicate that a three-cluster solution appeared to be appropriate, the moderately experienced group (n = 57) a group which had participated in the regatta on two to five occasions, were mainly under 24-year-olds, spending less than 1,500 euros, and staying two weeks at the destination. The less experienced group (n = 41), participating for the first time, were mainly under 24-year-olds, spending less than 1,500 euros, and spending two weeks at the destination. The more experienced group (n = 40), was composed of mainly 46-year-olds or over, spending more than 4,001 euros, and mostly spending two weeks at the destination. Furthermore, the effect of experience of the event (number of participations in recent years) and its influence on the total expenditure at destination was evaluated. Significant differences were observed between those attending the event for the first time as opposed to those with more experience who declared having attended more than seven times. Expenditure was considerably higher for the more experienced. The analysis revealed the existence of significant differences between those who had attended the event between 2 and 4 times, and those who had attended more than 7 times. Consequently, it can be stated that the experience of participating in the event increased the total expenditure at the destination.

It was concluded that small- and medium-sized sports events, such as the regatta in question, could contribute to the reduction of the effects of seasonality, and to the improvement of the economic and social revitalisation for host cities, significantly in events held during the months of lower tourism activity. The analysis of the participants in the 47th annual S.A.R. Princess Sofia race, and the analysis of motivations and levels of satisfaction should contribute towards improving the efficiency and effectiveness of the organisation of future events. This type of event, with international participation and global media coverage, could help to reposition the Balearic destination and offer alternative products to the hegemonic sun and beach.

In order to promote a tourist destination through its suitability for sailing, emphasis must be placed on the motivations which lead sailing tourists to choose a particular destination. The results of this study have shown that sailing sports tourism is heterogenous, and they could be used to develop business strategies aimed at improving the marketing of the segments identified. As a sports activity, sailing races can be used as a pull factor in tourism.

As with all research, this study has limitations which could serve as the basis for further research. One of the main limitations of the study is that the sample analysed is only composed of sailors in one regatta in the Balearic Islands. This means that the results obtained in terms of the characteristics and motivations of nautical tourists when choosing a nautical tourism destination may be difficult to extrapolate. For future research, the size of the study sample should be increased, and observations taken throughout the whole year and across different events.

References

Agarwal, S. (1994). *The resort cycle revisited: Implications for resorts*. In C. P. Coope & A. Lockwood (Eds.), *Progress in tourism, recreation and hospitality management* (pp. 194–208).

Agarwal, S. (2006). Restructuring seaside tourism: The resort lifecyle. In R. Bulter (Ed.), *The tourism area life cycle: Conceptual and theoretical issues* (Vol. 2, pp. 201–218.). Clevendon, Channel View: Elsevier.

Agha, N., & Taks, M. (2015). A theoretical comparison of the economic impact of large and small events. *Internatioanl Journal of Sport Finance, 10*(3), 199–216.

Alcover, A., Alemany, M., Jacob, M., Payeras, M., García, A., & Martínez-Ribes, L. (2011). The economic impact of yacht charter tourism on the Balearic economy. *Tourism Economics, 17*(3), 625–638.

Añó Sanz, V., Calabuig Moreno, F., & Parra Camacho, D. (2012). Impacto social de un gran evento deportivo: el Gran Premio de Europa de Fórmula 1. *Cultura, Ciencia y Deporte, 7*(19), 53–65.

Antón Clavé, S. (2004). De los procesos de diversificación y cualificación a los productos turísticos emergentes. Cambios y oportunidades en la dinámica reciente del turismo litoral. *Papeles de Economía Española, 102,* 316–333.

Ávila, M. A., & Gandara, J. M. G. (2007). Oportunidades y propues-tas para la diversificación de un tradicional destino de sol y playa a un destino de ocio activo: un análisis de la ciudad de Florianópolis-Brasil. In *Turismo en los espacios litorales: sol, playa y turismo residencial/9° Congreso de Turismo, Universidad y Empresa* (pp. 221–259).

Baade, R. A., Baumann, R., & Matheson, V. A. (2008). Selling the game: Estimating the economic impact of professional sports through taxable sales. *Southern Economic Journal, 74*(3), 794–810.

Barajas, A., & Sanchez, P. (2011). Aplicación del análisis coste-beneficio (ACB) al Campeonato de España de Natación Master 2011. I Gijón Workshop de Economía del Deporte: El Impacto Económico en el Deporte, Gijón, Universidad de Oviedo.

Butler, R. (1980). The concept of a tourist area cycle of evolution: Implications for management of resources. *The Canadian Geographer/Le Géographe, 24*(1), 5–12.

Cassar, M., & Dias, R. (2005). *Fundamentos do marketing turístico*. São Paulo.

Ceballos, G. (2010). *Estudio sobre el Turismo de Montaña en España*. Madrid: Turespaña.

CITTIB, & Centro de Promoción de la Investigación y las Tecnologías Turísticas. (2009). *Tourism in the Balearic Islands, Yearbook 2008* (Centro de.). Conselleria de Turismo, Govern de les Illes Balears (2009).

Crompton, J. L. (1979). Motivations for pleasure vacation. *Annals of Tourism Research, 6*(4), 408–424.

Crompton, J., & McKay, S. (1994). Measuring the economic impact of festivals and events: Some myths, misapplications and ethical dilemmas. *Festival Management and Event, 2*(1), 33–43.

Dann, G. M. S. (1977). Anomie, ego-enhancement and tourism. *Annals of Tourism Research, 4*(4), 184–194.

Exceltur. (2014). Impactur 2014. Retrieved from http://www.exceltur.org/wp-content/uploads/2015/10/IMPACTUR-Baleares-2014-informe-completo.pdf.

Filo, K. R., Funk, D. C., & O'Brien, D. (2008). It's really not about the bike: Exploring attraction and attachment to the events of the Lance Armstrong Foundation. *Journal of Sport Management, 22*(5), 501–525.

Fodness, D. (1994). Measuring tourist motivation. *Annals of tourism research, 21*(3), 555–581.

Garau-Vadell, J. B. (2008). *El Turismo del golf en las Islas Baleares* (Govern de les Illes Balears, Ed.). Palma.

Herzog, T. R., Black, A. M., Fountaine, K. A., & Knotts, D. J. (1997). Reflection and attentional recovery as distinctive benefits of restorative environments. *Journal of environmental psychology, 17*(2), 165–170.

Hodgetts, R. M., & Altman, S. (1991). *Organizational behavior*: Theory and practice. Merrill.

Iet, I. D. E. T. (2012). Balance del turismo año 2011. Resultado de la actividad Turística en España, 112.

Kaplanidou, K., & Gibson, H. (2012). Differences between first time and repeat spectator tourists of a youth soccer event: Intentions and image approaches. *Current Issues in Tourism, 15*(5), 477–487.

Ko, T. G. (2005). Development of a tourism sustainability assessment procedure: A conceptual approach. *Tourism Management, 26*(3), 431–445.

Kruger, M., Botha, K., & Saayman, M. (2012). The relationship bet-ween visitor spending and repeat visits: An analysis of spectators at the Old Mutual Two Oceans Marathon. Acta Commercii.

Maas, J., Verheij, R., & Groenewegen, P. (2006). Green space, urbanity, and health: How strong is the relation? *Journal of Epidemiology and Community Health, 60*(7), 587–592.

Matheson, V. (2012). Assessing the infrastructure impact of mega-events in emerging economies. (N°. 1203). *College of the Holy Cross*, Department of Economics.

Miller, G., & Twining-Ward, L. (2005). *Monitoring for a sustainable tourism transition: The challenge of developing and using indicators*. Cabi.

Mowen, J. C. (2000). *The 3M model of motivation and personality: Theory and empirical applications to consumer behavior*. Springer Science & Business Media.

Mullin, B. J., Hardy, S., & Sutton, W. A. (2000). *Sport marketing* (2nd ed.). Champaign, IL: Human Kinetics.

NewMan, A. (2011). *Estudio de mercado. Campos de golf en España*. Departamento de análisis e investigación de mercados). The world of property. Madrid: Aguirre Newman.

Ntloko, N. J., & Swart, K. (2008). Sport tourism event impacts on the host community a case study of Red Bull Big Wave Africa. *South African Journal for Research in Sport, Physical Education and Recreation, 30*(2), 79–93.

Parra Camacho, D., Calabuig Moreno, F., Añó Sanz, V., Ayora Pérez, D., & Núñez Pomar, J. M. (2014). El impacto de un evento deportivo mediano: percepción de los residentes de la comunidad de acogida. *Retos. Nuevas tendencias en Educación Física, Deporte y Recreación, 26*, 88–93.

Parra-Camacho, D., Añó-Sanz, V., Calabuig-Moreno, F., & Ayora-Pérez, D. (2016). Percepción de los residentes sobre el legado de la America's Cup. *Cuadernos de Psicología del Deporte, 16*(1), 325–338.

Pillay, U., & Bass, O. (2008). *Mega-events as a response to poverty reduction: The 2010 FIFA World Cup and its urban development implications*. Urban Forum.

Priestley, G., & Mundet, L. (1998). The poststagnation phase of the resort cycle. *Annals of tourism research, 25*(1), 85–111.

Pulido-Fernández, J. I., & Sánchez-Rivero, M. (2010). Attitudes of the cultural tourist: A latent segmentation approach. *Journal of Cultural Economics, 34*(2), 111–129.

Ramírez Hurtado, J. M., Ordaz Sanz, J. A., & Rueda Cantuche, J. M. (2007). Evaluación del impacto económico y social de la celebración de grandes eventos deportivos a nivel local: el caso del Campeonato de Tenis femenino de la ITF en Sevilla en 2006. *Revista de Métodos Cuantitativos para la Economía y la Empresa, 3*(3), 20–39.

Rejón-Guardia, F., García-Sastre, M. A., & Alemany-Hormaeche, M. (2017). Hikers as cultural tourists: Differences between hard and soft behaviours. *Anatolia, 29*(2), 267–277.

Rejón-Guardia, F., García-Sastre, M. A., & Alemany-Hormaeche, M. (2018). Motivation-based behaviour and latent class segmentation of cycling tourists: A study of the Balearic Islands. *Tourism Economics, 24*(2), 204–217.

Ritchie, J. R. B., & Crouch, G. I. (2003). *The competitive destination: A sustainable tourism perspective*. Cabi.

Salom, M. B., Mas, I. M., Montaner, J. M. G., & Mateu, C. A. (2002). *El tercer boom: indicadors de sostenibilitat del turisme de les Illes Balears 1989–1999*. Centre dInvestigació i Tecnologies Turístiques de les Illes Balears (CITTIB).

Sancho, A., Garcia, G., & Rozo, E. (2007). Comparativa de indicadores de sostenibilidad para destinos desarrollados, en desarrollo y con poblaciones vulnerables. *Annals of Tourism Research, 9*(1), 150–177.

Sturgess, B., & Brady, C. (2006). *Hosting the FIFA World Cup*. World Economics.

Suárez Acosta, M. Á., Manrique, Zoghbi, de Lara, P., & Aguiar Quin-tana, T. (2013). Motivación del turista hacia la práctica de deportes náuticos: un estudio en el destino turístico de Gran Ca-naria. *Revista de análisis turístico, 15,* 37–48.

Taks, M. (2013). Social sustainability of nonmega sport events in a global world 1. *European Journal for Sport and Society, 10*(2), 121–141.

Thrane, C. (2002). Music quality, satisfaction, and behavioral intentions within a jazz festival context. *Event Management, 7*(3), 143–150.

Um, S., Chon, K., & Ro, Y. (2006). Antecedents of revisit intention. *Annals of Tourism Research, 33*(4), 1141–1158.

Uysal, M., & Hagan, L. A. R. (1993). Motivation of pleasure travel and tourism. *Encyclopedia of Hospitality and Tourism*, 798, 810.

Veltri, F. R., Miller, J. J., & Harris, A. (2009). Club sport national tournament: Economic impact of a small event on a mid-size community. *Recreational Sports Journal, 33*(2), 119–128.

Vera-Rebollo, J. F. (2001). Planificación y gestión del desarrollo turístico sostenible: propuestas para la creación de un sistema de indicadores. *Working paper – Instituto Universitario de Geografía*, Universidad de Alicante, n°1, 75.

Vera-Rebollo, J. F., & Baños Castiñeira, C. J. (2010). Renovación y reestructuración de los destinos turísticos consolidados del litoral: las prácticas recreativas en la evolución del espacio turístico. *Boletín de la Asociación de Geógrafos Españoles, 53*(2), 329–353.

Vera-Rebollo, J. F., & Ivars-Baidal, J. (2003). Sistema de indicadores aplicado a la planificación y gestión del desarrollo turístico sostenible. In *Experiencias públicas y privadas en el desarrollo de un modelo de turismo sostenible* (pp. 105–129).

Waitt, G. (2003). Social impacts of the Sydney Olympics. *Annals of Tourism Research, 30*(1), 194–215.

Weed, M., & Bull, C. (2012). *Sports tourism: Participants, policy and providers*. Routledge.

Wood, L., Snelgrove, R., & Danylchuk, K. (2010). Segmenting volunteer fundraisers at a charity sport event. *Journal of Non-profit & Public Sector Marketing, 22*(1), 38–54.

Chapter 4
Tourists' City Trip Activity Program Planning: A Personalized Stated Choice Experiment

Astrid Kemperman, Theo Arentze and Petr Aksenov

4.1 Introduction

Cities are important destinations for tourists. Nowadays, new digital technologies support tourists in planning their city trips (e.g., Buhalis, 1998; Rodriguez, Molina, Perez, & Caballero, 2012; Steen Jacobsen & Munar, 2012). Specifically, a personalised recommender system can assist a tourist who wants to make a tour that comprises a scheduled list of activities and points of specific interest (POIs; e.g., museums, heritage sites, shops, parks) as well as the trips needed to travel from one point to the other (e.g., Gretzel, Mitsche, Hwang, & Fesenmaier, 2004). To generate useful program recommendations the system must use information about specific needs, preferences, and budget constraints the tourist may have regarding the content and duration of their trip. In commonly used approaches, the recommendation of activities is based on a ranking of points of interests with the more advanced systems taking into account personal interests of the tourist (e.g., Yeh & Cheng, 2015). However, a selection based on separate evaluations of interest points, even if personal interests are accounted for does not necessarily result in a most preferred program (e.g., Gibson & Yiannakis, 2002; Vansteenwegen, Souffriau, Vanden Berghe, & Van Oudheusden, 2011).

A. Kemperman (✉) · T. Arentze · P. Aksenov
Eindhoven University of Technology, Urban Systems & Real Estate,
P.O. Box 513, 5600MB Eindhoven, The Netherlands
e-mail: a.d.a.m.kemperman@tue.nl

T. Arentze
e-mail: t.a.arentze@tue.nl

P. Aksenov
e-mail: paksenov@gmail.com

© Springer Nature Switzerland AG 2019
A. Artal-Tur et al. (eds.), *Trends in Tourist Behavior*,
Tourism, Hospitality & Event Management,
https://doi.org/10.1007/978-3-030-11160-1_4

Therefore, to develop a smart system that can give tourists an optimized complete activity program for their trip, we do not only need to know the preferences and interests of tourists but also whether they like combinations of activities/POIs or not. Thus, the recommender system should be able to suggest and present a program that is related to the selection and sequence of activities and POIs to follow. The aim of this study is to measure and predict tourists' preferences for combinations of activities in planning a program during a city trip.

A personalized stated choice experiment is developed and presented in an online survey to a random sample of a Dutch national panel. Subsequently, binary mixed logit models are estimated on the choice data collected. An advantage of this discrete choice modeling approach is that it allows estimation of covariances between city trip activities indicating whether they would act as complements or substitutes for a specific tourist in his/her city trip activity program for the day.

4.2   Related Work and Approach

In this section, to provide background information for our study, we review existing work in the areas of Travel Recommender Systems (TRS) and discrete choice analysis of user preferences. Our purpose is not to offer an extensive overview of these fields. Extensive recent reviews of the TRS literature can be found in Borras, Moreno, and Valls (2014) and Gavalas, Konstantopolous, Mastakas, and Pantziou (2014), and reviews of discrete choice analysis in tourism research in Crouch and Louviere (2000), Baltas (2007) and Morley (2014). Our purpose here is to indicate how our work is positioned in this literature.

The goal of TRS is to overcome the information overload that tourists experience when they search for travel and activity options for a trip. The systems are designed to offer personalized information by recommending points of interests (POIs) or services that match the personal preferences of the user. An ability to assess the personal preferences of a user, therefore, is an important component of the systems. Several methods have been used in TRSs for that purpose. Filtering methods generally assume that preferences for POIs are represented in the form of preference ratings of attractions or services offered. If so-called collaborative filtering is used, recommendations are based on the ratings that similar users have assigned to the POI before. If a contents-based filtering method is used, a user has provided information on his or her preferences for particular attributes and the system recommends POIs that match those preferences. Knowledge-based approaches have also received attention, especially, to overcome the so-called cold-start problem of collaborative and content-based filtering methods. If a knowledge-based approach is used, recommendations are derived based on reasoning about what items meet the user's requirements.

TRSs that use filtering methods are focused on the recommendation of city attractions (museums, archeological sites, churches etc.) or services (restaurant, hotel, transportation services etc.) as single items. Other TRSs focus on tourists that visit a city or another tourist destination and wish to make a day or multiple-day tour combining several POIs. These TRSs consider the problem of recommending a complete set of POIs as a program for a tour (e.g., an itinerary). In determining an activity program for a tour, routing characteristics and time and monetary budgets for the tour need to be taken into account as well. The problem of finding an optimal activity program is known as the Tourist Trip Design (TTD) problem (Wörndl & Hefele, 2017). In TRSs, the problem is typically solved in two steps. In the first step, the POIs that are of interest to the user are selected using a filtering method. In the second step, a combinatory algorithm is used to find the optimum sequence of visiting the locations and the point-to-point travel routes. Advanced systems take opening and closing times of attractions, multi-modal travel and the time tables of public transport into account (Aksenov, Kemperman, & Arentze 2014, 2016). Wörndl and Hefele (2016, 2017) provide an extensive overview of TRSs that consider the TTD problem.

In this study the focus is on the TTD problem and, more specifically, on the estimation of tourists' preferences for activity programs of a (city) tour. As reviewed in Wörndl and Hefele (2017), existing TRSs generally assume minimizing travel costs or maximizing a sum profit score across POIs as objective function for solving the TTD problem. Existing theories of tourist behavior indicate, however, that interactions may exist in preferences between activities that are combined on a trip, which suggests that a more refined objective function is needed. For example, as emphasized in recreation specialization theories (Bryan, 1977), a tourist may seek a very specific experience that can be realized by highlighting a particular theme in the selection of POIs (e.g., select the sites that highlight a particular architectural style). On the other hand, novelty seeking and variety seeking have been recognized as important drivers of tourists' choice behavior (Dellaert, Arentze, & Horeni 2013; Kemperman, Borgers, Oppewal, & Timmermans 2000; Nicolau 2010). If variety seeking rather than specialization is the dominant drive, the tourist would prefer a mix of diverse experiences (e.g., a museum and botanic garden) rather than a single specific experience. Although outcomes are different, both specialization and variety-seeking tendencies are about preferences defined on the level of combinations of activities rather than the separate items. If these tendencies play a role, current objective functions of TRSs should be extended to take into account interactions between activities.

Discrete choice analysis is a well-known method to estimate individuals' preferences. This method makes use of carefully designed choice experiments where individuals are asked to indicate their preferences in hypothetical choice situations. By systematically varying the attributes of the (hypothetical) choice alternatives presented the implicit preferences for attributes can be derived from the responses by statistical analysis. Preference values estimated in this way reveal how individuals value particular attributes of choice options. The discrete choice analysis method is also known as conjoint analysis or stated preference. It is well-known in tourism research. Many applications have been described in studies of tourists' choice of destination (e.g., Andrada, Rogelio, Deng, Pierskalla, & Brooks, 2014; Jeng & Fesenmaier, 1998; Nicolau & Más, 2006; Oppewal, Huybers, & Crouch, 2010), hotel accommodation (e.g., Huertas-Garcia, Laguna García, & Consolación, 2008; Román

& Martin, 2016), travel itinerary (e.g., Tsaur & Wu, 2005), transport mode (e.g., Hergesell & Dickinger, 2013) and combinations of travel choices (e.g., Grigolon, Kemperman, & Timmermans, 2012).

In the present study, we use discrete choice analysis, specifically, a binary mixed logit model, to estimate tourist's activity programming preferences for day trips to a city. We are particularly interested in estimating preferences for combinations of activities that relate to possible tendencies ranging from specialization to variety seeking. To estimate the preferences we collect choice data using a personalized stated choice experiment in a survey held among a large random sample of individuals. This study is complementary to an earlier study of the authors (Arentze, Kemperman, & Aksenov, 2018) where the focus was on how individuals make trade-offs between travel costs, time-use characteristics and attraction values of POIs in preferences for activity programs in city trips. Together with the previously obtained estimates, the results of the present study should allow the specification a complete user model for activity program recommendation.

4.3 A Personalized Stated Choice Experiment

A personalized stated choice experiment was developed to measure tourists' preferences for combinations of activities during a city trip. Note, that each activity in itself is a combination of a POI and a specific theme. In most tourist choice related research, generic static stated choice experiments are used. In these studies respondents are presented with hypothetical alternatives and they are asked to indicate their preferences for these alternatives or choose between a set of alternatives. These alternatives are described by a number of attribute levels and are created based on an experimental design (e.g., Hensher, Rose, & Greene, 2015). This allows efficient estimation of the parameters of interest and, moreover allows to predict for new, not yet existing alternatives how they are preferred by the tourists. Examples of research in tourism using such an approach are Choi, Ritchie, Papandrea, and Bennett (2010) who modeled the economic valuation of cultural heritage sites, and Sarman, Scagnolari, and Maggi (2015) who measured the acceptance of life-threatening hazards among young tourists. In this study, we also adopt the stated choice approach. However, to provide the tourists with more meaningful sets of possible city trip activities we use a personalized stated choice experiment.

To personalize the experiment and present respondents with meaningful sets of activities, they were first asked, in an online survey, to indicate their interest for a set of POIs that are typically available in tourist cities. The following POIs were included: attraction/theme park, museum/art gallery, monument/churches, music/festival/concert, film/theater, park/water/gardens, going out/nightlife, eating/restaurants, shopping, and touring. A 6-point scale ranging from very uninterested to very interested was used.

Subsequently, they were asked to indicate their interest for specific themes that are often related to the POIs including: archeology, architecture, religion, heritage, history, old art and culture, modern art and culture, war, science, sport, animals, nature, food and drinks, design and fashion. A similar 6-point scale was used.

Then, per respondent all POIs and themes that were of interest (scores neutral-very interested) were selected and combined into city trip program activities (this was programmed in the online survey). Also 'no specific theme' was added as a possibility because some POIs do not have a specific theme. Furthermore, as some combinations of POIs and themes make no sense they were excluded from the list of possible combinations, leading to a maximum of 69 possible combinations.

To develop the personalized stated choice experiment first, per respondent a random set of ten combinations of POI's and themes was selected from the set of interest to that respondent. This set represents the tourist activities available in a specific city for a day trip. As previous research has shown that attraction value is an important factor for tourists to select an activity, Michelin starts were used to classify the attraction value for each combination of POI and theme, where * = of interest, ** = worth a detour, *** = worth the trip. The stars were randomly assigned to each combination.

The task for the respondents was to imagine that they were going to plan a city trip to an unknown, safe, not too crowded and well accessible city. They are traveling together with a person who has the same interests. It is good weather for visiting the city, and the walking distances in between activities are small. Moreover, they have a city pass-partout that allows them to visit all activities/POIs for free. The time spending for the city trip program planning was controlled for and the respondent needed to spend the exact indicated time over all activities including the possibility to take a break. The time spending options were 4, 6 or 8 h and they were randomly assigned to the choice task. For each respondent this task was repeated four times, meaning that each of them planned four city trips. Note that for each trip planning they were presented with a new set of combinations of POIs and themes.

In addition, the survey included questions to record relevant background variables of the persons, such as gender, age, household type, education and income level and work status.

Invitations to participate in the survey were sent to a random sample of an existing national panel which should be representative for the Dutch population in March, 2016. Only respondents that have made at least one city trip in the last two years proceed with the questionnaire. A city trip is defined as a visit to a city in leisure time with the aim to explore the city. A city trip lasts minimally 4 h and do not include more than 3 nights. By this filter, we make sure that the relevant segment of the population is selected.

4.4 Binary Mixed Logit Model

Binary mixed logit models (Hensher et al., 2015), a specific type of discrete choice modeling, are used to estimate the probability that tourists will choose a certain activity to be part (yes or no) of the activity program for a day trip to a city. The activity is described as a POI with a specific theme and attraction value.

The formal model (based on Hensher et al., 2015) can be described as follows. A tourist i chooses at occasion t whether an activity available in the city will be part of the activity program for that day. Note that because the tourist makes subsequently several choices of activities to add to the program the time aspect needed to be included in the model estimation. The utility that tourist i would obtain from choosing activity j to be part of the activity program on choice occasion t is:

$$U_{ijt} = \beta_i' X_{ijt} + \varepsilon_{ijt} \tag{4.1}$$

where,

X_{ijt} is a vector of observed variables (POIs, themes, attraction value, and available time)

β_i is a vector of coefficients that is unobserved for each i and varies randomly over the tourists representing each tourists' preferences, and

ε_{ijt} is an unobserved random term that is distributed iid extreme value, independent of β_i and X_{ijt}.

The coefficients β_i are allowed to vary across tourists, and this variance induces correlation in utility over activities and choice occasions (note that due to the limitation of number of random parameters in a model a selection is made which variables are included as random variables). Each random parameter β_i is defined as the average preference, b, and an individual deviation, η_i, which represents the tourists' preference relative to the average preference for a particular activity in the city. The utility is:

$$U_{ijt} = b' X_{ijt} + \eta_i' X_{ijt} + \varepsilon_{ijt} \tag{4.2}$$

The unobserved part of the utility is $\eta_i' X_{ijt} + \varepsilon_{ijt}$, and this term is correlated over activities and choice occasions. Therefore, the (binary) mixed logit model does not exhibit the independence from irrelevant alternatives property of standard logit. Hence, covariances between random variables can be obtained. Positive covariances suggest that larger parameter estimates for tourists along the distribution on one variable are in general associated with larger parameter estimates for that same tourist in the parameter space for the second variable (Hensher et al., 2015). Meaning that the larger the covariance the greater the relationship between two random parameters. For example, in case of a positive covariance between two POIs, this means that if one POI is added to the activity program the other one is more likely to be added as well. Negative covariances work the other way around, meaning that two POIs are less likely to be chosen in the same activity program.

For model estimation simulated maximum likelihood estimation, using Halton draws, was used (Bhat, 2001). The number of Halton draws was set to 1000. The data for estimation were prepared as follows. The dependent variable was the choice whether an activity will be selected or not for the activity program for a one day city trip. As there are 11 activities (including the 'break' option) available to choose from per day, each respondent made 11 choices. Per respondent this was repeated for four days. For the POIs and themes dummy coding was used, with the 'break' serving as the base for the POIs and 'no theme' as the base for the themes. Attraction value was effect-coded and the available time was coded as a continuous variable (in half hours).

4.5 Analyses and Results

To answer the research question, what are the preferences of tourists for POIs and themes and their combinations in planning a program during a city trip, first character-istics of the respondents are described, followed by preferences for POIs and themes, and time spending on activities. Finally, the preferences for including combinations of activities during a city trip are presented.

4.5.1 Sample

The personalized stated choice experiment was implemented in an on-line question-naire. In total 283 persons completed the survey. See Table 4.1 for the distribution of the sample for some key socio-demographic characteristics. It shows that the respondents are fairly representative for the (Dutch) population.

4.5.2 Personal Interests for POIs and Themes

The descriptive analyses regarding tourists' interest in city trip activities, pre-sented in Table 4.2, show that the top three of preferred POIs is eating/restaurants, park/water/gardens and shopping. The top three of most preferred themes is food and drinks, nature, and history. Surprisingly, visiting an attraction during a city trip is not preferred by the tourists. This might be due to the fact that an attraction is possibly seen as a stand-alone tourist attraction that will be visited for a day trip, but not as part of a city trip.

4.5.3 Preferred Time Spending

Table 4.3 presents the preferred time spending by the respondents on the POIs, themes and combinations of those, which they have selected for their trip programs. Note that some combinations were excluded from the experiment as they make no sense. The

Table 4.1 Sample characteristics ($N = 283$)

Variables	Levels	%
Gender	Male	59.5
	Female	50.5
Age	$0 \leq 24$ years	11.3
	$15 \leq 44$ years	43.8
	$45 \leq 64$ years	35.0
	65+ years	9.9
Household type	Single	19.4
	Couple	44.5
	Family with children	36.0
Education level	Low	15.2
	Medium	36.0
	High	48.8
Income level	Unknown	15.5
	Low	19.1
	Medium	49.8
	High	15.5
Work status	Not	26.5
	Part-time	24.7
	Full-time	48.8

results show that shopping activities, going out, or visiting a theme park/attraction have the longest activity duration. In general, respondents like to spend 1 h per activity, and when they take a break it on average lasts for three quarters of an hour. Themes that they like to spend most of their time on are food and drinks, design and fashion, followed by animals. Least preferred themes in terms of time spending are modern art and culture, followed by old art and culture, heritage and religion.

Looking at the time spending on combinations of POIs and themes it shows that some combinations are clearly preferred over other ones. For example, the respondents spend most time on attractions with the themes war or animals, science and history museums, war monuments, music festival with food and drinks, animal and nature parks, and touring in green and nature.

4.5.4 Preferences for Combinations of Activities

Binary mixed logit models (Hensher et al., 2015) were estimated based on the data collected with the personalized stated choice experiment. The model estimation results are shown in Tables 4.4, 4.5 and 4.6. Table 4.4 presents on the left hand side the results for model 1 including the standard deviations for the POIs and on

Table 4.2 Indicated personal interests of respondents for POIs and themes on a 6-point scale

	Mean	Standard deviation
POI		
Eating/restaurants	4.98	0.916
Park/water/gardens	4.45	0.93
Shopping	4.44	1.104
Touring (walking/biking/boating)	4.34	1.07
Monument/churches	4.23	1.176
Music/festival/concert	4.06	1.137
Film/theater	3.96	1.172
Museum/art gallery	3.95	1.305
Going out/nightlife	3.64	1.349
Attraction/theme park	3.36	1.37
Theme		
Food and drinks	4.81	0.947
Nature	4.38	1.063
History	4.25	1.128
Architecture	4.12	1.18
Old art and culture	4.1	1.225
Heritage	3.84	1.288
Archeology	3.82	1.301
Animals	3.77	1.193
Design and fashion	3.73	1.325
Science	3.73	1.226
Modern art and culture	3.67	1.221
Sport	3.55	1.261
War	3.49	1.295
Religion	3.18	1.314

the right hand side the results for model 2 including the standard deviations for the themes (note that because of a restriction on the number of random parameters two models were estimated). The corresponding correlations matrices for both models are presented in Tables 4.5 and 4.6. Model statistics are also presented in Table 4.4. Both models are performing fine although the goodness of fit presented in pseudo R^2s are low. This is due to the fact that the experiment already included the preferred activities; the models were specifically estimated to find preferences for the combinations of POIs/themes.

Table 4.4 also includes the most significant interaction effects between POIs and themes. They show that tourists prefer certain POIs for certain themes: museums for

Table 4.3 Time spending on chosen POIs and themes in minutes

Themes POIs	Archaeology	Architecture	Religion	Heritage	History	Old art and culture	Modern art and culture	War	Science	Sport	Animals	Nature	Food and drinks	Design and fashion	No theme	Total-Mean
Attraction	82.34			56.51	79.62			88.33	58.57	75.96	87.83	73.06			80.37	76.72
Museum	53.64	46.48	43.40	48.17	56.33	52.73	50.56	59.45	57.89		52.64	46.90	50.36	55.63	57.27	52.24
Monument	53.02	55.95	52.88	48.27	53.80	52.17	42.35	60.51							46.86	51.75
Music			57.50										68.74		65.31	65.87
Film					54.12	45.00	51.54	72.35	60.70	49.25	56.13	51.58	62.55	55.29	57.50	56.45
Park		52.09		51.5	47.62	47.06	44.23				64.84	63.52			56.98	54.58
Nightlife													84.22		80.64	82.50
Eating													73.22		67.77	70.73
Shopping													72.86	77.95	71.97	73.66
Touring		60.58	48.00	50.77	57.53	51.07	48.68	53.04				73.40			58.58	58.17
Break																48.95
Total-mean	60.15	54.01	50.27	50.47	55.98	50.22	47.02	63.79	58.94	61.80	66.14	63.94	70.76	67.87	59.82	59.64

Table 4.4 Estimation results of the binary logit model for POIs (model 1) and themes (model 2)

Variables	Model 1			Standard deviation	Model 2			Standard deviation
	Parameters	t-value			Parameters	t-value		
POIs								
Attraction/theme park	−0.276	−3.62		1.157	−0.500	−7.50		
Museum/art gallery	−0.488	−7.34		1.693	−0.597	−10.70		
Monument/churches	−0.173	−2.39		1.556	−0.360	−5.87		
Music/festival/concert	−0.259	−3.04		0.932	−0.407	−5.15		
Film/theater	−0.660	−8.79		1.420	−0.740	−11.47		
Park/water/gardens	−0.099	−1.43		1.227	−0.315	−5.18		
Going out/nightlife	0.148	1.41		0.894	−0.042	−0.46		
Eating/restaurants	0.602	6.07		0.997	0.319	3.86		
Shopping	0.611	5.79		1.200	0.329	3.56		
Touring	−0.137	−1.95		1.231	−0.359	−5.95		
Break (base)	0							
Themes								
Archeology	0.097	0.95			159	1.63		0.953
Architecture	0.066	0.86			0.108	1.59		
Religion	−0.549	−4.05			−0.579	−4.07		1.636
Heritage	0.172	2.25			0.276	3.61		1.410
History	0.119	1.81			0.114	1.95		
Old art and culture	0.012	0.14			0.137	1.59		1.241
Modern art and culture	−0.378	−4.75			−0.185	−2.75		
War	0.004	0.05			0.047	0.58		0.994
Science	−0.012	0.09			0.046	0.39		

(continued)

Table 4.4 (continued)

Variables	Model 1		Standard deviation	Model 2		Standard deviation
	Parameters	t-value		Parameters	t-value	
Sport	0.288	2.18		0.301	2.61	
Animals	0.471	4.93		0.501	5.02	1.301
Nature	0.156	1.85		0.166	2.03	0.946
Food and drinks	0.296	4.66		0.326	5.15	0.839
Design and fashion	−0.336	−3.64		−0.224	−2.31	1.671
No theme (base)	0					
Interactions						
Museum * Religion	0.643	2.65		0.785	3.18	
Museum * Old art	0.640	3.70		0.439	2.72	
Monument * Religion	0.844	3.60		1.111	4.44	
Film * Old Art	−0.622	−3.00		−0.625	−3.13	
Film * Science	−0.477	−2.21		−0.302	−1.60	
Film * Animals	−0.428	−2.32		−0.410	−2.20	
Film * Nature	−0.637	−3.87		−0.606	−3.84	
Park * Nature	0.504	3.37		0.463	3.18	
Shopping * Food	−0.464	−2.97		−0.427	−2.82	
Attraction value						
1star	−0.115	−5.32		−0.099	−4.90	
2stars	0.036	1.57		0.036	1.72	
3stars (base)	0.079	10.50		0.063	15.84	
Available time						
In half hours	0.029			0.038		

(continued)

Table 4.4 (continued)

Variables	Model 1			Standard deviation	Model 2			Standard deviation
	Parameters	t-value			Parameters	t-value		
Chi-square value	729.204				196.754			
Significance level	0.000				0.000			
DoF	91				81			
LL(0)	−8165.547				−0.8165.547			
LL(B)	−7800.945				−8067.170			
Pseudo-R²	0.045				0.012			

Sample size is 12,452 choices: 4 days, 11 choices per day from 283 respondents

Table 4.5 Correlation matrix for the POIs—model 1

POIs	Attraction	Museum	Monument	Music	Film	Park	Nightlife	Eating	Shopping	Touring
Attraction	1.000	−0.570	−0.136	0.966	−0.885	−0.337	0.510	−0.156	0.037	−0.302
Museum		1.000	0.690	−0.438	0.587	0.432	−0.305	0.308	−0.144	0.415
Monument			1.000	−0.031	0.301	0.794	−371	0.644	−0.403	0.523
Music				1.000	−0.824	−0.350	0.384	−159	−0.005	−0.399
Film					1.000	0.523	−0.761	0.443	−0.414	0.323
Park						1.000	−0.473	0.834	−0.552	0.750
Nightlife							1.000	−0.507	0.616	0.013
Eating								1.000	−0.890	0.717
Shopping									1.000	−0.385
Touring										1.000

Table 4.6 Correlation matrix for the themes—model 2

Themes	Archaeology	Religion	Heritage	OldArt	War	Animals	Nature
Archaeology	1.000	−0.449	−0.637	−0.789	0.922	−0.126	0.617
Religion		1.000	0.567	0.815	−0.638	−0.445	−0.337
Heritage			1.000	0.884	−0.692	−0.540	−0.761
OldArt				1.000	−0.834	−0.336	−0.622
War					1.000	0.171	0.732
Animals						1.000	0.555
Nature							1.000

religion or old art; a monument and religion; parks and nature. On the other hand, some combinations are not preferred such as: films with the themes old art, science or animals. The parameters for the attraction value indicate that POIs with more Michelin stars are most preferred.

Tables 4.5 and 4.6 presents the correlation matrices related to respectively models 1 and 2. A significant, positive covariance between two POIs or themes implies that when one activity is chosen the other activity is more likely to be chosen during the same day trip to a city, thus would complement each other in the activity program. A significant negative covariance means that the two activities are not likely to be selected for a city trip program by the same tourist during a one day visit. Thus, the estimated correlation matrices indicate which POIs and which themes tourists wish to combine on a city trip. The positive correlations between museum, film, park and eating out, for example, indicate that these activities are particularly favored combinations and hence would constitute a good program for a city trip. Negative correlations indicate the opposite. For example, tourists on average do not prefer to combine a film and nightlife, or a film with an attraction or music festival on a same day. Combinations of themes that are preferred in the program for a city trip are religion, old art and heritage. Also war, archeology and nature are themes that show a good match in an activity program. While nature for example does not match with the themes heritage or old art.

4.6 Conclusion and Implications

To provide tourists with a complete user model for activity program recommendation it is important to not only know the preferences and interests of tourists but also whether they like combinations of activities/POIs or not. Therefore, the aim of this study was to describe and predict tourists' preferences for combinations of POIs and related themes in planning a program for a city trip.

To measure and predict tourists' preferences specifically a personalized stated choice experiment was developed and presented in a survey to a random sample of 238 respondents. Binary mixed logit models for POIs and activity themes were estimated. A special feature of this model is that preferences for specific combinations of POIs or themes, can be estimated. The model parameters provide information on combinations of activities and themes that tourists prefer during their city trip and that the recommender system can use to further fine-tune the recommendations of city trip programs and optimize the tourist experience.

Several problems remain for future research. First, tourists' city trip activities are often conducted by individuals in a group and preferences for selecting combinations of POIs and themes are the result of a group decision process. This social aspect was not taken into account in our experiment and model estimation. To take group preferences into account, and optimize the user model for TRSs, the discrete choice analysis need to be expanded in future research.

Furthermore, data was only collected among a random sample in the Netherlands, while foreign tourists might have different preferences. It would be of interest to collect data in different countries to also be able to include the cultural background of the visitors.

Finally, the binary mixed logit models were estimated based on the choices of the respondents to include an activity to the program of the day or not. Estimating a model including both this binary choice and the time spent on an activity is a future challenge.

Acknowledgements The research leading to these results has received funding from the European Community's Seventh Framework Program (FP7/2007–2013) under the Grant Agreement number 611040. The author is solely responsible for the information reported in this paper. It does not represent the opinion of the Community. The Community is not responsible for any use that might be made of the information contained in this paper.

References

Aksenov, P., Kemperman, A. D. A. M., & Arentze, T. A. (2014). Toward personalized and dynamic cultural routing: A three-level approach. *Procedia Environmental Sciences, 22,* 257–269.

Aksenov, P., Kemperman, A.D.A.M., Arentze, T.A. (2016). A personalized recommender system for tourists on city trips: concepts and implementation. In *International Conference on Smart Digital Futures, KES International*, Tenerife, Spain, 15–17 June.

Andrada, I. I., Rogelio, T., Deng, J., Pierskalla, C., & Brooks, J. (2014). A conjoint approach in estimating the importance of urban forests versus other major tourism attractions in urban tourism destinations: Insights from Washington, DC. *Tourism Analysis, 19,* 301–310.

Arentze, T., Kemperman, A., & Aksenov, P. (2018). Estimating a latent-class user model for travel recommender systems. *Information Technology & Tourism, 19*(1–4), 61–82.

Baltas, G. (2007). Econometric models for discrete choice analysis of travel and tourism demand. *Journal of Travel & Tourism Marketing, 21,* 25–40.

Bhat, C. R. (2001). Quasi-random maximum simulated likelihood estimation of the mixed multinomial logit model. *Transportation Research, 35B*(7), 677–695.

Borras, J., Moreno, A., & Valls, A. (2014). Intelligent tourism recommender systems: A survey. *Expert Systems with Applications, 41,* 7370–7389.

Bryan, H. (1977). Leisure value system and recreational specialization: The case of trout fishermen. *Journal of Leisure Research, 9,* 174–187.

Buhalis, D. (1998). Strategic use of information technologies in the tourism industry. *Tourism Management, 19*(5), 409–421.

Choi, A. S., Ritchie, B. W., Papandrea, F., & Bennett, J. (2010). Economic valuation of cultural heritage sites: a choice modeling approach. *Tourism Management, 31*(2), 213–220.

Crouch, G.I. Louviere, J.J. (2000). A review of choice modelling research in tourism, hospitality, and leisure. *Tourism Analysis, 5*(2–4), 97–104(8).

Dellaert, B. G. C., Arentze, T. A., & Horeni, O. (2013). Tourists' mental representations of complex travel decision problems. *Journal of Travel Research, 53,* 3–11.

Gavalas, D., Konstantopolous, C., Mastakas, K., & Pantziou, G. (2014). Mobile recommender systems in tourism. *Journal of Network and Computer Applications, 39,* 319–333.

Gibson, H., & Yiannakis, A. (2002). Tourist roles, needs and the life course. *Annals of Tourism Research, 29*(2), 358–383.

Gretzel, U., Mitsche, N., Hwang, Y. H., & Fesenmaier, D. R. (2004). Tell me who you are and I will tell you where to go: Use of travel personalities in destination recommendation systems. *Information Technology & Tourism, 7,* 3–12.

Grigolon, A. B., Kemperman, A. D. A. M., & Timmermans, H. J. P. (2012). The influence of low-fare airlines on vacation choices of students: Results of a stated portfolio choice experiment. *Tourism Management, 33,* 1174–1184.

Hensher, D. A., Rose, J. M., & Greene, W. H. (2015). *Applied choice analysis* (2nd ed.). Cambridge: Cambridge University Press.

Hergesell, A., & Dickinger, A. (2013). Environmentally friendly holiday transport mode choices among students: the role of price, time and convenience. *Journal of Sustainable Tourism, 21,* 596–613.

Huertas-Garcia, R., Laguna García, M., & Consolación, C. (2008). Conjoint analysis of tourist choice of hotel attributes presented in travel agent brochures. *International Journal of Tourism Research, 16,* 65–75.

Jeng, J. M., & Fesenmaier, D. R. (1998). Destination compatibility in multidestination pleasure travel. *Tourism Analysis, 3,* 77–87.

Kemperman, A. D. A. M., Borgers, A. W. J., Oppewal, H., & Timmermans, H. J. P. (2000). Consumer choice of theme parks: A conjoint choice model of seasonality effects and variety seeking behavior. *Leisure Sciences, 22,* 1–18.

Morley, C. (2014). Discrete choice analysis and experimental design. In: L. Dwyer, A. Gill & N. Seetaram (Eds.) *Handbook of research methods in tourism: Quantitative and qualitative approaches* (pp. 113–126). Edward Elgar Publishing.

Nicolau, J. L. (2010). Variety-seeking and inertial behaviour: The disutility of distance. *Tourism Economics, 16,* 251–264.

Nicolau, J. L., & Más, F. J. (2006). The influence of distance and prices on the choice of tourist destinations: The moderating role of motivations. *Tourism Management, 27,* 982–996.

Oppewal, H., Huybers, T., & Crouch, G. I. (2010). *How do Australians choose holiday destinations and experiences?*. Gold Coast, Australia: CRC for Sustainable Tourism Pty Ltd.

Rodríguez, B., Molina, J., Pérez, F., & Caballero, R. (2012). Interactive design of personalised tourism routes. *Tourism Management, 33*(4), 926–940.

Román, C., & Martin, J. C. (2016). Hotel attributes: Asymmetries in guest payments and gains—A stated preference approach. *Tourism Management, 52,* 488–497.

Sarman, I., Scagnolari, S., & Maggi, R. (2015). Acceptance of life-threatening hazards among young tourists: A stated choice experiment. *Journal of Travel Research, 55*(8), 979–992.

Steen Jacobsen, J. K., & Munar, A. M. (2012). Tourist information search and destination choice in a digital age. *Tourism Management Perspectives, 1*(1), 39–47.

Tsaur, S. H., & Wu, D. H. (2005). The use of stated preference model in travel itinerary choice behaviour. *Journal of Travel & Tourism Marketing, 18,* 37–48.

Vansteenwegen, P., Souffriau, W., Vanden Berghe, G., & Van Oudheusden, D. (2011). The city trip planner: An expert system for tourists. *Expert Systems with Applications, 38,* 6540–6546.

Wörndl, W., Hefele, A. (2016). Generating paths through discovered places-of-interests for city trip planning. In: A. Inversini & R. Schegg (Eds.), Information and Communication Technologies in Tourism (pp. 441–453). Springer International Publishing.

Wörndl, W., & Hefele, A. (2017). Recommending a sequence of interesting places for tourist trip. *Information Technology & Tourism, 17,* 31–54.

Yeh, D. Y., & Cheng, C. H. (2015). Recommendation system for popular tourist attractions in Taiwan using Delphi panel and repertory grid techniques. *Tourism Management, 46,* 164–176.

Chapter 5
The Youth Tourism Market: A Structural Equation Model of Determinants and Impacts of Social Interactions

Maria João Carneiro, Celeste Eusébio and Ana Caldeira

5.1 Introduction

The supply of enriching tourism experiences is a crucial factor for the competitiveness of tourism destinations. Satisfying encounters among visitors and between hosts and visitors can have an important role in creating rewarding and memorable tourism experiences. Social interaction in tourism is a very complex concept that has been analysed both from the perspective of visitors (e.g. Eusébio & Carneiro, 2012; Fan, Zhang, Jenkins, & Tavitiyaman, 2017; Kastenholz, Carneiro, & Eusébio, 2018; Pizam, Uriely, & Reichel, 2000) and of residents (e.g. Andereck, Valentine, Knopf, & Vogt, 2005; Sinkovics & Penz, 2009; Weaver & Lawton, 2001). However, a limited number of published studies analyse the encounters that each visitor has with residents and with other visitors in a tourism destination (Eusébio & Carneiro, 2012; Fan et al., 2017). Moreover, although the literature (e.g. Eusébio & Carneiro, 2012; Pizam et al., 2000; Sinkovics & Penz, 2009) highlights the existence of several factors influencing the intensity, type and nature of social encounters in tourism, a limited number of studies has analysed these factors empirically.

Several theories related to social contact in tourism suggest that encounters between people of different characteristics and cultural backgrounds may result in positive outcomes (e.g. cultural enrichment, mutual appreciation, understanding, tolerance). However, these encounters may also generate negative outcomes (e.g.

M. J. Carneiro · C. Eusébio · A. Caldeira
GOVCOPP Research Unit, Universidade de Aveiro, Aveiro, Portugal
e-mail: celeste.eusebio@ua.pt

A. Caldeira
e-mail: anacaldeira@ua.pt

M. J. Carneiro (✉) · C. Eusébio · A. Caldeira
DEGEIT, Universidade de Aveiro, 3810-193 Aveiro, Portugal
e-mail: mjcarneiro@ua.pt

© Springer Nature Switzerland AG 2019   71
A. Artal-Tur et al. (eds.), *Trends in Tourist Behavior*,
Tourism, Hospitality & Event Management,
https://doi.org/10.1007/978-3-030-11160-1_5

development of negative attitudes, increase in tension and hostility, development of stereotypes) (Reisinger & Turner, 2003). The type and nature of the outcomes are strongly related to the intensity and nature of the social encounters. The great challenge for the agents responsible for the planning and management of a tourism destination is the implementation of strategies to maximize the positive outcomes and minimize the negatives outcomes of social encounters. To design these strategies, it is of utmost relevance to have insights from empirical studies regarding the factors influencing social interactions and also the outcomes of these interactions.

The youth tourism market is recognized as a very important tourism segment that is at the beginning of a long travel career (Eusébio & Carneiro 2012, 2015). The intensity and the types of social interaction in this market have received little attention in the tourism literature (Eusébio & Carneiro, 2012). Moreover, the identification of the factors influencing these interactions and also the identification of outcomes of these interactions have been almost neglected in published studies.

The present chapter extends the previous studies carried out on social interaction in tourism in the youth tourism market in three areas. First, different types and intensities of social encounters between visitors and residents and between visitors and other visitors in a tourism destination are analysed. Second, both positive and negative consequences of these encounters for young visitors are examined. Third, the direct and indirect effects of several travel motivations of the young visitors on various types of social encounters and on the consequences of these social encounters are analysed through a structural equation model.

In order to accomplish the above-mentioned objectives, the present chapter is structured into six sections. After this introduction, a literature review on social contact in tourism is presented in terms of concepts, characteristics and relevance to the youth market. In section three, the research model proposed is described, specifically analysing the determinants of social contact in tourism and the potential consequences (outcomes) of these interactions. The methodology of the empirical study carried out is presented in section four, concerning data collection and analysis methods. The results obtained from tests of the model proposed are presented and discussed in section five. Finally, the chapter ends with the theoretical and practical contributions of this research and also with some limitations and recommendations for further research to extend knowledge in this under researched area.

5.2   Social Contact in the Youth Tourism Market

Social contact in tourism is a complex construct influenced by several factors and with various consequences, namely for satisfaction of both residents and visitors. During a trip, each visitor may interact with other visitors and with hosts and consequently social contact has the power of influencing visitors' behaviours and the visitors' attitudes and perceptions toward the destination (Fan et al., 2017; Kastenholz et al., 2018; Pizam et al., 2000; Sharpley, 2014). Although the study of the effects of intergroup contact, mainly between groups with different cultural background, has a long history in the social psychology field, in the scope of tourism this issue has been almost neglected (Eusébio & Carneiro, 2012; Fan et al., 2017; Pizam et al., 2000). However, in recent years, the literature in this field has increased.

Various definitions of social contact have been used in the tourism literature. De Kadt (1979) was one of the first authors who analysed host-tourist encounters, reporting that these encounters occur in three main contexts: when visitors purchase products from the hosts; when visitors and hosts find themselves side by side in a tourism attraction or facility; and when visitors and hosts come face-to-face with the objective of exchanging information and ideas. Different outcomes will result from these different kinds of encounters. Reisinger and Turner (2003, p. 37) define social contact in tourism as "the personal encounter that takes place between a tourist and a host". However, during a trip, a visitor may interact not only with the local population but also with other visitors. Fan et al. (2017) adopted the concept of cross-cultural social contact proposed by Cushner and Brislin (1996) and Yu and Lee (2014). This concept is defined as "the face-to-face contacts between people of different cultural backgrounds" (Fan et al., 2017, p. 358). In this line of thought, in this chapter social contact is defined as the face-to-face contact that occurs during a tourism trip between visitors and hosts and between visitors and other visitors. To date, some studies have applied social contact from the perspective of visitors (Eusébio & Carneiro 2012, 2015; Fan et al., 2017; Kastenholz et al., 2018). However, a limited number of studies simultaneously analyses tourist-host interactions and interactions between tourists (e.g. Kastenholz et al., 2018).

In the majority of tourism destinations, visitors stay for a short and well-structured period of time (Fan et al., 2017). Consequently, encounters between visitor and host tend to be more formal, superficial, brief, unbalanced, limited in terms of spontaneity, unequal and transitory (Eusébio & Carneiro, 2012; Reisinger & Turner, 2003; Reisinger, 2009; Sharpley, 2014). De Kadt (1979) and Krippendorf (1987) highlight that in some situations interactions are frequently open to deceit, exploitation and mistrust. However, in some types of tourism and contexts, encounters tend to be more informal, close and intense. Different outcomes will be obtained from these different kinds of interactions.

Social encounters between visitors and hosts and between visitors and other visitors tend to provide positive and negative outcomes, mainly when these encounters occur between people from different cultural backgrounds. According to Reisinger and Turner (2003), contact hypotheses express that social contact between individuals from different cultures may originate mutual appreciation, understanding, respect, tolerance and positive attitudes and reduce ethnic prejudices, stereotypes and racial tension. Fan et al. (2017) also point out that social encounters in tourism tend to reduce anxiety, enhance understanding of others, reduce misunderstandings and stereotypes, further improve intergroup relations and enhance empathy between people. However, social encounters in tourism may also contribute, according to Reisinger and Turner (2003, p. 39), to the development of "negative attitudes, stereotypes, prejudices and increase tension, hostility, suspicion and often violent attacks". Some studies reveal the existence of a positive relationship between the intensity and quality of interaction and the occurrence of positive outcomes (Reisinger & Turner, 2003). Therefore, in order to maximize positive and minimize negative outcomes, the agents responsible for the planning and management of tourism destinations should implement strategies to stimulate pleasant encounters in tourism. However, the studies that examine the outcomes of social encounters in tourism are very limited. Moreover, few empirical studies analyse the factors influencing these outcomes.

The youth market is, nowadays, an important and growing segment that has time to travel (Eusébio & Carneiro 2012, 2015). In 2020, it is expected that there will be about 300 million international youth trips per year (UNWTO & WYSE w.d.). Moreover, these individuals are in the initial stage of their travel career (Eusébio & Carneiro, 2012). Furthermore they are highly resilient (Tourism Research & Marketing, 2013; UNWTO & WYSE w.d.), are not easily discouraged from travelling by terrorism or natural disasters, and are pioneers in discovering new destinations (UNWTO & WYSE w.d.), and so have an important role in the development of tourism destinations.

The results of some research also suggest that young people may want to socialize during tourism trips. The study of Morgan and Xu (2009) showed that, for 23% of the students surveyed, having fun with family and friends was the reason for having memories of their holidays. In the research undertaken by Tourism Research and Marketing (2013) on youth travellers, meeting local people emerged as one important motivation for travel, being mentioned by about 80% of respondents. Appreciating or exploring new cultures also emerged as important travel behaviours for young people (Morgan & Xu, 2009; Tourism Research & Marketing, 2013), which may also indicate that young visitors will be likely to contact the residents of tourism destinations to know their culture better. Given that young visitors seek to meeting new people, be with friends, expand knowledge and experience a different culture in their travels (Eusébio & Carneiro, 2012; Morgan & Xu, 2009; Tourism Research & Marketing, 2013) there is a high probability of their engagement in encounters with local people and with other visitors to satisfy these travel motivations. Knowing the travel behaviour of this segment, mainly social encounters with local people and other visitors, the outcomes of these social encounters and the factors influencing these outcomes is of utmost relevance to better satisfy this segment and to turn young visitors into loyal customers. However, the few empirical studies on social contact in the youth market (e.g. Eusébio & Carneiro 2012, 2015) showed a limited frequency of interaction. The model proposed in this research may provide important insights in this scope. The model will be presented in more detail in the next section.

5.3   Conceptual Model Proposed

In order to thoroughly understand the crucial role of social interaction in tourism and what tends to influence this kind of contact, it is essential to analyse the determinants and the outcomes of this interaction. Several factors may influence the intensity, type and nature of social contact in tourism. The characteristics of both parties involved in the process (visitors and hosts), type of tourism destination, travel behaviour and travel motivations (Eusébio & Carneiro, 2012; Pizam et al., 2000; Sinkovics & Penz, 2009) are the factors more frequently referred to. However, only a limited number of studies analyses the influence of these factors on intensity of social interaction from the perspective of visitors (e.g. Eusébio & Carneiro, 2012). Moreover, positive and negative outcomes may occur in consequence of social contact between visitors and both hosts and other visitors. However, this topic is highly neglected in the empirical research. In order to expand the knowledge in these fields, a conceptual model is proposed in the next sections in order to examine the relationships between travel motivations, interactions with other visitors and hosts and also visitors' perceptions of the outcomes of these interactions.

5.3.1   Travel Motivations as Determinants of Social Interaction

Travel motivations are thus one crucial determinant of social contact in tourism. In fact, when one need arises leading to a disequilibrium in the motivational systems of visitors, this drives visitors to act in order to satisfy that need (Crompton, 1979). A motivation is, therefore, a state where people feel certain needs that lead them to act in such a way that they believe they will become satisfied (Moutinho 1987). According to Iso-Ahola (1982) a tourism motivation corresponds to "a meaningful state of mind which adequately disposes an actor or a group of actors to travel" (p. 257). In some instances, visitors' interaction with other people at the destination—either local residents or other visitors—is important to reach an equilibrium and satisfy the visitors' needs. However, several motivations can originate different intensities and types of interaction (Eusébio & Carneiro, 2012; Reisinger, 2009).

Several researchers (e.g. Beard & Ragheb, 1983; Crompton, 1979; Iso-Ahola, 1982; Manfredo, Driver, & Tarrant, 1996) proposed diverse categorizations of motivations for engaging in leisure and tourism which may provide important insights on motivations for undertaking leisure trips. Increase knowledge, challenge, novelty and escape are among the most frequently mentioned dimensions of motivations in these categorizations.

Expand knowledge is one of the most important motivations for engaging in leisure trips. Educational motivations such as learning about things or satisfying curiosity or, more specifically, learning about things around or about other cultures are recognized as important motivators of leisure trips (Beard & Ragheb, 1983; Iso-Ahola, 1982; Manfredo et al., 1996).

Underlying the leisure trip is also frequently a motivation for novelty. This motivation is often expressed as a desire to see something different, discover something new and have a new experience (Beard & Ragheb, 1983; Crompton, 1979; Manfredo et al., 1996). Many people specifically express the wish to meet new people, other people or even to meet new people from outside the usual environment (including local people and other visitors) (Beard & Ragheb, 1983; Crompton, 1979; Manfredo et al., 1996).

Tourism, involving trips to destinations outside the usual environment of the visitor, offers good opportunities to go to places with different characteristics, namely with different natural environments and cultural atmospheres, enabling new information to be gathered, perspectives to be enlarged and knowledge to be expanded in some areas. When staying in destinations with different characteristics from the usual environment, visitors have also more possibilities of experiencing new atmospheres, discovering new things and living new experiences. As remarked by White and White (2008), a full understanding of the destination is not possible without the visitors' contact with local residents and the help of the local community. Manfredo et al. (1996) also remark that, in this context, some important motivations for engaging in leisure are to observe and talk to other people, probably because, among other reasons, this is a way to obtain more information and, thus, to expand knowledge, or to have a different experience. Both hosts' and other visitors' advice can also be very useful for exploring the destination (Su, Long, Wall, & Jin, 2016; White & White, 2008). However, the empirical research in this field is mostly scarce. Nevertheless, some reveals that the visitors' interaction with other visitors and the local populations enriches the visitors' understanding of the destination (White & White, 2008) and that those visitors wanting to thoroughly explore the destination tend to have very intense contact with hosts (Fan et al., 2017).

Challenge seems to be also an important motivation for carrying out leisure activities. Some visitors report that they want to engage in tourism to challenge their abilities (Beard & Ragheb, 1983), to test their abilities and develop skills (Beard & Ragheb, 1983; Manfredo et al., 1996). Some researchers highlight that some visitors even want to have thrills and take risks (Manfredo et al., 1996). Frequently, social contact in tourism involves challenge, due to the existing differences between the visitors and both the hosts and other visitors, often associated with the provenance from different contexts frequently with different cultural backgrounds (Fan et al., 2017; Reisinger & Turner, 2003). Even communication with other visitors and hosts can imply challenge given that different languages are often used by both parties in contact. Considering this literature, it is expected that visitors most motivated for this challenge are also those who are more likely to contact hosts and other visitors, given the challenge involved in much of this kind of contact.

On another hand, escape has also emerged as an important motivation for undertaking leisure trips. In fact, many people participate in these trips to be in a calm environment (Beard & Ragheb, 1983; Manfredo et al., 1996) and to experience tranquillity and peace (Manfredo et al., 1996). These visitors want to avoid crowds or escape from stressful environments, avoiding the hustle and bustle of daily life (Beard & Ragheb, 1983; Iso-Ahola, 1982). Some of these visitors express the desire to get away from other people, and even to have more privacy and be isolated (Manfredo et al., 1996). Taking into account that visitors with more motivations for escape are most likely to visit destinations with a quiet environment, probably with not many people, and tend to search for more privacy, it is considered that these visitors are likely to have a lower intensity of interactions with other visitors and hosts than those with fewer motivations for escape.

Despite recognizing that motivations may play a crucial role as determinants of visitors' interactions with hosts and other visitors, as already mentioned, few studies analyse this kind of influence. Eusébio and Carneiro (2012) already found that motivations other than those of escape had a positive influence on young visitors' interaction with residents in all the places considered in the study. Nevertheless, this positive influence was not observed in all the specific places analysed, escape motivations did not show any significant influence on interaction and the study is confined to interaction with residents. Therefore, more research is needed in this scope. Nevertheless, the previous literature review leads us to posit the following:

H1—Travel motivations influence the intensity of visitors' interactions with other visitors and hosts
H1a—The travel motivations of knowledge, challenge and novelty have a positive effect on the intensity of visitors' interactions with other visitors and hosts
H1b—The travel motivation of escape has a negative effect on the intensity of visitors' interactions with other visitors and hosts.

5.3.2 The Outcomes of Social Interaction

As already discussed in section two, social interaction in the context of tourism may have several distinct outcomes. Several theories related to social contact in tourism suggest that encounters between people of different cultural backgrounds may result in negative outcomes (e.g. development of negative attitudes, increase in tension and hostility, development of stereotypes) (Reisinger & Turner, 2003) but may also originate positive outcomes (e.g. cultural enrichment, mutual appreciation, understanding, respect, tolerance). Some research (e.g. White & White, 2008) also reveals that visitors' interaction with other visitors and with the local community have played a crucial role in the visitors' touristic experience, providing comfort while at the destination—a place perceived as unknown and hostile. These outcomes are strongly related to the intensity, type and nature of the social encounters. In this context, the great challenge of the tourism industry is the implementation of strategies to maximize the positive outcomes and minimize the negative outcomes of social encounters. Nevertheless, empirical research on the consequences of visitors' interactions with other visitors and with hosts is extremely scarce.

Although recognizing that social contact between visitors and both visitors and hosts can have either positive or negative outcomes, these encounters will always involve some negotiation. According to social exchange theory, when people perceive that the costs of the contact outweigh its benefits, they do not establish contact or try to end it (Sharpley, 2014). Bimonte and Punzo (2016) also argue that visitors, when interacting with others, will try to maximize their wellbeing. Furthermore, it is also

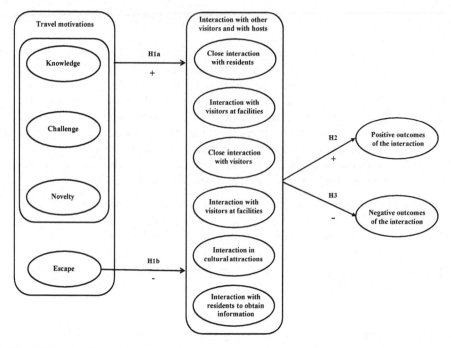

Fig. 5.1 Proposed research model

posited that, when interaction increases, it will contribute to mutual understanding (Su et al., 2016). Considering all these arguments it is hypothesized that:

H2—The intensity of visitors' interactions with other visitors and hosts contributes to increasing the positive outcomes of the interaction
H3—The intensity of visitors' interactions with other visitors and hosts contributes to decreasing the negative outcomes of the interaction.

Based on the literature reviewed, a research model is proposed (Fig. 5.1).

5.4 Methodology

A questionnaire survey was carried out among undergraduate and graduate students of the University of Aveiro (Portugal). Respondents were selected using a quota sampling approach based on the area of studies and gender. Students were asked to consider the longest trip made in the last three years and to answer questions about it. Respondents were asked to state whether they agreed that 12 features, selected from previous research (Kim et al., 2007; Richards, 2007), motivated their trip, using a scale from 1 "completely disagree" to 7 "completely agree". Students had to report how often they had specific types of interactions (e.g. sharing meals, exchanging gifts) with local residents and other visitors and had contact with them in different places (e.g. in the street, in monuments), using a scale from 1 "very rarely" to 7 "very frequently". A total of 24 items (from De Kadt, 1979; Eusébio & Carneiro, 2012; Reisinger & Turner, 1998) were used. Respondents were also required to report positive and negative effects of the interaction expressing their agreement with eight items (based on Reisinger & Turner, 2003), using the same Likert-type scale adopted for motivations. Finally, the questionnaire included questions on sociodemographic characteristics.

A pilot test of the questionnaire was conducted with 18 students. In consequence of the pilot test, few changes were introduced in the questionnaire in order to improve its clarity and content validity. The final version of the questionnaire was administered face-to-face in March and April 2013.

In order to analyse data, first a descriptive analysis was carried out. Then, three Principal Component Analyses (PCA) were undertaken—one on motivations for travel, other on interactions with other visitors and local residents and, another on the positive and negative effects of these interactions. Finally, a partial least squares structural equation modelling (PLS_SEM) was carried out to test the conceptual model proposed.

5.5   Analysis and Discussion of Results

5.5.1   Characterization of the Sample

The sample was composed by students (N = 399) with an average of 21 years old and by only slightly more women (54%). Four dimensions of motivations emerged from the PCA—knowledge, challenge, escape and novelty. There was a prevalence of novelty motivations (5.64 in average) but people also showed very high knowledge and escape motivations, with 4.97 and 4.81 on average, respectively. Challenge motivations were considerably lower (4.00).

The PCA on interactions permitted six dimensions of interactions to be identified: close interaction with residents, interaction with visitors at recreational attractions and facilities, close interaction with visitors, interaction with residents at recreational attractions and facilities, interaction in cultural attractions and interaction to obtain information. Visitors' interaction with local residents and other visitors is low. The interactions with residents, both in facilities (4.09 in average) and to obtain information (3.82), are the most frequent. The least frequent interactions are close interactions with residents (2.49) and interaction in cultural attractions (2.90).

The PCA on the outcomes of interaction generated two factors, one representing positive outcomes (e.g. visitors' enrichment, ability of interaction, increase in respect) and another the negative outcomes (e.g. increase in stress, development of feelings of inferiority). The interaction has more positive outcomes (4.39) than negative (2.16).

5.5.2   Testing the Model Proposed

The PLS estimation assessment comprises two stages: the evaluation of the estimation (outer model), which refers to the connection between the indicators and the constructs, and the analysis of the structural (inner model), which concerns the hypothesized relationships amongst constructs.

First, when assessing the reliability and validity of the outer model, the requirements were clearly met: composite reliability (>0.7, varying from 0.79 to 0.92), outer loadings (>0.6), average variance extracted (>0.5, ranging from 0.55 to 0.75) (Table 5.1). Furthermore, the discriminant validity of all constructs was also established, with the heterotrait-monotrait ratio of correlations <0.85 (Table 5.2).

Then, once the outer model was validated, the inner model estimates were examined, considering the path coefficients and corresponding significance levels. The indirect and total effects of the independent constructs on the dependent ones were also analysed.

Regarding the impact of motivations on interaction (hypotheses H1a and H1b), knowledge motivations stand out, showing a positive significant influence on all interaction dimensions (Table 5.3 and Fig. 5.2), corroborating what is discussed by Fan et al. (2017), Reisinger and Turner (2003), Su et al. (2016) and White and White (2008). Challenge motivations and novelty motivations only have a significant direct influence on a small number of dimensions of interaction, but this effect is always positive. Therefore, H1a is strongly supported.

As far as escape motivations are concerned, these motivations only have a negative influence on one kind of interaction—close interaction with visitors ($\beta = -0.139$, $p < 0.01$). These results reveal that when people travel in order to escape from their usual environments, they are less likely to have close encounters with other visitors, as expected. Therefore, H1b is slightly supported.

Three of the six interaction dimensions exercise a statistically significant impact on both outcomes of interaction (positive and negative) (hypotheses H2 and H3). As expected, interaction to obtain information registers a negative impact on negative outcomes ($\beta = -0.216$, $p < 0.001$) and a positive one on positive outcomes ($\beta = 0.233$, $p < 0.001$), while close interaction with residents and interaction in cultural attractions show contradictory impacts (contributing to an increase in both positive and negative outcomes). Since the majority of the dimensions of interaction (four in six) have a significant contribution to the positive outcomes of interaction and these contributions are positive, H2 is strongly supported. These findings provide empirical evidence to support what is suggested by Bimonte and Punzo (2016), Reisinger and Turner (2003), Sharpley (2014) and Su et al. (2016).

The influence of interaction on negative outcomes is not so clear. While close interaction with residents and interaction in cultural attractions have a positive influence, leading to negative outcomes, only interaction with residents seems to reduce potential negative outcomes of interaction, as posited. Consequently, H3 is only slightly supported. These results suggest that additional researched is required in order to analyse why, when the intensity of certain kinds of interaction increase, neg-

Table 5.1 Measurement model assessment

Construct/indicators	Mean	Stand dev.	Item loading	t-value[a]	Composite reliability	AVE	Discriminant validity[b]
Knowledge motivations (KM)	4.97	1.27			0.858	0.601	Yes
Expand knowledge	5.06	1.56	0.731	20.37			
Interact with local residents	4.58	1.60	0.783	27.97			
Get to know other cultures	5.26	1.72	0.799	27.24			
Meet other people	4.97	1.64	0.787	29.97			
Challenge motivations (CM)	4.00	1.29			0.834	0.558	Yes
Develop physical abilities	3.55	1.72	0.694	15.80			
Learn more about oneself	4.00	1.76	0.743	18.76			
Have an experience that involves thrills, taking risks	3.81	1.72	0.744	20.53			
Have an experience that involves surprise	4.63	1.70	0.802	26.13			
Novelty motivations (NM)	5.64	1.13			0.855	0.747	Yes
Be in a different environment	5.70	1.23	0.696	4.26			
Learn new things	5.59	1.38	0.952	7.43			
Escape motivations (EM)	4.81	1.43			0.817	0.696	Yes
Be in a calm environment	4.51	1.65	0.826	16.83			
Rest	5.11	1.72	0.901	36.28			
Close interaction with residents (CIR)	2.49	1.52			0.898	0.639	Yes

(continued)

Table 5.1 (continued)

Construct/indicators	Mean	Stand dev.	Item loading	t-value[a]	Composite reliability	AVE	Discriminant validity[b]
Practised sports with residents	2.17	1.66	0.701	16.55			
Participated in celebrations with residents	3.17	2.12	0.798	38.43			
Exchanged gifts with residents	1.84	1.57	0.772	27.62			
Shared meals with residents	2.99	2.19	0.874	62.18			
Was invited to local residents' home	2.28	1.92	0.841	42.39			
Interaction with visitors at recreational attractions and facilities (IVRAF)	3.67	1.42			0.868	0.570	Yes
Interaction with other visitors in discos, clubs and bars	4.10	2.04	0.792	29.73			
Interaction with other visitors in nature places	3.76	1.92	0.696	17.81			
Interaction with other visitors in other commercial establishments	3.42	1.81	0.807	33.71			
Interaction with other visitors in food & beverage establishments	3.86	1.85	0.799	28.40			
Interaction with other visitors in the street	3.22	1.80	0.668	18.01			

(continued)

Table 5.1 (continued)

Construct/indicators	Mean	Stand dev.	Item loading	t-value[a]	Composite reliability	AVE	Discriminant validity[b]
Close interaction with visitors (CIV)	3.32	1.63			0.892	0.673	Yes
Participated in recreational activities with other visitors	3.23	1.98	0.777	27.74			
Had the opportunity to get to know other visitors	3.85	1.98	0.851	52.05			
Exchanged information about the place with other visitors	3.19	1.90	0.824	38.69			
Shared meals with other visitors	3.02	2.09	0.829	41.29			
Interaction with residents at recreational attractions and facilities (IRRAF)	4.09	1.56			0.865	0.681	Yes
Interaction with residents in discos, clubs and bars	4.08	2.00	0.764	18.31			
Interaction with residents in other commercial establishments	3.86	1.92	0.853	38.84			
Interaction with residents in food & beverage establishments	4.32	1.76	0.855	39.75			
Interaction in cultural attractions (ICA)	2.90	1.41			0.855	0.595	Yes
Interaction with residents in events	2.82	1.83	0.789	28.58			
Interaction with residents in monuments	2.80	1.80	0.745	21.86			
Interaction with other visitors in events	2.94	1.79	0.773	26.05			

(continued)

Table 5.1 (continued)

Construct/indicators	Mean	Stand dev.	Item loading	t-value[a]	Composite reliability	AVE	Discriminant validity[b]
Interaction with other visitors in monuments	3.03	1.90	0.777	28.26			
Interaction with residents to obtain information (IRI)	3.82	1.44			0.785	0.550	Yes
Obtained information about this place from local residents	3.77	2.02	0.719	16.32			
Interaction with residents in nature places	3.53	1.89	0.678	13.78			
Interaction with residents in the street	4.18	1.94	0.821	32.21			
Positive outcomes of interaction (POI)	4.39	1.47			0.917	0.689	Yes
Cultural enrichment	4.69	1.86	0.806	37.12			
Development of respect and understanding	4.53	1.75	0.875	58.33			
Development of positive attitudes	4.60	1.70	0.859	47.88			
Improved ability to interact	4.50	1.68	0.854	50.80			
Reduction of prejudice	3.66	1.86	0.749	25.85			
Negative outcomes of interaction (NOI)	2.16	1.18			0.847	0.649	Yes
Development of feelings of inferiority	1.79	1.32	0.804	19.97			
Development of superficial relationships	2.74	1.67	0.780	17.93			
Increased stress	1.95	1.41	0.833	26.61			

[a]t-values were obtained with the bootstrapping procedure (5000 samples) and are significant at the 0.001 level (two-tailed test)
[b]Discriminant validity of all contracts is established since the heterotrait-monotrait ratios of correlations are <0.9

Table 5.2 Discriminant validity of the constructs—Heterotrait-Monotrait Ratio (HTMT)

	KM	CM	NM	EM	CIR	IVRAF	CIV	IRRAF	ICA	IRI	POI	NOI
KM												
CM	0.746											
NM	0.726	0.451										
EM	0.102	0.166	0.124									
CIR	0.402	0.324	0.186	0.127								
IVRAF	0.411	0.367	0.174	0.107	0.397							
CIV	0.379	0.344	0.246	0.170	0.543	0.663						
IRRAF	0.435	0.289	0.292	0.072	0.489	0.557	0.391					
ICA	0.412	0.273	0.176	0.071	0.456	0.559	0.506	0.468				
IRI	0.614	0.444	0.479	0.225	0.606	0.572	0.52	0.796	0.615			
POI	0.713	0.586	0.452	0.087	0.461	0.507	0.587	0.452	0.512	0.663		
NOI	0.195	0.385	0.141	0.164	0.348	0.224	0.225	0.181	0.352	0.170	0.332	

Table 5.3 Hypotheses testing

Hypotheses path	Coefficient	t-value[a]	p value	Support
H1. Motivations → Interaction				Strongly supported
H1a. KM, CM and NM → Interaction				
KM → CIR	0.307	5.132	0.000	Positive influence
KM → IVRAF	0.281	4.467	0.000	Positive influence
KM → CIV	0.201	3.414	0.001	Positive influence
KM → IRRAF	0.291	4.482	0.000	Positive influence
KM → ICA	0.328	5.152	0.000	Positive influence
KM → IRI	0.325	5.310	0.000	Positive influence
CM → CIR	0.107	1.849	0.064	–
CM → IVRAF	0.151	2.636	0.008	Positive influence
CM → CIV	0.150	2.662	0.008	Positive influence
CM → IRRAF	0.040	0.688	0.492	–
CM → ICA	0.037	0.643	0.52	–
CM → IRI	0.074	1.308	0.191	–
NM → CIR	−0.046	0.918	0.359	–
NM → IVRAF	−0.071	1.265	0.206	–
NM → CIV	0.044	0.851	0.395	–
NM → IRRAF	0.055	0.992	0.321	–
NM → ICA	−0.055	1.064	0.287	–
NM → IRI	0.106	2.002	0.045	Positive influence
H1b. EM → Interaction				Slightly supported
EM → CIR	−0.072	1.264	0.206	–
EM → IVRAF	−0.017	0.313	0.754	–
EM → CIV	−0.139	2.597	0.009	Negative influence
EM → IRRAF	−0.041	0.815	0.415	–
EM → ICA	−0.020	0.348	0.728	–
EM → IRI	0.064	1.202	0.229	–
H2. Interaction → POI				Strongly supported
CIR → POI	0.099	2.241	0.025	Positive influence
IVRAF → POI	0.085	1.521	0.128	–
CIV → POI	0.268	4.860	0.000	Positive influence
IRRAF → POI	0.044	0.843	0.399	–
ICA → POI	0.123	2.574	0.010	Positive influence
IRI → POI	0.233	4.300	0.000	Positive influence
H3. Interaction → NOI				Slightly supported
CIR → NOI	0.237	3.933	0.000	Positive influence
IVRAF → NOI	0.046	0.780	0.435	–
CIV → NOI	0.018	0.283	0.777	–
IRRAF → NOI	0.052	0.884	0.377	–
ICA → NOI	0.222	4.161	0.000	Positive influence
IRI → NOI	- 0.216	3.616	0.000	Negative influence

[a]t-values were obtained with the bootstrapping procedure (5000 samples) and are significant at the 0.001 level (two-tailed test)

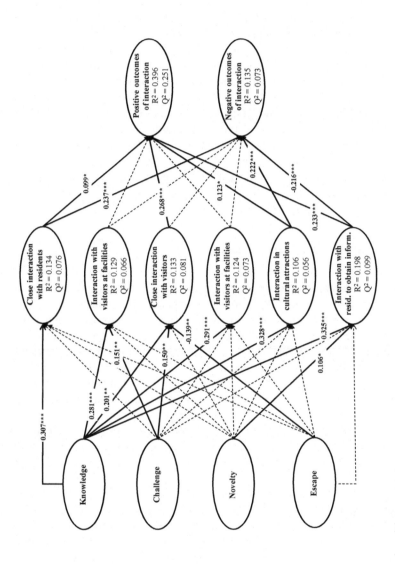

Fig. 5.2   Structural model assessment

ative outcomes occur. These findings also suggest that an appropriate management of these types of interaction, to promote pleasant encounters that lead to positive outcomes, is needed. However, it is worth noticing that the close interaction with residents and interaction in cultural attractions are still very low, corresponding to the least frequent types of interaction. This low frequency of interaction can lead to superficial encounters that do not fulfil the expectations of young visitors and that can even result in misunderstandings and stereotypes.

Beyond the results presented above, indirect effects should also be analysed (Table 5.4). Only knowledge motivations, with influence on both positive and negative outcomes ($\beta = 0.237$, $p<0.001$ and $\beta = 0.107$, $p<0.01$, respectively), and challenge motivations, on positive effects of interaction ($\beta = 0.087$, $p<0.01$), register a statistically significant indirect impact on outcomes of interaction. Knowledge motivations stand out again as the most influential of the model.

The coefficients of determination (R^2) range from 0.106 (interaction in cultural attractions) to 0.396 (positive outcomes of interaction), indicating that the model has moderate predictive value and is capable of explaining endogenous constructs (Fig. 5.2).

5.6   Conclusion and Implications

The study suggests that the interaction of young visitors with hosts and other visitors during tourism trips is still low. Motivations are important determinants of the interactions of young visitors, with motivations for increasing knowledge being the most likely to induce interaction with both hosts and visitors. This research corroborates previous research, showing that superficial contact tends to occur more frequently than close interaction (Eusébio & Carneiro, 2012; Reisinger, 2009). Nevertheless, close interactions with visitors and contact with residents to obtain information are the most powerful in increasing positive outcomes of interaction. Findings also remark that the intensity of interaction has more impact in increasing the positive outcomes of the interaction than in decreasing the negative ones. Moreover, the social contact of young visitors tends to have more positive outcomes than negative, which highlights the important role that interaction during tourism trips may have in the life of young visitors.

This study provides important theoretical and practical contributions. From a theoretical perspective, three important contributions may be highlighted in an under-researched area. First, this study gives more thorough knowledge concerning the influence of travel motivations on visitors' interactions with hosts and other visitors. Second, important insights are provided in terms of different kinds of interactions that take place in the youth market during a tourism trip. Finally, the impact of both travel motivations and different kinds of interactions on visitors' perceptions of outcomes of these interactions are analysed through a structural equation model.

The findings obtained in this research also provide important guidelines for public and private agents responsible for the planning and management of tourism desti-

Table 5.4 Direct, indirect and total effects

Path	Direct	Indirect	Total	t values	p values
KM → CIR	0.307***		0.307***	5.132	0.000
KM → IVRAF	0.281***		0.281***	4.467	0.000
KM → CIV	0.201**		0.201**	3.414	0.001
KM → IRRAF	0.291***		0.291***	4.482	0.000
KM → ICA	0.328***		0.328***	5.152	0.000
KM → IRI	0.325***		0.325***	5.31	0.000
KM → NOI		0.107**	0.107**	3.393	0.001
KM → POI		0.237***	0.237***	5.760	0.000
CM → CIR	0.107		0.107	1.849	0.064
CM → IVRAF	0.151**		0.151**	2.636	0.008
CM → CIV	0.150**		0.150**	2.662	0.008
CM → IRRAF	0.040		0.040	0.688	0.492
CM → ICA	0.037		0.037	0.643	0.520
CM → IRI	0.074		0.074	1.308	0.191
CM → NOI		0.029	0.029	1.138	0.255
CM → POI		0.087*	0.087*	2.573	0.010
NM → CIR	−0.046		−0.046	0.918	0.359
NM → IVRAF	−0.071		−0.071	1.265	0.206
NM → CIV	0.044		0.044	0.851	0.395
NM → IRRAF	0.055		0.055	0.992	0.321
NM → ICA	−0.055		−0.055	1.064	0.287
NM → IRI	0.106*		0.106*	2.002	0.045
NM → NOI		−0.046	−0.046	1.915	0.056
NM → POI		0.022	0.022	0.733	0.464
EM → CIR	−0.072		−0.072	1.264	0.206
EM → IVRAF	−0.017		−0.017	0.313	0.754
EM -→ CIV	−0.139**		−0.139**	2.597	0.009
EM → IRRAF	−0.041		−0.041	0.815	0.415
EM → ICA	−0.020		−0.020	0.348	0.728
EM → IRI	0.064		0.064	1.202	0.229
EM → NOI		−0.041	−0.041	1.590	0.112
EM → POI		−0.035	−0.035	1.038	0.300
CIR → NOI	0.237***		0.237***	3.933	0.000
CIR → POI	0.099*		0.099*	2.241	0.025
IVRAF → NOI	0.046		0.046	0.780	0.435
IVRAF → POI	0.085		0.085	1.521	0.128

(continued)

Table 5.4 (continued)

Path	Direct	Indirect	Total	t values	p values
CIV → NOI	0.018		0.018	0.283	0.777
CIV → POI	0.268***		0.268***	4.860	0.000
IRRAF → NOI	0.052		0.052	0.884	0.377
IRRAF → POI	0.044		0.044	0.843	0.399
ICA → NOI	0.222***		0.222***	4.161	0.000
ICA → POI	0.123*		0.123*	2.574	0.010
IRI → NOI	−0.216***		−0.216***	3.616	0.000
IRI → POI	0.233***		0.233***	4.300	0.000

***$p < 0.001$; **$p < 0.01$; *$p < 0.05$ for a two-tailed test based on 5000 bootstraps

nations to design strategies to maximize positive outcomes of social interactions. In this context, it is of utmost relevance to promote opportunities of interaction between young visitors and both local residents and other visitors in the scope of tourism trips and manage these interactions appropriately. It seems especially important to offer opportunities for close interactions with visitors and residents. One strategy is to design organized trips or organized activities (e.g. events) for young visitors, where they contact other visitors for a longer period, sharing meals and talking with them, in order to have a more in-depth knowledge about them. It is also very important to promote opportunities for contact with residents where residents assume an active role in providing information, since these kinds of interaction are among the most likely to generate high positive outcomes. It is also relevant to sensitize residents to be friendly and helpful to young visitors, mainly when providing information, and to involve local people in the provision of tourism information to visitors, both in tourism attractions and tourism facilities (e.g. tourism offices).

Although the present research provides relevant contributions and implications, it also has some limitations. First, only a limited range of determinants of interactions, namely motivations for travel, are considered in the model. In future studies it would be important to consider other potential determinants of interactions such as place attachment, activities undertaken in the destination visited, length of stay at the destination and type of destination visited. Moreover, the research is also limited in terms of geographical scope. It is undertaken only in Portugal and only with students of one university. Extending this research to young people of other countries would also be useful to observe whether the results obtained concerning the model proposed are confirmed. Finally, only a quantitative approach was adopted. Using qualitative approaches would permit to obtain a more in-depth perception of the reasons why motivations have some influence on interactions and why these interactions have certain kinds of consequences .

Acknowledgements This work was financially supported by the research unit on Governance, Competitiveness and Public Policy (project POCI-01-0145-FEDER-008540), funded by FEDER funds through COMPETE 2020—Programa Operacional Competitividade e Internacionalização (POCI)—and by national funds through FCT—Fundação para a Ciência e a Tecnologia.

References

Andereck, K. L., Valentine, K. M., Knopf, R. C., & Vogt, C. A. (2005). Residents' perceptions of community tourism impacts. *Annals of Tourism Research, 32,* 1056–1076.

Beard, J. G., & Ragheb, M. G. (1983). Measuring leisure motivation. *Journal of Leisure Research, 15*(3), 219–228.

Bimonte, S., & Punzo, L. F. (2016). Tourist development and host-guest interaction: An economic exchange theory. *Annals of Tourism Research, 58,* 128–139.

Crompton, J. L. (1979). Motivations for pleasure vacation. *Annals of Tourism Research, 6*(4), 408–424.

Cushner, K., Brislin, R. W. (1996). Intercultural interactions: A Practical Guide. Thousand Oaks, CA: Sage Publications.

De Kadt, E. (1979). *Tourism: Passport to development? Perspectives on the social and cultural effects of tourism in developing countries.* New York: Oxford University Press.

Eusébio, C. A., & Carneiro, M. J. A. (2012). Determinants of tourist–host interactions: An analysis of the university student market. *Journal of Quality Assurance in Hospitality & Tourism, 13*(2), 123–151.

Eusébio, C. A., & Carneiro, M. J. A. (2015). How diverse is the youth tourism market? An activity-based segmentation study. *Tourism, 63*(3), 295–316.

Fan, D. X. F., Zhang, H. Q., Jenkins, C. L., & Tavitiyaman, P. (2017). Tourist typology in social contact: An addition to existing theories. *Tourism Management, 60,* 357–366.

Iso-Ahola, S. E. (1982). Toward a social psychological theory of tourism motivation: A rejoinder. *Annals of Tourism Research, 9*(2), 256–262.

Kastenholz, E., Carneiro, M. J., & Eusébio, C. (2018). Diverse socializing patterns in rural tourist experiences—A segmentation analysis. *Current Issues in Tourism, 21*(4), 401–421.

Krippendorf, J. (1987). *The holidaymakers: Understanding the impact of leisure and travel.* London, UK: Heinemann.

Kim, K., Oh, I.-K., & Jogaratnam, G. (2007). College student travel: A revised model of push motives. *Journal of Vacation Marketing, 13*(1), 73–85.

Manfredo, M. J., Driver, B. L., & Tarrant, M. A. (1996). Measuring leisure motivation: a meta-analysis of the recreation experience preference scales. *Journal of Leisure Research, 28*(3), 188–213.

Morgan, M., & Xu, F. (2009). Student travel experiences: Memories and dreams. *Journal of Hospitality Marketing and Management, 18,* 216–236.

Moutinho, L. (1987). Consumer behaviour in tourism. *European Journal of Marketing, 21*(10), 5–43.

Pizam, A., Uriely, N., & Reichel, A. (2000). The intensity of tourist-host social relationship and its effects on satisfaction and change of attitudes: The case of working tourists in Israel. *Tourism Management, 21*(4), 395–406.

Reisinger, Y. (2009). *International tourism: Cultures and behavior.* Oxford, UK: Butterworth Heinemann.

Reisinger, Y., & Turner, L. (1998). Cultural differences between Mandarin-Speaking tourists and Australian hosts and their impact on cross-cultural tourist-host interaction. *Journal of Business Research, 42*(2), 175–187.

Reisinger, Y., & Turner, L. W. (2003). *Cross-cultural behavior in tourism*. Oxford, UK: Elsevier Butterworth Heinemann.

Richards, G. (2007). *New horizons II: The young independent traveller 2007*. Amsterdam, The Netherlands: WYSE Travel Confederation.

Sharpley, R. (2014). Host perceptions of tourism: A review of the research. *Tourism Management, 42*, 37–49.

Sinkovics, R. R., & Penz, E. (2009). Social distance between residents and international tourist-implications for international business. *International Business Review, 18*, 457–469.

Su, M. M., Long, Y., Wall, G., & Jin, M. (2016). Tourist–community interactions in ethnic tourism: Tuva villages, Kanas Scenic Area, China. *Journal of Tourism and Cultural Change, 14*(1), 1–26.

Tourism Research and Marketing (2013). *New Horizons III: A global study of the youth and student traveler*. New South Wales: WYSE Travel Confederation. Retrieved 27 March, 2016 from https://wysetc.files.wordpress.com/2013/09/newhorizonsiii-v7-execsummary-v4s.pdf.

UNWTO & WYSE (sd.). *The power of youth travel*. Madrid: World Tourism Organization.

Weaver, D. B., & Lawton, L. L. (2001). Resident perceptions in the urban–rural fringe. *Annals of Tourism Research, 28*(2), 439–458.

White, N. R., & White, P. B. (2008). Travel as interaction: Encountering place and others. *Journal of Hospitality and Tourism Management, 15*, 42–48.

Yu, J., Lee, T. J. (2014). Impact of tourists' intercultural interactions. *Journal of Travel Research, 53*(2), 225–238.

Chapter 6
Wine Tourism: Constructs of the Experience

Arlindo Madeira, Antónia Correia and José António Filipe

6.1 Introduction: Conceptualizing Wine Tourism, State of the Art

Charters and Ali-Knight (2002), defined wine tourism as a travel for the purpose of experiencing wineries and wine regions and their links to lifestyle, and as encompassing both service provision and destination marketing. Earlier, Hall (1996) putted the focus of wine tourism on the cultural experience, hence wine is related with heritage of the place, stating that it is a form of tourism with ancestral roots related to the cultivation of vines and wine and combines culture, territory and lifestyle in the context of the rural universe, although it may exist in the urban context. According to Getz and Brown (2006), the concept of wine tourism should be examined from three points: as a form of consumer behaviour, as a regional development strategy, and as a winery opportunity to sell their products directly to the final consumer. All these definitions proposed by the different authors on wine tourism have in common of a direct or indirect form the guest's motivation to travel and the experiences provided by the hosts in the place where the experience happens, as argued by Capitello, Begalli, and Agnoli (2013).

A. Madeira (✉)
Instituto Universitário de Lisboa, Universidade Europeia,
Rua Laura Ayres, nº 4, 1600-510 Lisbon, Portugal
e-mail: arlindo.madeira@universidadeeuropeia.pt

A. Correia
CEFAGE, Universidade do Algarve, Universidade Europeia,
Rua Antonio Henrique Balte, lote 78, 8005-328 Faro, Portugal
e-mail: antonia.correia@universidadeeuropeia.pt

J. A. Filipe
Instituto Universitário de Lisboa, Av das Forças Armadas, 1649-026 Lisbon, Portugal
e-mail: jose-filipe@iscite.pt

© Springer Nature Switzerland AG 2019
A. Artal-Tur et al. (eds.), *Trends in Tourist Behavior*,
Tourism, Hospitality & Event Management,
https://doi.org/10.1007/978-3-030-11160-1_6

The research on wine tourism started in the 80's (Becker, 1984; Spawton, 1986; Edwards, 1989), although only in the beginning of the 90s articles started to be published in a significant way (Gilbert, 1992; Corigliano, 1996; Hall, 1996; Macionis, 1996; Dodd & Bigotte, 1997; Beverland, 1998; Carlsen & Dowling, 1998). The Australian Wine Tourism Conference in 1998 was the first relevant academic meeting on wine tourism. At this conference, there was an emphasis on descriptive and comparative studies that sought to explore the dimensions of this new field of tourism.

From the turn of the century there was a proliferation of several international tourism conferences about this topic. At the same time, Hall et al. (2000) and Getz (2000) published the first two research books on wine tourism.

Nowadays, most of the literature on wine tourism is still coming from the countries designated as new world, mainly from Australia and USA, although in the last few years many old-world researchers have begun to publish especially from France, Italy and Spain. In the literature review carried out by Carlsen in 2004, the author states that three broad themes have emerged in the academic literature on wine tourism: development and promotion of regional wine destinations, policy and environmental sustainability of wine destinations, and winery activities for the public to increase wine sales. In 2006, Mitchell and Hall organized in detail the research in wine tourism by topics that can be grouped in seven different groups: enotourism product; enotourism and regional development; quantification of the demand; segmentation of the wine tourist; visitors' behaviour; nature of visits to wineries; food safety and wine tourism.

Another perspective of wine tourism studies is from the supply and demand perspective. The studies on the demand contemplate: analysis of demographic features (Bruwer, Li, & Reid, 2002, Charters & Ali-Knight, 2002); analysis of perceptions and expectations of wine tourists (Bruwer, Prayag, & Disegna, 2018; Charters & Ali-Knight, 2000), wine tourist motivations (Alant & Bruwer, 2004; Johnson & Bruwer, 2007), tourists behaviour (Mitchell & Hall, 2004; Galloway, Mitchell, Getz, Crouch, & Ong, 2008), brand loyalty (O'Neill & Charters, 2006; Johnson & Bruwer, 2007), wine tourism experiences (Quadri-Felitti & Fiore, 2012; Pikkemaat, Peters, Boksberger, & Secco, 2009), to taste and purchase wine at the wineries (Bruwer, 2003; Lee & Chang, 2012); to receive information about wine and its elaboration process (O'Neill, Palmer, & Charters, 2002; Getz & Brown, 2006); to visit wineries (Cambourne, Macionis, Hall, & Sharples, 2000; Mitchell & Hall, 2006); to visit vineyards, (Frochot, 2000; Sparks, 2007) and taste local gastronomy (Gillespie, 2002; Duarte Alonso & Liu, 2010).

The studies on the supply include: analysis of a combination of wine production and tourism (Carmichael, 2005, Byrd, Canziani, Hsieh, Debbage, & Sonmez, 2016); a product analysis (Carlsen & Dowling, 2001, Getz & Brown, 2006), wine routes (Bruwer, 2003; Hashimoto & Telfer, 2003); festivals (Hall & Sharples, 2008; Fountain, Fish, & Charters, 2008); sustainability of a destination (Poitras & Donald, 2006; Grimstad & Burgess, 2014) regional destination image (Williams, 2001, Bruwer & Joy, 2017), cellar door sales (Dodd, 1999; O'Neill & Charters, 2006), cellar door activities (Mitchell & Hall, 2001), wine market (Brown, Havitz, & Getz, 2006), wine marketing (Dodd, 1995; Espejel & Fandos, 2009), strategies for winery managers

(Telfer, 2001; Williams & Dossa, 2003), Wine tourism life cycle (Getz, 2000; Dodd & Beverland, 2001), small wineries (Edwards, 1989), regional development (Hall & Mitchell, 2000; Frochot, 2003) and the business dimensions of wine tourism (Carlsen & Charters, 2004; Bruwer & Johson, 2010). Although the experience is indirectly present in a large number of wine tourism studies, only a few specifically focus on this subject (Carmichael, 2005; Pikkemaat et al., 2009; Cohen & Ben-Nun, 2009; Quadri-Felitti & Fiore, 2012).

6.2 Enogastronomy as the Core Product

Wine and gastronomy are naturally the core products that sustain this form of tourism (Kivela & Crotts, 2006). Wine tourism is also seen as a particular form of gastronomic tourism, lying closely linked to local gastronomy and wine and the place where the experience unfolds (Getz, 2000). This idea is supported by Gillespie (2002) when argues that gastronomy is about the recognition of a variety of factors relevant to the foods and beverages eaten and consumed by a group, in a locality, region or even a nation. Santich (2004), adds to the discussion culture as a complementary product of this type of tourism, referring that gastronomy involves everything from guidance on proper food and drink, as a historical topic, and as a reflection of a society's culture. Although the need for food is common to all types of tourism, the development of wine tourism suggests the idea that gastronomy, wine and culture often are the main attractions leading tourists to visit a specific region and not necessarily a secondary or complementary attraction (Stewart, Bramble, & Ziraldo, 2008). The relationship between consumers' travel and their involvement with wine and food has demonstrated the strength of their dependence, not only because of an obvious need for food but also for hedonism (Sparks, 2007; Bruwer & Alant, 2009). This hedonistic perspective is highlighted by Getz (2000) who states that it wine tourism has different characteristics from other forms of tourism in that it heavily involves all the senses: taste, smell, touch, sight and hearing. Duarte Alonso and Liu (2010) underline the power of local cuisines and wines as powerful tools to elevate or enhance a region's profile as a destination, especially among culinary, wine and tourism enthusiasts.

6.3 Defining the Wine Tourism Experience

According to Williams (2001), wine tourism involves more than just visiting wineries and purchasing wine: it is the culmination of a number of unique experiences composed by: the ambience, atmosphere, surrounding environment, regional culture, local cuisine and wine with its intrinsic characteristics (grapes, techniques and characteristics). Therefore, a visit to a winery involves an holistic experience (Mitchell & Hall, 2006) that include: an aesthetic appreciation of the natural environment, the winery and its cellar door (Charters et al., 2009); the cultural and historical context of the wine region (Frochot, 2000), the production methods (Roberts & Sparks, 2006), a search for education and diversity (Charters & Ali-Knight, 2002), a sense of connection with the winery (Fountain et al., 2008), and the search for authenticity (Charter et al., 2009). Bruwer and Alant (2009) complement this idea by stating that wine tourism represents a journey for the purpose of experiencing wineries, wine regions, and their links to a lifestyle, encompassing both service provision and destination marketing. This hedonistic experience is only possible if the winescape is prepared to meet the needs of the guests (Bruwer & Alant, 2009). Thus, creating enogastronomic experiences implies that wine producers in a region intentionally use their services as a stage and its products as props to involve tourists individually and thus create conditions for a memorable event (Pine & Gilmore, 1999).

In order to create experiences is essential understand the key elements of the experience by analysing the tourist's motivation to visit a certain area (Charters & Ali-Knight, 2002). Visiting a winery is also a key factor for wine distribution, customer satisfaction, and positive brand image for the winery as well as for the region (Hall et al., 2000; Mitchell, Hall, & McIntosh, 2000). O'Neill and Charters (2006), determinates four attributes on the cellar door experiences: empathy (the ability of staff to make visitors feel welcome), reliability (providing a consistent level of service), response (ability of staff to meet guests' needs) and assurance (providing a sense of security to customers). Roberts and Sparks (2006) defined key factors that enhance the experience from the wine tourist's perspective: authenticity of experience, value for money, service interactions, setting and surroundings, product offerings, information dissemination, personal growth (learning experiences) and indulgence (lifestyle). The Pine and Gilmore experience economy model (1998) presents four dimensions of the experience, adaptable to wine tourist's expectations: entertainment (wine events, wine tours in vineyards with tastings, cultural events), education (learning about wine and its production, about wine history, culture and gastronomy), escape (guided tours through vineyards, participating in the wine production process, sport activities combined with wine), and aesthetics (landscape is dominated by wine, good signage and information in the region, well-tended wine bars and wine shops). This work aims to define the fundamental constructs of the experience, that occurs from the interaction of the Guests with the Place and the Hosts as, based on the model of Pine and Gilmore (1998), as presented in the model below (Fig. 6.1).

6.4   Wine Tourist as the Guest

Wine tourists are the centrepiece of the process because without tourists there is no wine tourism. The wine tourist naturally assumes the role of guest when visiting a wine region, being fundamental its segmentation and characterization for those involved in the wine tourism process, in order to structure their products better and facing the expectations of the visitors (Bruwer et al., 2002). Charters and Ali-Knight (2002) ask the essential question: who is the wine tourist? The segmentation and characterization of wine tourists is not consensual among the researchers and must also be seen according to the old world/new word dichotomy, from one winery to

Fig. 6.1 The constructs of the experience. *Source* Own elaboration

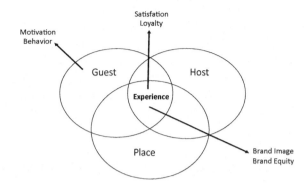

another, or from one region to another within the same country, taking into account cultural values of the visitors (Frochot, 2000).

The studies on the characterization of the wine tourists may be divided in demographic (Hall, 1996; Corigliano, 1996; Dodd & Bigotte, 1997; Mitchell & Hall, 2006; O'Neill & Charters, 2006), or motivational and behavioural (Johnson, 1998; Mitchell & Hall, 2006; Johnson & Bruwer, 2007). The first profiles of wine tourists used the psychographic characteristics as the criteria for segmenting wine tourists. Hall (1996) highlighted three categories of wine tourists: The Wine Lovers, the Wine Interested and Curious Tourists. Corigliano (1996), defined the wine tourists as Wine-Interested, Wine-Curious, Professional, Passionate Newcomer, Follower and Drinker. Dodd and Bigotte (1997) also used demographic data to determine consumer perceptions and suggest two segments based only on age and income: older people with high income and younger people with low income. Johnson (1998), distinguishes two types of wine tourists: the "specialist winery tourist" and the "generalist" visitor, based on the purpose of the visit. Dodd (1999), classifies the wine tourists into two main groups regarding their knowledge: "advanced or specialist" and "basic or intermediate". Charters and Ali-Knight (2002) presented a characterization of wine tourists based not only on their knowledge, but also in their interest about wine. This categorization results in four types of wine tourists: "Wine Lovers" (with a sub segment called "Connoisseurs"); "Wine Interested" and "Wine Novice". In the same study the authors point out that for the producers, visitors are either Sophisticated Drinker, corresponding to a low percentage of visitors, Casual Tourist or even in the intermediate category, individuals who have no specific knowledge about wine but who regularly drink wine and who are interested in learning and passing through that experience.

Williams and Dossa (2003) presented a segmentation of the non-resident wine tourist into two distinct groups: The Generalists and the Immersionists (visitors who gives a greater emphasis on increasing knowledge about the wine region and participates in various cultural activities). Gatti and Maroni (2004), classified wine tourists into four distinct groups on their motivations: The Professional, the Cultured, the Enthusiastic and the Wine Tourist by Change. Galloway et al. (2008) presented a segmentation of the wine tourists based on a median split of their sensation showing that, compared with the group of lower sensation seekers, higher sensation seekers have a higher monthly expenditure on wine, purchase more bottles of wine per month, drink more bottles of wine per month, engaged in more visits to wineries, are more likely to use the internet as a source of information about wineries, participated in more activities during a visit to a wine region and rated wine and winery-related learning, as well as stimulation and indulgence experiences and emotions as stronger incentives in deciding whether to visit a wine region.

6.5   The Interaction Between Guest and Host

The most important aspect to the guest when visiting wine regions is the cellar door experience (Alant & Bruwer, 2004). This experience provides the opportunity for visitors (guests) to sample the winery's products, by interact with staff (hosts) and thus form an opinion about the producer and the region (O'Neill et al., 2002). The importance of the interaction between guests and hosts is highlighted by Marlowe, Brown, and Zheng (2016) by stating that visitors (guests) have high expectation regarding the winery and the region and placed considerable importance on, the staff (hosts) being friendly, knowledgeable, undertaking of visitor needs, and capable of providing individual attention. This idea is defended by Roberts and Sparks (2006) who stress the importance of personal interactions with winery staff in creating memorable experiences and a connection with the winery and the region. Charters et al. (2009) suggested that the authenticity and quality of the visitor's experience is increased when winery staff show a passion for their products. O'Neill and Charters (2006) identified four intangible service quality dimensions: Empathy (the ability of staff to make visitors feel welcome), Reliability (providing a consistent level of service), Response (ability of staff to meet guests needs) and assurance (providing a sense of security to customers).

6.5.1   Guest Motivations

Wine tourism as a tourist product has several points of interest, which generate different types of motivations, according to the purpose of each guest to visit a region (Byrd et al., 2016). The visitation to vineyards, wineries and wine festivals for wine tasting and/or experiencing the attributes of a grape wine region are the prime motivating factors for visitors (Hall et al., 2000). Bruwer (2003) ranked the follow motivations through surveying wine tourists: tasting wine and purchasing wine, visiting the country setting/vineyards, participating in a wine tour, learning about wine and winemaking, meeting the winemaker, socializing with family/friends, attending wine-related festivals or events and eating at the winery. Alant and Bruwer (2004) organized the motivations on three framework dimensions: to visit a wine region: the visitor's preferences and traits, the region's facilities and attractions and the dynamic of the visit itself.

According to Bruwer (2003) motivations in wine tourism can be identified as primary and secondary. Primary motivators include wine tasting, purchasing and have a pleasant tasting experience (Hall et al., 2000). Secondary motivators are socializing, learning about wine, entertainment, rural setting and relaxation (Bruwer & Alant, 2009). Other researchers distinguish between pull and push motivational factors (Alebaki & Iakovidou, 2011). Pull factors include the general features or activities of the winery: tasting and buying wine, participating in guided tours, staying overnight, drinking wines paired with food, participating in activities with family or friends (Cohen & Ben-Nun, 2009). Push factors include the desire to broaden one's social network, relax, learn about wine and enhance one's understanding of its cultural significance (Galloway et al., 2008).

6.5.2   Guest Behaviour

Understanding the patterns of wine consumption plays a critical role in the wine marketing process and allows wineries and other wine business to effectively target their market (Mitchell & Hall, 2006). Wine tourist behaviour has an inherent element of hedonism, because the tasting of wine involves alcohol and there are links with food, socializing and relaxation, which point to indulgent activity (Beverland, 1998). This line of thought is also advocated by Sparks (2007) by stating that involvement with food and wine activities in general is likely to influence intentions to partic- ipate in a specific wine tourism vacation. Getz and Brown (2006) emphasizes two major factors regarding behaviour: the appeal of wine tourism destinations and fac- tors shaping their attractiveness and who are the wine tourists and what they want from a wine tourism experience. Alebaki et al. (2015), underlined the following fac- tors as behaviour influencers: the travel distance (tourism demand varies depending on whether travel distance increases or decreases), the wine product involvement (visitor's motivational state of mind with wine related activities), the wine product knowledge (the level of visitor's knowledge regarding the world of wine), the wine tourist identity (a person who places more importance on his/her wine consumer identity is more likely to dedicate time and money to wine related activities, includ- ing visitation to wineries) and the past wine tourism experience (the influence of past experience in a particular wine region affects the visitor's future choices).

6.6   Wine Region as the Place

Getz and Brown (2006) argues that attributes of a wine region, such as the scenery and open spaces, also provide an incentive to visit the region. Hall et al. (2000) have asserted that visitation to a wine region is frequently motivated by 'the attributes of a grape wine region, referred to as the winescape. Winescape are characterised by three main elements: the presence of vineyards, the winemaking activity and the wineries where the wine is produced and stored (Bruwer and Alant, 2009).

Hall et al. (2002) brought to the discussion the concept of tourist terroir, which they define in terms of the "unique combination of the physical, cultural and natural environment that gives each region its distinctive tourist appeal. To Marzo-Navarro and Pedraja-Iglesias (2012), wine products are now enjoyed by a much wider socio-economic range of increasingly sophisticated consumers who seek information about where their wines come from and value a wine more when it comes from somewhere specific, such as a known regional destination or origin.

6.6.1 Brand Equity

Brand equity may be defined as the value that a brand adds to a product or service (Lockshin & Spawton, 2001). From a business perspective, brand equity is a useful instrument with which to calculate a brand's value (Gómez, Lopez, & Molina, 2015). The formation of brand equity is essential for wine regions that seek to differentiate themselves from their competitor's destination because the guest relates with the place based on his/her perceived brand equity (Lockshin & Spawton, 2001; Gómez et al., 2015). The recognition that countries, regions, places, and other geographical entities behave rather like brands is gaining acceptance and the value of branding places is now better understood (Gómez et al., 2015). Preferences for wine from different origins differ significantly with respect to the benefits perceived by consumers regarding the wine region equity dimensions, that is quality, price, social, emotional, environmental, and humane value (Orth, McGarry Wolf, & Dodd, 2005). Everyone involved in the wine tourism process, from governance to producers, are beginning to understand just how much equity can be added to their brands (Orth et al., 2005). In order to develop and enhance brand equity through wine tourism, it is necessary to understand the concept and its complexity, that is, brand equity is a sum total of the attributes of a brand (Lockshin & Spawton, 2001). Thus, destination brand equity should be addressed as a multidimensional construct through the analysis of five dimensions, based on Aaker's work (1996) and adapted for wine tourism by Gómez et al. (2015): brand awareness (the consumer's ability to recall and recognize a wine destination), brand loyalty (the consumers' preference for the destination, intention to repeat the visit, and likelihood of recommending the destination), brand image (the cognitive and affective associations that consumers link to the destination), perceived quality (the consumer's perception of the overall service quality) and other proprietary (wine destination brand assets, such as historic buildings, unique processes, channel management methods, and customer relationship management, can determine brand equity).

6.6.2 Brand Image

The strategic goal for wine of tourism is to become not only a region promotor but also a tool to improve the image and reputation of the regional wines and by extension, the region itself (Frochot, 2003). The study of the wine region destination image has its roots in the need to better understand the characteristics and motives of wine tourists (Getz & Brown, 2006). As it was pointed out before, the wine region can be defined as a pack of products offered, which encompasses the activities related to the world of wine, a tourist impeller of the area in which it is implanted, that allows to revalue the image of the rural, to increase the knowledge about the architectural heritage of the place, to preserve the cultural and gastronomic tradition, and at the same time satisfy the expectations demanded by the consumer (Frochot, 2000; Kivela & Crotts, 2006). Consequently, a wine and food route contributes to the reputation and image of wine regions and their wines by highlighting a set of regional features, which gives a brand identity and a distinctive note or something that makes it unique (Cambourne et al., 2000). At the same mean, wine, food and tourism rely on regional branding for market leverage and promotion and thus the appellation, or the regional brands become an important source of differentiation and value added for rural regions (Frochot, 2003).

6.7 Winery Staff as Hosts

As hosts, service staff have a determinant roll in order to engage the guest with the place. The ability to connect with the guest goes beyond just good service, rather, staff must also enable visitors to have a sense of linkage with the winery; they must convey passion about it and they have to provide a "story", or a myth, which can engage the visitor with the place (Charters, Fountain, & Fish, 2009). The ability of the winery and its staff to engage the visitor at the tasting room is therefore crucial component in establishing brand loyalty (Alant & Bruwer, 2004). In this way, winery staff can establish in the winery visitor an emotional connection to the brand. The importance of this personal connection to the overall winery experience was very apparent in the current research project and manifested itself in a number of ways (Marlowe et al., 2016). Providing training to the tasting-room staff is essential to deliver a better service and thus increasing sales of wine at wineries (Marlowe et al., 2016). Tasting-room staff are better able to sell wines to visitors when their level of understanding of the wines being offered are high (Thach & Olson, 2003). Implementing a customer-service training program is fundamental in order to the staff feel more empowered and confident in speaking with sophisticated wine consumers (Marlowe et al., 2016). Learning the basics of viticulture and winemaking by employees in the tasting room, as well as the major grape varietals and regions is pointed out by Thach and Olson (2003) as the most critical training needed for the success of tasting-room employees.

6.8   Service Quality as the Determinant of Satisfaction and Loyalty

Service quality is the determinant for customer satisfaction in wine tourism. The increased significance and growing competitiveness of this sector has led to a heightened concern by producers and consumers for the quality of services being offered, and has forced many within the industry to invest in the delivery of higher levels of service quality as a means to achieving competitive differentiation (O'Neill & Charters, 2006). The service scape concept holds that the design of the physical environment can be an extremely important element of the perception of service quality and satisfaction and influence consumption, patterns and practices (Bitner, 1992, cited in Bruwer & Joy, 2017). The service scape refers to the physical facility (wine region, winery tasting rooms) in which a service is delivered and in which the service provider and customer interact, and to any tangible commodities that facilitate that service (Bitner, 1992, cited in Bruwer & Joy, 2017). Customer perceptions of the quality of a cellar door's physical environment contribute to the formation of visitors' first impressions of a cellar door prior to interacting with the staff for purchasing its products (Chen, Bruwer, Cohen, & Goodman, 2016). In tasting room, service quality is the key to the affective attachments a visitor develops for a particular producer which, by extension, can have an impact on their subsequent brand loyalty (O'Neill & Charters, 2006). The tasting room experience and associated memories are influential in the post-visit behaviour of consumers, and thus a memorable experience will more likely to result in a future purchase (Mitchell & Hall, 2004).

6.8.1   Guest Satisfaction

The question of customer satisfaction regarding services related to wine tourism was addressed by different authors (Carmichael, 2005; Getz & Brown, 2006). Satisfaction is believed to impact on destination image (Bruwer & Joy, 2017), service quality, post- purchase perceptions, future purchase decisions and long-term customer loyalty (O'Neil & Charters, 2006) who should ultimately translate into higher sales and revenue (Yuan & Jang, 2008). Wine tourists enjoy a high level of satisfaction for services experienced during wine tourist vacation. These include visits to cellars, wine tastings and the quality of the wine tasted (Carmichael, 2005). Thus, wineries should create pleasant experiences in order to generate higher satisfaction levels and to positively influence visitors' behavioural intentions (Charters et al., 2009).

6.8.2   Guest Loyalty

Measuring tourists' loyalty has become vitally important to understanding the success of particular destinations. Tourist loyalty intentions refer to future behavioural intentions of tourists in relation to tourism experiences (Mason & Paggiaro, 2012). It is consensual that the intention to revisit a destination, recommend it to others and spread positive word-of-mouth reflect tourist loyalty intentions for a particular destination (Mitchell & Hall, 2004). Furthermore, these repeat visitors tend to spend more on wine, accessory items and souvenirs than first time visitors (Alant & Bruwer, 2004). Mitchell and Hall (2004) similarly report that repeat visitors to a winery are more likely to make a post-visit purchase off site. Loyalty in wine tourism, terms must include the purchase of wine both during the visit and the intention/likelihood of purchasing wine made by that particular winery in the future (Lee & Chang, 2012). Loyalty intentions are naturally related to destination image (Williams, 2001), leisure activities (Getz & Brown, 2006), involvement (Brown et al., 2006) and service quality (O'Neill & Palmer, 2004). In short, loyalty to destination is a natural reflection of the satisfaction of lived experiences and is reflected in the brand equity and brand image of the producer and the destination (Lee & Chang, 2012).

6.9   Conclusion and Implications

This work analyses the constructs that interfere with the experience given to the visitors of a wine region from the interaction of Guest-Place-Host trilogy: motivation, behaviour, quality of service, satisfaction, loyalty, brand equity and brand image. Motivations for visiting wineries are important to understand the nature of the visitor, as they can be used to explain visitor's behaviour and thus to define market segments. The conceptual relationship established between motivation and involvement is fundamental to explain the behaviour and the consequent satisfaction of the visitor towards the destination. Guest satisfaction should be analysed regarding all the attributes and services available during the wine experience: entertainment, aesthetics, educational and escapist. A wine region that counts with positive winescape attributes shapes favourable wine tourist evaluations and behavioural intention toward it. Satisfaction in tasting room experience potentially generate loyalty among visitors. The winery visitation is a key factor for wine distribution, customer satisfaction, and positive brand image for the winery as well as for the region. The underlying assumption is that is possible to reach a higher level of customer satisfaction, and thus generate customer loyalty by understanding the effects of different attributes on customer satisfaction. This line of thought argues that satisfaction with an event is affected by perceptions that are formed before and after the experience and that will be decisive for loyalty, future visit and for the catapulting of the brand equity and image of the destination and its products. The visit is composed of tangible and intangible features, the most obvious tangible factors being those that led to the decision of the visit: tasting and/or buying wine and tasting food. In order to increase visitor's loyalty, more attention should be made to enhance visitors' satisfaction of the intangible service because pleasure contributes dramatically to the satisfaction of the intangible service. Service quality and the ability of the staff to connect with the guest plays a key role on the service encounter found a positive association between pleasure and satisfaction. The more pleasurable experience visitors had, the more likely they were to be satisfied by both tangible and intangible service attributes of the wine region. This research has three main theoretical contributions. First, the study states the relevance of the Pine and Gilmore's experience economy model adapted to the wine tourism context. Secondly, it brings to the discussion a new organization of the main constructs of the enogastronomic experience, based on the trilogy Guest-Host-Place and finally this work additionally contributes to a review of the literature on wine tourism from a new organization of the constructs that compose the experience. The growing body of research has validated the relevance of the studies on wine tourism, with more authors addressing specific topics from the perspective of demand and supply. Although the experiences provided to tourists are the main argumet for the existence of this type of tourism, only a few studies directly address this issue. From the existing studies on the experience almost all of them adopted the model of the ecomomy experience of Pine and Gilmore, although none of them organize the constructs from the Guest-Host-Place trilogy. The study of the wine tourism experience requires a careful analysis due to the specificities of each wine region, each country and wine tourist segmentation. Thus, the complexity of the products that composed the holistic wine tourism experience deserves a detailed study, which equates how to approach wine tourism in that country (there are huge differences between wine tourism in the new and old world, in terms of products, (local grapes, techniques, local gastronomy) the purpose and duration of the visit, the motivations and knowledge of each type the tourist, its cultural tourist background, among other factors. It is therefore recommended that future studies adopting this approach take account of all these specificities, in order to obtain more accurate results, according to the region/country under study and those of its visitors.

References

Aaker, D. (1996). Measuring brand equity across products and markets. *California Management Review, 38*(3), 102–120.

Alant, K., & Bruwer, J. (2004). Wine tourism behaviour in the context of a motivational framework for wine regions and cellar doors. *Journal of Wine Research, 15*(1), 27–37.

Alebaki, M., & Iakovidou, O. (2011). Market segmentation in wine tourism: A comparison of approaches. *Tourismos, An International Multidisciplinary Journal of Tourism, 6*(1), 123–140.

Alebaki, M., Menexes, G., & Koutsouris, A. (2015). Developing a multidimensional framework for wine tourist behavior: Evidence from Greece. *Wine Economics and Policy, 4*(2), 98–109.

Becker, C. (1984). Der Weintourismus an der Mosel. *Berichte zur deutschen Landeskunde, 58*(2), 381–405.

Beverland, M. (1998). Wine tourism in New Zealand—Maybe the industry has got it right. *International Journal of Wine Marketing, 10*(2), 24–33.

Bitner, M. (1992). Servicescapes: The impact of physical surroundings on customers and employees. *The Journal of Marketing, 56*(2), 57–71.

Brown, G., Havitz, M., & Getz, D. (2006). Relationship between wine involvement and wine related travel. *Journal of Travel & Tourism Marketing, 2*(1), 31–46.

Bruwer, J. (2003). South African wine routes: some perspectives on the wine tourism industry's structural dimensions and wine tourism product. *Tourism Management, 24*(4), 423–435.

Bruwer, J., & Alant, K. (2009). The hedonic nature of wine tourism consumption: An experiential view. *International Journal of Wine Business Research, 21*(3), 235–257.

Bruwer, J., & Johnson, R. (2010). Place-based marketing and regional branding strategy perspectives in the California wine industry. *Journal of Consumer Marketing, 27*(1), 5–16.

Bruwer, J., & Joy, A. (2017). Tourism destination image (TDI) perception of a Canadian regional winescape: A free-text macro approach. *Tourism Recreation Research, 42*(3), 367–379.

Bruwer, J., Li, E., & Reid, M. (2002). Segmentation of the Australian wine market using a wine-related lifestyle approach. *Journal of Wine Research, 13*(3), 217–242.

Bruwer, J., Prayag, G., & Disegna, M. (2018). Why wine tourists visit cellar doors: Segmenting motivation and destination image. *International Journal of Tourism Research, 20*(3), 355–366.

Byrd, T., Canziani, B., Hsieh, J., Debbage, K., & Sonmez, S. (2016). Wine tourism: Motivating visitors through core and supplementary services. *Tourism Management, 52,* 19–29.

Cambourne, B., Macionis, N., Hall, M., & Sharples, L. (2000). The future of wine tourism. In C. M. Hall, L. Sharples, B. Cambourne, & N. Macionis (Eds.), *Wine tourism around the world*. Oxford: Butterworth-Heinemann.

Capitello, R., Begalli, D., & Agnoli, L. (2013). Tourism experiences and wine experiences: a new approach to the analysis of the visitor perceptions for a destination. The case of Verona. In *7th Academy of Wine Business Research International Conference.*

Carlsen, J., & Charters, S. (2004). International wine tourism research. In *Proceedings of the International Wine Tourism Conference*. Cambridge: CAB International Publisher.

Carlsen, J., & Dowling, R. (1998). Wine tourism marketing issues in Australia. *International Journal of Wine Marketing, 10*(3), 23–32.

Carlsen, J., & Dowling, R. (2001). Regional wine tourism: A plan of development for Western Australia. *Tourism Recreation Research, 26*(2), 45–52.

Carmichael, B. (2005). Understanding the wine tourism experience for winery visitors in the Niagara Region, Ontario, Canada. *Tourism Geographies, 7*(2), 185–204.

Charters, S., & Ali-Knight, J. (2000). Wine tourism—A thirst for knowledge? *International Journal of Wine Marketing, 12*(3), 70–80.

Charters, S., & Ali-Knight, J. (2002). Who is the wine tourist? *Tourism Management, 23*(3), 311–319.

Charters, S., Fountain, J., & Fish, N. (2009). "You felt like lingering…" Experiencing "real" service at the winery tasting room. *Journal of Travel Research, 48*(1), 122–134.

Chen, X., Bruwer, J., Cohen, J., & Goodman, S. (2016). A wine tourist behaviour model for Australian winery cellar doors. *Tourism Analysis, 21*(1), 77–91.

Cohen, E., & Ben-Nun, L. (2009). The important dimensions of wine tourism experience from potential visitors' perception. *Tourism and Hospitality Research, 9*(1), 20–31.

Corigliano, M. (1996). *Caratteristiche della Domanda Strategie di Offerta e Aspetti Territoriali e Ambientali*. Franco Angeli: Milano.

Dodd, T. (1995). Opportunities and pitfalls of tourism in a developing wine industry. *International Journal of wine marketing, 7*(1), 5–16.

Dodd, T. (1999). Attracting repeat customers to wineries. *International Journal of Wine Marketing, 11*(2), 18–28.

Dodd, T., & Beverland, M. (2001). Winery tourism life-cycle development: A proposed model. *Tourism Recreation Research, 26*(2), 11–21.

Dodd, T., & Bigotte, V. (1997). Perceptual differences among visitor groups to wineries. *Journal of Travel Research, 35*(3), 46–51.

Duarte Alonso, A., & Liu, Y. (2010). Wine tourism development in emerging Western Australian regions. *International Journal of Contemporary Hospitality Management, 22*(2), 245–262.

Edwards, F. (1989). The marketing of wine from small wineries: Managing the intangibles. *International Journal of Wine Marketing, 1*(1), 14–17.

Espejel, J., & Fandos, C. (2009). Wine marketing strategies in Spain: A structural equation approach to consumer response to protected designations of origin (PDOs). *International Journal of Wine Business Research, 21*(3), 267–288.

Fountain, J., Fish, N., & Charters, S. (2008). Making a connection: Tasting rooms and brand loyalty. *International Journal of Wine Business Research, 20*(1), 8–21.

Frochot, I. (2000). Wine tourism in France: A paradox?. Wine tourism around the world: Development, management and markets. In C. M. Hall, L. Sharples, B. Cambourne, & N. Macionis (Eds.), *Wine tourism around the world*. Oxford: Butterworth-Heinemann.

Frochot, I. (2003). An analysis of regional positioning and its associated food images in French tourism regional brochures. *Journal of Travel & Tourism Marketing, 14*(3–4), 77–96.

Galloway, G., Mitchell, R., Getz, D., Crouch, G., & Ong, B. (2008). Sensation seeking and the prediction of attitudes and behaviours of wine tourists. *Tourism Management, 29*(5), 950–966.

Gatti, S., & Maroni, F. (2004). A profile of wine tourists in some Italian region vineyards: An application of the multiple correspondence analysis. In *Colloque Oenométrie XI*, Dijon.

Getz, D. (2000). *Explore wine tourism: Management, development & destinations*. New York: Cognizant Communication Corporation.

Getz, D., & Brown, G. (2006). Critical success factors for wine tourism regions: A demand analysis. *Tourism Management, 27*(1), 146–158.

Gilbert, D. (1992). Touristic development of a viticultural region of Spain. *International Journal of Wine Marketing, 4*(2), 25–32.

Gillespie, C. (2002). European gastronomy into the 21st century. *Food Service Technology, 2*(2), 107–107.

Gómez, M., Lopez, C., & Molina, A. (2015). A model of tourism destination brand equity: The case of wine tourism destinations in Spain. *Tourism Management, 51*, 210–222.

Grimstad, S., & Burgess, J. (2014). Environmental sustainability and competitive advantage in a wine tourism micro-cluster. *Management Research Review, 37*(6), 553–573.

Hall, M. (1996). Wine tourism in New Zealand. In G. Kearsley (Ed.) *Proceedings of tourism down under II: A tourism research conference*, Dunedin: Centre for Tourism, University of Otago.

Hall, M., Johnson, G., Cambourne, B., Macionis, N., Mithcell, R., & Sharples, L. (2000). Wine tourism: An introduction. In C. M. Hall, L. Sharples, B. Cambourne, & N. Macionis (Eds.), *Wine tourism around the world*. Oxford: Butterworth-Heinemann.

Hall, M., Longo, A. M., Mitchell, R., & Johnson, G. (2002). Wine tourism in. *Wine tourism around the world: development, management and markets*, 150.

Hall, M., & Mitchell, R. (2000). Wine tourism in the Mediterranean: A tool for restructuring and development. *Thunderbird International Business Review, 42*(4), 445–465.

Hall, M., & Sharples, L. (2008). *Food and wine festivals and events around the world: Development, management and markets*. Oxford: Butterworth-Heinemann.

Hashimoto, A., & Telfer, D. (2003). Positioning an emerging wine route in the Niagara region: Understanding the wine tourism market and its implications for marketing. *Journal of Travel & Tourism Marketing, 14*(3–4), 61–76.

Johnson, G. (1998). *Wine tourism in New Zealand—A national survey of wineries*. Unpublished Dip. Tour. Dissertation. University of Otago.

Johnson, R., & Bruwer, J. (2007). Regional brand image and perceived wine quality: The consumer perspective. *International Journal of Wine Business Research, 19*(4), 276–297.

Kivela, J., & Crotts, J. C. (2006). Tourism and gastronomy: Gastronomy's influence on how tourists experience a destination. *Journal of Hospitality & Tourism Research, 30*(3), 354–377.

Lee, T., & Chang, Y. (2012). The influence of experiential marketing and activity involvement on the loyalty intentions of wine tourists in Taiwan. *Leisure Studies, 31*(1), 103–121.

Lockshin, L., & Spawton, T. (2001). Using involvement and brand equity to develop a wine tourism strategy. *International Journal of Wine Marketing, 13*(1), 72–81.

Macionis, N. (1996). Wine tourism: Just what is it all about? Wine tourism in Australia. In G. Kearsley (Ed.) *Proceedings of tourism down under II: A tourism research conference*, Dunedin: Centre for Tourism, University of Otago.

Marlowe, B., Brown, E., & Zheng, T. (2016). Winery tasting-room employee training: Putting wine first in Oregon. *Journal of Quality Assurance in Hospitality & Tourism, 17*(2), 89–100.

Marzo-Navarro, M., & Pedraja-Iglesias, M. (2012). Critical factors of wine tourism: Incentives and barriers from the potential tourist's perspective. *International Journal of Contemporary Hospitality Management, 24*(2), 312–334.

Mason, M., & Paggiaro, A. (2012). Investigating the role of festivalscape in culinary tourism: The case of food and wine events. *Tourism Management, 33*(6), 1329–1336.

Mitchell, R., & Hall, C. (2001). Lifestyle behaviours of New Zealand winery visitors: Wine club activities, wine cellars and place of purchase. *International Journal of Wine Marketing, 13*(3), 82–93.

Mitchell, R., & Hall, C. (2004). The post-visit consumer behaviour of New Zealand winery visitors. *Journal of Wine Research, 15*(1), 39–49.

Mitchell, R., & Hall, C. (2006). Wine tourism research: The state of play. *Tourism Review International, 9*(4), 307–332.

Mitchell, R., Hall, C., & McIntosh, A. (2000). Wine tourism and Wine tourism around the world: Development, management and markets. In C. M. Hall, L. Sharples, B. Cambourne, & N. Macionis (Eds), *Wine tourism and consumer behaviour.* Oxford: Butterworth-Heinemann.

O'Neill, M., & Charters, S. (2006). Managing tourism and hospitality services: Theory and international applications. In Prideaux, B., Moscardo, G, & Laws, E. (Eds), *Service quality at the cellar door: A lesson in services marketing from Western Australia's wine-tourism sector.* Cambridge: CAB International Publisher.

O'Neill, M., & Palmer, A. (2004). Wine production and tourism: Adding service to a perfect partnership. *Cornell Hotel and Restaurant Administration Quarterly, 45*(3), 269–284.

O'Neill, M., Palmer, A., & Charters, S. (2002). Wine production as a service experience—The effects of service quality on wine sales. *Journal of Services Marketing, 16*(4), 342–362.

Orth, U. R., McGarry Wolf, M., & Dodd, T. H. (2005). Dimensions of wine region equity and their impact on consumer preferences. *Journal of Product & Brand Management, 14*(2), 88–97.

Pikkemaat, B., Peters, M., Boksberger, P., & Secco, M. (2009). The staging of experiences in wine tourism. *Journal of Hospitality Marketing & Management, 18*(2–3), 237–253.

Pine, J., & Gilmore, J. (1998). Welcome to the experience economy. *Harvard Business Review, 76*(4), 97–105.

Pine, J., & Gilmore, J. (1999). *The experience economy: Work is theatre & every business a stage.* Boston: Harvard Business Press.

Poitras, L., & Donald, G. (2006). Sustainable wine tourism: The host community perspective. *Journal of Sustainable Tourism, 14*(5), 425–448.

Quadri-Felitti, D., & Fiore, A. (2012). Experience economy constructs as a framework for understanding wine tourism. *Journal of Vacation Marketing, 18*(1), 3–15.

Roberts, L., & Sparks, B. (2006). *Enhancing the wine tourism experience: The customers' viewpoint.* In J. Carlsen & S. Charters (Eds.), *Global wine tourism research management and marketing.* Cambridge: CAB International Publisher.

Santich, B. (2004). The study of gastronomy and its relevance to hospitality education and training. *International Journal of Hospitality Management, 23*(1), 15–24.

Sparks, B. (2007). Planning a wine tourism vacation? Factors that help to predict tourist behavioural intentions. *Tourism Management, 28*(5), 1180–1192.

Spawton, T. (1986). Understanding wine purchasing: Knowing how the wine buyer behaves can increase sales. *Australian Wine Industry Journal, 1*(3), 89–91.

Stewart, J., Bramble, L., & Ziraldo, D. (2008). Key challenges in wine and culinary tourism with practical recommendations. *International Journal of Contemporary Hospitality Management, 20*(3), 303–312.

Telfer, D. (2001). Strategic alliances along the Niagara wine route. *Tourism Management, 22*(1), 21–30.

Thach, E., & Olsen, J. (2003). Customer service training in winery tasting rooms: Perceptions of effectiveness by tasting room personnel'. In *Third Australian Wine Marketing Conference*, Adelaide.

Williams, P. (2001). Positioning wine tourism destinations: An image analysis. *International Journal of Wine Marketing, 13*(3), 42–58.

Williams, P., & Dossa, K. (2003). Non-resident wine tourist markets: Implications for British Columbia's emerging wine tourism industry. *Journal of Travel & Tourism Marketing, 14*(3–4), 1–34.

Yuan, J., & Jang, S. (2008). The effects of quality and satisfaction on awareness and behavioral intentions: Exploring the role of a wine festival. *Journal of Travel Research, 46*(3), 279–288.

Chapter 7
EBSCode—Eco Based Surf Code—Surfing for a Sustainable Development of Beaches: The Portuguese Case

Fernanda Oliveira, Sofia Eurico and João Paulo Jorge

7.1 Introduction

The primary focus of this paper is to understand in which way a Code of Conduct (CC) may be designed and used to promptly answer the concept of sustainable development of Tourism regarding a very specific context, namely beaches. The main aim is the creation of a CC that establishes a set of rules to guide and discipline the behaviour of beaches' users, more specifically surfers. For this study, we have considered the case of Peniche, a Portuguese city well known and looked for the practice of surf. It still does not have a CC as the general national panorama regarding this topic.

Peniche is a small city located 80 km from Lisbon, which was initially an island but then with the wind and tidal current become a peninsula. Its strategic coast and specific natural features offer 8 beaches which regularly are chosen by surfers due to their tubular and long waves. Likewise Peniche, we have similar spots throughout the coast which are well-known by national and international surfers. One of the most famous is Ericeira, which was entitled the first World Surfing Reserve in Europe by UNESCO. Besides Ericeira, there are only two more places with this same sort of category.

Surf has been an extremely promoted and supported activity by national and local authorities, reflecting the raising demand of surfers for Portuguese beaches with excellence characteristics for the practice of surf. Considering the extreme fragility

F. Oliveira (✉) · S. Eurico · J. P. Jorge
CITUR - Tourism Applied Research Centre, ESTM - Polytechnic Institute of Leiria,
Santuário Nª Senhora dos Remédios, 2520–641 Peniche, Portugal
e-mail: foliveira@ipleiria.pt

S. Eurico
e-mail: sofia.eurico@ipleiria.pt

J. P. Jorge
e-mail: jpjorge@ipleiria.pt

of the natural areas where these spots are situated, there is an urgent need to create tools of different nature to regulate and guideline its users to a proper use of these territories, aligned with the sustainable approach.

This code is therefore a tool that can be used to ensure that the use of Peniche's beach areas by the surfers' community is guide lined in order to protect and the preserve their environment, but also a national instrument that can be adapted to these different places.

This CC is to be assumed as a voluntary instrument for sustainable tourism (UNWTO/UNEP, 2005), which aims to provide a basis for the development of a responsible use of beaches. Not disregarding the country's legislation, and for this specific study, the CC aims to establish a set of principles and values for the sustainable use of the natural resource that a beach constitutes. Furthermore, it intends to serve as a reference for the surfers, guiding behaviours and actions that encourage trust, mutual respect, transparency and the preservation of the natural resources involved.

The methodology procedures consist of literature review and the analysis of specialized technical documents that address this topic and an insightful analysis of CsC throughout the world, via Internet official sites.

7.2 Literature Review

Outdoor sport and recreation has gathered in the past few years the attention of several authors (Agarwal, 2002; Jurado, Damian, & Fernandez-Morales, 2013). Being an adventure sport tourism product, and considering that first surfing references date back to the 19th century (Esparza, 2016), surfing has increasingly been analysed as a niche market that takes place worldwide and is growing fast and creating an impact on tourism development of different countries with coasts which have waves (Ponting & O'Brien, 2015). Even if not widely covered by literature review, an emergent attention is being given to this phenomenon by researchers (Martin, & Assenov, 2012) and more and more studies regarding different perspectives of it are accessible. Nevertheless, there is a gap in literature as far as CsC are concerned within surf Tourism, even though carrying capacity, environmental impacts, problems with local communities and local surfers are the subject of some of these studies (Scarfe, Healy, Rennie, & Mead, 2009; Fletcher, Bateman, & Emery, 2011; Jurado, Damian, & Fernandez-Morales, 2013).

Frame worked by the paradigm of sustainable development of Tourism, the Global Code of Ethics for Tourism (GCET) (UNWTO, 1999) emphasises tourism's responsibilities to local communities and their natural, social and cultural environments. It is a reference for responsible and sustainable tourism and contains a comprehensive set of principles designed to guide the various actors and develop the industry. The 'Eco Based Beaches Code' will therefore try to answer this gap in literature review seeking the protection and preservation of the beach environment, regarding ecological, recreational and cultural values and following the GCET indications.

7.3 Methodology

Literature review and the analysis of specialized technical documents were part of the study's methodological procedures. Besides this, a careful analysis of CsC throughout the world, via Internet official sites, was put forward using Google as the search engine.

The choice of using the internet to obtain the desired information for this study—that is, the collection of existing codes of conduct in the practice of surf-ing—become the only possible option after having verified the weak data supply available on the websites and search engines in the field of scientific production. In this first attempt of our research, we used sciencedirect.com and the B-on, the Online Knowledge Library (a Portuguese National online tool) which offers higher education and research institutions unlimited and permanent access to thousands of journals and e-books from some of the leading providers of international scientific content.

Considering the specificity of the theme and the fact that the surf/surfing/surfers' codes of conduct are instruments essentially associated with surf schools, federations and surf destinations management, the Worldwide dimension is nowadays the most used communication platform by them.

As such, and being the internet an opportune form of communication and self-presentation of individuals and organizations, this was considered an added value and the unique opportunity to have access to the needed data for this research, in the digital world. However, some barriers were felt, namely in terms of managing the large volume of documents, the constant modifications on web contents, and the complexity of using different search engines and triangulate its outputs. As so, and according to Flick (2009), when analysing documents on Internet, one should considered the following:

General Aspects: large volume of documents on the Web with connections to each other or between specific sites; impermanence and infinity of texts on the Web (characterized by non-linearity);

Problems in conducting this search technique: difficulty in defining the limits of web pages, which are changing and some may even disappear, and also regarding the different structure of texts that may include other forms of data (images, sounds, text, links, etc.);

Contribution to the general methodological discussion: because documents on the Web are an opportune form of communication and self-presentation for individuals and organizations;

Fitting the search techniques in the research process: requiring the adaptation of the analytical tools and demanding a theoretical or intentional sampling;

Limitations of this search technique: concerning that Web pages represent a specific context that includes technical barriers; and, as so, a common recommendation is to triangulate with other methods to reach the real on the people or institutions.

The research was conducted in four different languages (English; French; Por-tuguese; Spanish) in order to cover the main geographic areas where surf is recognized as an international reference. The expressions used for this analysis were: "surf code of conduct" and "surf ethic code" and Google.com software was used to conduct the

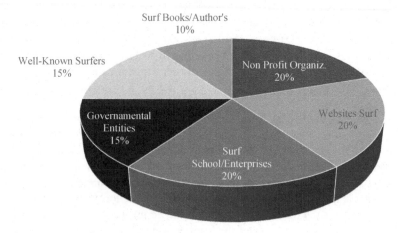

Fig. 7.1 Surf codes by authorship. *Source* Own elaboration

research. In all, 19 codes targeted to surfers were analysed: 12 in English (mainly from South Africa, Australia, Canada and Great Britain); 1 in French (from France); 2 in Portuguese (from Portugal); 4 in Spanish (from Spain). The obtained CsC come from different sources (see Fig. 7.1), including surf schools, non-profit organizations and governmental entities (national, regional and local), specialized websites and individual authors (former well-known Surfers and writers).

In addition, we often found that occasionally the same code (with the same principles) was used by different entities or companies. In these cases, only one code was considered in our final scheme (Table 7.1), regardless of the number of entities/companies that use and promote it. This is the case of the *Surfers' Code of Conduct* found on the institutional website of New South Wales, Australia (http://www.surfthecoast.com.au). This same code can also be found on the Official Website of San Sebastián Tourism and Convention Bureau (https://www.sansebastianturismo.com) and on the council official website of Deba (http://www.deba.eus), a town in the autonomous community of the Basque Country, Spain, where surfing is one of the main tourism attractions. The same situation was verified with the Surfing Great Britain—SGB Code of Conduct for Surfers, found on the website of the National Governing Body for the Sport of Surfing in England (https://www.surfingengland.org/) which is also promoted by local surf shops' websites. Other situations are identified in Table 7.1.

After identifying the 19 CsC listed before, a content analysis of each code and its principles was carried out. The use of this method is justified by its transparency as mentioned by Bryman (2012) and due to the fact that the "coding scheme and the sampling procedures can be clearly set out so that replications and follow-up studies are feasible" (Idem: 304). The structuring of a scheme with all the codes and all the principles allowed us to identify principles that were repeated in several codes or principles whose title was not exactly the same but whose meaning was similar.

Table 7.1 Studied CsC

1. Surfers' code of conduct http://www. surfthecoast.com.au; http://www. sansebastianturismo.com; http://www.deba. eus)	11. Surfers code of conduct http://www. stokedsurfschool.com/blog/2012/06/02/ surfers-code-conduct
2. NSSIA surfing code of ethics http://www. nssia.org/surfing_ethics.html	12. Los 10 Mandamientos del surf (http:// escueladesurflasdunas.com; https://www. artsurfcamp.com; www.todosurf.com)
3. Surfing Etiquette (http://www. surfinghandbook.com; Peter Spacek (2014). Wetiquette.)	13. Surf code French Federation of surf http://www.surfingfrance.com
4. Surfrider foundation's—the surfer's code; https://www.konaboys.com (SurfShop in Hawaii)	14. Surf code of conduct—algarve surf school association (http://www. algarvesurfschoolsassociation.com/etiquette. html)
5. A Surfer's code by Tomson and Moser (2006a, b)	15. Randwick lifeguard surf Etiquette—Randwick city council, Australia www.randwick.nsw.gov.au
6. Nat Young's code of Ethics—Give Respect To Gain Respect	16. SURF CATALUNHA
7. Surfer's Code of Ethics via Louise Southerden	17. Wisewell (2013). The surfer coach—the ten universal commandments of surfing etiquette
8. Surfing great Britain—SGB code of conduct for surfers http://surfinggb.com; *Surfing England code of conduct for surfers*; http://www.pjsurfshop.co.uk/info_conduct.cfm	18. Codigo surfero: 15 reglas básicas para practicar surf https://totalsurfcamp.com
9. Eleven rules every new surfer needs to know before paddling out http://www.surfer.com	19. Barefoot surf travel http:// barefootsurftravel.com/surf-ethics-10-rules- beginner-needs-know
10. SBC surf MAgazine http://sbcsurf.com	

Source Own elaboration

The content analysis was the method selected to analyse the 187 principles of the 19 codes and was followed by a categorization process, usually associated to this type of analysis. According to Bardin (2015), the categories are seen as rubrics or classes that aggregate certain elements with common characteristics. In this study, each category adds all principles that have the same meaning. Therefore, the process of choosing categories followed the semantic criterion (associated to the central theme of each principle) and also the lexical criterion (regarding the meaning of each principle description and its inherent message). Table 7.2 exemplifies this aspect through the category *Paddling Rules*, by discriminating the various principles found in the studied CsC and which have been integrated in this category.

In order to analyse the contents of the different CsC, a word cloud tool was also used to depict keyword metadata and categorize the main issues covered. A free online software was used (wordclouds.com) and the obtained results were used to understand if the studied CsC already considered an ecological approach and, if so, to what extent.

Table 7.2 The 19 principles contained on the category *Paddling Rules*

1. Paddle wide	11. If a collision between a Paddler and a rider looks imminent, paddlers should "keep their line" and let the rider be the one to take evasive action
2. When paddling out, stay out of the way of riding surfers	
3. and 4. Paddling Rules (appear in two different codes)	12. Read the Lineup; Beware the zone—the impact zone is one place you don't want to be. Paddle out to the shoulder and around the back
5. I Will Paddle around the impact zone; I will Paddle back out	
6. Paddling out: Paddle wide. Caught inside stay in the white water	14. Paddle around the wave, not through it
7. Paddle; caught inside	15. Paddle back out safely—when you are paddling back out after a wave, do not paddle in front of someone riding a wave
8. When paddling out avoid surfers who are riding waves	
9. Paddle around the lineup, not through it	16. Keep out of the way—when paddling out, stay out of the surfing zone
10. Always study the lineup before you paddle out. If the conditions are beyond your abilities, go somewhere else or surf another day	17. It is your responsibility not to obstruct other surfers when paddling towards the peak when paddling out
	18. Avoid getting in the way of other surfers
	19. Paddle wide and avoid other surfers' Lines

Source Own elaboration

7.4 Results

Considering the 19 codes, 187 principles (or rules) were analysed. The number of principles per code ranges from 5 to 19. In general, most of them aim a healthy practice of surfing, ensuring safety and respect among all surfers. Indications about the need for communication among surfers, the importance of not surfing alone, respecting other surfers and recognizing the level of surfing are the most common items. They also include very specific rules on how and when to start riding a wave and how to use the board.

Only one of the codes—that from the École Française de Surf (surf schools' network certified by the French Surfing Federation)—sets standards exclusively for an ecological approach of the Surfer, including examples of environmentally responsible practices throughout the journey before reaching the surf destination, once at the beach, and specifically considering natural resources (the sea and the beach) and when in direct contact with the local community.

From the analysis of all the principles, we realised that many of them were repeated in several codes and, as such, the categorization of the principles was carried out. We identified 19 different categories as presented in Table 7.3.

Of these 19 categories, 14 specifically concern surfing and the rules that must be followed when more than one surfer is at sea and sharing the same wave zone. These categories aggregate 75% of the gathered principles. The remaining 25% principles are distributed in four categories (5, 8, 18 and 19) that focus on aspects related to the importance of the surfer having a respectful attitude towards:

Table 7.3 Categories of the principles/rules gathered on the selected codes

Principles/rules categories	n	%
1. Paddling rules	19	10,2
2. Be conscious of your surf skills and limits and prevent collisions	19	10,2
3. Don't drop in	18	9,6
4. Keep control of your equipment—Hold on to your board	17	9,1
5. Respect the beach, the ocean and others	15	8,0
6. Observe right of way	12	6,4
7. Stay positive	10	5,3
8. Dealing with "locals" surfers	9	4,8
9. Don't snake" waves—don't maneuver around another surfer about to take off to claim the inside position	8	4,3
10. Don't be a "wave hog"—don't take every wave in crowded conditions	6	3,2
11. Share the water, your knowledge and your stoke	6	3,2
12. Trade off with the waves, so that everyone gets a share of the surf	5	2,7
13. Be aware of currents, jetties and other surfers	5	2,7
14. Always consider other water users	5	2,7
15. Avoid crowded conditions	4	2,1
16. First to his or her feet has priority	3	1,6
17. Communicate with other surfers while surfing	3	1,6
18. Be responsible during your trip and your stay	3	1,6
19. Other recommendations to ensure safe surfing	20	10,7
Total	187	100,0

Source Own elaboration

- other beach and sea users;
- (being a visiting surfer) the local surfers;
- other spaces that the surfer uses in the chosen destination to surf.

In addition, category 19, which will be discussed later in this study, combines principles regarding the need for the surfer to have a set of attitudes before and during surfing that ensure their physical well-being.

Of these 4 categories, the main highlight is for Category 5 (*Respect the beach, the ocean and others*) since it is the one that concentrates a set of principles whose main concern is the natural environment and how it should be cared for and protected. Here we find recommendations for a more responsible attitude of surfers regarding the waste they can do (or find) on the beach. This category compiles 8% of the analysed principles, which were found in 13 codes.

Some of the principles (6) present a very simple message (but also, somewhat vague), referring only to "Respect the beach, the ocean and others", "Respect the beach" or "You will not pollute the beaches". But most (8) of the principles are clearer and more specific regarding the attitude that every surfer should have while on the beach. The main message focuses essentially on the need not to leave garbage on the beaches:

- Keep the beach clean—Throw rubbish into the bin (Code 15)
- Be environmentally friendly. Always leave the beach and other areas as you would wish to find them (Code 8)
- Don't litter. Simple as that. (Code 3)
- You will not pollute the beaches (Code 12)
- Leave the site clean and thank the locals for letting you share their waves (Code 16)

Others, call for a more proactive attitude associated with collecting garbage made by others:

- Pick up your trash, and try to pick up a few pieces of trash before you leave even if it is not yours. (Code 3)
- Leave only footprints. If on your way out of the water back to the car you stumble across some trash, pick it up. Every bit helps. (Code 11)
- Clean up after yourself and others less thoughtful (Code 4)

Finally, the principle found in code 18. (Table 7.1) (*Codigo de Surfero: 15 reglas básicas para practicar Surf*) in addition to recommend the need not to leave trash on the beach, it also informs about the impacts of leaving trash on the beach and the consequences for surfing practice:

> Care for the environment - Even if you are not an environmentalist and you do not care about the disastrous state of beaches and seas, you must take care of the environment for your own interest and for the future of surfing. Because when all the trash that is poured into the sea prevents you from surfing, it will be late. Also, take care of the beach and pick up some trash whenever you leave the water to thank the nature the good waves you just enjoyed.

In addition to the environmental perspective, surfing ethics is also approached from its social perspective in code 19 (Table 7.1)—The 10 rules Beginners need to know from Barefoot Surf Travel. This code presents a principle that focuses on equality and equity issues:

> There are no differences in Surfing. Do not judge anyone by their sex, their appearance, their skin color, their race, their way of rowing or their way of dressing. None of that matters in surfing, because all surfers deserve your respect, as long as they follow the basic rules. He remembers that Duke Kahanamoku, the legend of Hawaiian surf, recognized for modernizing this water sport, chose like first disciple to a woman.

The subject of localism[1] in surfing is not forgotten in the studied codes. Category 8. *Dealing with "locals" surfers* has 9 principles, all related to this subject. The examples given below illustrate some of the principles that have a broader content, which is not limited to the basic message "Respect the locals":

---

[1](…) A balanced view positions localism as a continuum of values and behaviours, ranging from benign or even positive expressions of local identity to actual acts of violence towards 'outsiders' or their property. Moreover, localism has contextually specific features in particular locations as well as shared features across locations (…) Beaumont and Brown (2014, p. 280).

- Respect the beach locals, don't be a wave hog and respect more experienced surfers than yourself. Do your bit to keep the beach and ocean clean. (Code 1)
- Respect the locals—Show respect and you will get your fair share of waves. The ocean is for everyone to enjoy in a safe and respectful manner. (Code 11)
- Respect the locals—They have the local knowledge. Watch and learn (Code 15)
- Respect the customs and rights of local surfers; Let the locals set the pace of the session and never try to catch more waves than they (Code 16)

Another category related to local communities and rules established at the surf destination is Category 18. *Be responsible during your trip and your stay.* Included here are principles that request for safe driving by surfers who have to travel by car to surf locations, especially when those locations are close to residential areas.

- Drive responsibly—The locals who live in the residential areas near the beach deserve your respect. Don't speed or drive recklessly. (Code 3)
- Drive with care—Before you hit the road, make sure that your boards are tied down securely. There's no need to speed, even if the waves are cranking. Be careful in parking lots at the beaches. (Code 11)

The third principle of this category refers to the very specific conditions to consider when in a protected area. The example given has to do with beaches which are located in a specific Portuguese natural park, marked by the Surfing Label of the Association of surf schools of the region. For this reason, there was a need to include a principle that warns for the prohibited activities within the park:

- Camping is illegal at the beach and in the carpark on the National Park. Respect the country's laws, do not do it. (Code 14)

Category 19 (Table 7.4) includes 20 principles which, most part (85%), belong to only 3 codes. In general, it contains principles that demonstrate a concern for the surfer's physical well-being (while at sea) and the guarantee that he is safe. Each of these 20 principles is only mentioned once and was pointed out only by one of the codes.

Finally, the analysis of the 19 CsC has shown us that except for the CC from the École Française de Surf which presents an ecological approach to responsible practices by surfers, all the other codes, and based on the results obtained with the word cloud tool, scarcely mention this aspect. The frequency of use is very low associated with words like environment (5 references), trash (6), litter (2), rubbish (1), nature (1), clean (1).

With the obtained results, the EBSCode (Eco Based Surf Code) was elaborated suggesting 17 principles for surfers. From the 19 categories of the principles gathered on the selected codes (Table 7.1), six were considered for the EBSCode due to their direct connection to its objective: to promote a responsible use of beaches by surfers, preserving this natural resource to future generations. To *respect the beach, the ocean and others* (5); to *stay positive* (7); to *deal with "locals" surfers* (8); to *always consider other water users* (14); to *be responsible during the trip and stay* (18); to *ensure safe surfing* (19) were the 6 categories highlighted from the studied codes

Table 7.4 Category 19. Other recommendations to ensure safe surfing

Source of the code	Principles	n
NSSIA[a] surfing code of Ethics	Leashes are not life-saving devices	1
	Improving your surfing: practice	1
A surfer's code by shaun tomson	I Will Never Turn My Back on the Ocean	1
	I Will Never Fight a Rip Tide	1
	I Will Catch a Wave Every Day (even in my mind)	1
	I Will Honor the Sport of Kings	1
Surfing great Britain—SGB code of conduct for surfers	All surfers must be able to swim at least 50 m in open water	1
	Recommended that you are covered by Public Liability Insurance for surfing	1
	Keep your surfing equipment in good condition	1
	Never surf alone	1
	Never surf immediately after eating a meal	1
	Always return to the beach before nightfall	1
	Never mix surfing with alcohol or drugs	1
	Always wear a wetsuit when surfing in Britain	1
	When possible use a lifeguard patrolled beach. Obey the life-guards instructions and be prepared to assist them if required	1
	Where possible surf in a recognised surfing area	1
Surf Code—French surfing federation	Do not panic if you are taken by the current (Do not try to swim back to the edge; rest on your board; again arms to alert relief)	1
	Never surf during a storm	1
	Protect yourself from the sun	1
Surfers' Code—Randwick city council	Learn from a professional—join a surf school	1

[a]NSSIA—National Surf Schools and Instructors Association
Source Own elaboration

Table 7.5 Relationship between categories of the principles gathered on the studied codes and those for EBSCode

Categories of the principles gathered on the studied codes	Categories of the principles for the EBSCode
5. Respect the beach, the ocean and others 8. Dealing with "locals" surfers 14. Always consider other water users	1. Respect communities and other users
18. Be responsible during your trip and your stay	2. Minimal impact beach and surroundings' use
	3. Education
	4. Natural resources/biodiversity protection
19. Other recommendations to ensure safe surfing	5. Safety
7. Stay positive	6. Enjoy

Source Own elaboration

to plan new major and broader categories for the EBSCode. Table 7.5 shows this relationship.

Taking into account these new six categories, the 17 principles for the EBSCode have been thought in order to exemplify how it manages to deal directly with environmental aspects, either during the surfing activity or general use of the beach and its surroundings (Table 7.6).

In view of the subjectivity of the principles regarding the environment, which we came upon in the studied codes, we felt the need to elaborate precise and clear actions that would leave no doubt to the surfer about what he/she was expected to do. Moreover, the Portuguese reality of beaches which make part of protected natural areas, namely natural parks, justify the focus of some principles in the protection of natural resources and biodiversity.

As far as "while surfing" related principles is concerned, these were mainly inspired by those we came across in the studied codes. The respect for communities and other users is directly linked to the responsible use of the beach and the tolerance needed to avoid conflicts and intolerance while surfing. Finally, the principles joined in the Education category mirror the Portuguese reality and its need to permanently and consistently stress the importance for sensitising and raising the awareness of people about the conservation and protection of natural resources.

The EBSCode has a dichotomous nature, as it has been organized in two parts. One suggesting a common set of principles for surfers while users of the beach and its surroundings, and one other that guidelines them in the surf activity. It is also structured in two languages, with one version in Portuguese and one in English, so that it can be accessible to a greater number of beach users.

The direct connection between principles and categories is shown in Table 7.7 and, from there, one can identify that four principles regard the "minimal impact beach and surroundings use", the categories "respect communities and other users",

Table 7.6 EBSCode principles	EBSCode—Eco based surf code guidelines for a responsible and Eco-friendly use of the beaches by surfers
	If you have chosen this beach, enjoy it the best you can and follow the rules that follow in order to maintain this beautiful natural area
	• Enjoy the beach and nature that surrounds it, always with respect
	• Respect the local community and do not park in areas that obstruct access to homes, garages, sidewalks and road crossings
	• Use specific identified walkways to get to the beach
	• In case of difficult access to beaches due to cliffs and rocks, only use the existing tracks for this purpose
	• Do not leave litter or cigarette butts on the beach
	• Avoid bringing glass objects to the beach
	• Do not park in the dunes. Use parking places, even if further from the beach
	• Do not pick up or step on the existing vegetation in the dunes and on the beach
	• Do not feed animals
	• Respect the local flora and fauna: do not pick up marine plants and animals
	• Respect other beach/water users and collaborate so that everyone can enjoy the beach
	While surfing
	• Be tolerant to the other surfers and avoid aggressive attitudes and unhealthy competition
	• Share knowledge and experience with beginners
	• Always aid another surfer or beach user in trouble danger in the water for any user, collaborate if possible in providing relief
	• Keep a safe distance from bathing areas, specifically if there are bath users in the water
	• Promote these guidelines among children that come with you
	• For non-locals, make your trip an opportunity to learn about the visited region
	Hi! Are you reading this message? If the adults who are with you haven't read it, call them and tell them it is important to do so!
	Reading these guidelines does not relieve you from knowing the information on the safety and general rules regarding the use of the beach space and respective access

Source Own elaboration

Table 7.7 EBSCode categories and principles

EBSCode categories	EBSCode principles
Minimal impact beach and surroundings use	• Use specific identified walkways to get to the beach • In case of difficult access to beaches due to cliffs and rocks, only use the existing tracks for this purpose • Do not leave litter or cigarette butts on the beach • Do not park in the dunes. Use parking places, even if further from the beach
Respect communities and other users	• Respect the local community and do not park in areas that obstruct access to homes, garages, sidewalks and road crossings • Respect other beach/water users and collaborate so that everyone can enjoy the beach • Be tolerant to the other surfers and avoid aggressive attitudes and unhealthy competition
Natural resources/biodiversity protection	• Do not pick up or step on the existing vegetation in the dunes and on the beach • Do not feed animals • Respect the local flora and fauna: Do not pick up marine plants and animals
Safety	• Avoid bringing glass objects to the beach • Always aid another surfer or beach user in trouble danger in the water for any user, collaborate if possible in providing relief • Keep a safe distance from bathing areas, specifically if there are bath users in the water
Education	• Share knowledge and experience with beginners • Promote these guidelines among children that come with you • For non-locals, make Your Trip an Opportunity to Learn About the visited region
Enjoy	• Enjoy the beach and nature that surrounds it, always with respect

Source Own elaboration

"natural resources/biodiversity protection", "safety" and "education" present three principles each and with one principle we have the "enjoy" category.

Usually this kind of CsC may be found in surf schools, shops related to surf practise, sports organizations, etc., but one can come across them in outdoor information, websites, apps and brochures. Aiming to target surfers but also those that may be with them, there is the need to include some clear messages that will also guide them to a user-friendly approach of the beach and its surroundings. This is why the EBSCode ends with two sentences, one targeting this specific segment (in this case children) and one other to all those that read it.

7.5   Conclusion and Implications

The EBSCode innovates from all the CsC studied because it introduces the ecological component in its principles. In fact, this is a code that promotes an eco approach of the surf activity, aiming a more respectful action regarding the natural, cultural and socioeconomic environment that characterizes each surf destination. As such, it is a code that does not replace the analysed surf codes. In relation to the only *ecocode* we found (that of the École Française de Surf) it differs from it if we consider the higher number of principles it contemplates, making it more applicable or adjustable to a greater diversity of surf destinations.

When considering the application of the EBSCode by surfers, we must not forget that it is a voluntary instrument, in which compliance is not mandatory. As such, and considering the importance of ensuring the natural values' stability and the socio-economic balance of surf destinations, it will be crucial that the adoption of this code is supported by other actions, namely: spreading the code either digital or in a printed format among tourism enterprises (surf schools, tourism accommodation, recreation operators) and among public or private entities operating at the destination (town halls, associations linked to surf etc.); creating awareness-raising actions about the benefits of applying and following the guidelines within the EBSCode; creating incentives for those who adopt some of its principles (for example, those who choose to purchase locally produced products). It is also important to ensure the translation of the code in different languages. This will enable it to target a higher number of surfers and entities.

From the methodological point of view, there's a limitation which regards the use of only one search engine—Google—to develop this research. This is an aspect to be improved since, as verified by Ho et al. (2002) and Dorsey, Steeves, and Porras (2004), the use of several search engines is desirable in order to increase the likelihood of approaching the total amount of websites.

References

Agarwal, S. (2002). Restructuring seaside tourism. The resort lifecycle. *Annals of Tourism Research*, *29*(1), 25–55.

Bardin, L. (2015). *Análise de Conteúdo*. Edições 70. ISBN 9789724415062.

Beaumont, E., & Brown, D. (2014). It's not something I'm proud of but it's … just how I feel': local surfer perspectives of localism. *Leisure Studies, 33,* 45–61.

Bryman, A. (2012). *Social Research Methods* (4th ed.). USA: Oxford University Press. ISBN 978-0-19-958805-3.

Dorsey, E. R., Steeves, H. L., & Porras, L. E. (2004). Advertising ecotourism on the internet: Commodifying environment and culture. *New Media and Society, 6,* 753–79.

Esparza, D. (2016). Towards a theory of surfing expansion: The beginnings of surfing in spain as a case study. *RICYDE Revista Internacional de Ciencias del Deporte, 44,* 199–215.

Fletcher, S., Bateman, P., & Emery, A. (2011). The governance of the Boscombe artificial surf reef, UK. *Land Use Policy, 28,* 295–301.

Flick, U. (2009). *Introdução à Pesquisa Qualitativa* (3rd ed., p. 9788536317113). ISBN: Bookman.

Ho, K. C., Baber, Z., & Khondker, H. (2002). 'Sites' of resistance: alternative websites and state-society relations. *British Journal of Sociology, 53*(1), 127–148. https://doi.org/10.1080/00071310120109366.

Jurado, E., Damian, I., & Fernandez-Morales, A. (2013). Carrying capacity model applied in coastal destinations. *Annals of Tourism Research, 43,* 1–19.

Martin, S., & Assenov, I. (2012). The genesis of a new body of sport tourism literature: A systematic review of surf tourism research (1997–2011). *Journal of Sport & Tourism, 17*(4), 257–287.

Ponting, J., & O'Brien, D. (2015). Regulating "Nirvana": Sustainable surf tourism in a climate of increasing regulation. *Sport Management Review, 18,* 99–110.

Scarfe, B., Healy, T., Rennie, H., & Mead, S. (2009). Sustainable management of surfing breaks: Case studies and recommendations. *Journal of Coastal Research, 25*(3), 684–703.

Spacek, P. (2014). *Wetiquette. How to hang ten without stepping on anyone's toes. An illustrated guide to surf etiquette.* Ditch Ink. ISBN 0991592905, 9780991592906.

Tomson, S., & Moser, P. (2006a). *Surfer's Code—12 Simple Lessons for Business & Life.*

Tomson, S., & Moser, P. (2006b). *Surfer's code—12 simple lessons for business & life* (1st ed.). UTAH/USA:Gibbs Smith Publisher. ISBN 978-1-14236-2227-7.

UTAH/USA: Gibbs Smith Publisher (1st ed.). ISBN 978-1-14236-2227-7.

UNWTO. (1999). Global code of ethics for tourism. Retrieved August 29, 2013 from http://ethics.unwto.org/en/content/global-code-ethics-tourism.

UNWTO/UNEP. (2005). *Making tourism more sustainable – a guide for policy makers.* France/Spain: UNEP/UNWTO.

Wisewell, A. (2013). *The Surfer Coach.* Lulu Press, Inc. ISBN1105610594, 9781105610592.

Part II
Tourism Experiences and Consumer Behaviour

Chapter 8
The Importance of Experience in Participant's Motivations in Recreational Sport Tourism Events in Portugal

Teresa Palrão and José António Filipe

8.1 Introduction

Nowadays tourism is increasingly claiming its role as one of the main sectors contributing for the economic development in many countries. In recent years there has been a remarkable increase of the touristic flow, as evidenced by Word Tourism Organization data, January 2017: "Demand for international tourism remained robust in 2016 despite challenges. Some 46 million more tourists (overnight visitors) travelled internationally last year compared to 2015".

Besides, in Portugal it is plain to see the major and increasing importance of the touristic sector for the national economy over the last years. Some internal factors were particularly important, such as the great commitment from both political and economic decision makers in the development of infrastructures as well as country's promotion abroad (cities of Lisbon and Oporto, and also Madeira and Azores Island, have been ranked as some of the best European destinies for tourism). Peculiar features like gastronomy are currently consensually considered relevant at international level. According to the Portuguese magazine *Evasões*, the number of Portuguese restaurants awarded with Michelin stars passed from fourteen in 2016 to twenty-one in 2017.

Also, a wide range of Portugal's features, like the weather, an extensive coast or yet the diverse countryside and Portugal's geographical position, project the tourism

T. Palrão (✉)
Universidade Europeia, Laureate International Universities ISCTE,
Instituto Universitário de Lisboa, Lisbon, Portugal
e-mail: tsrrp@iscte.pt

J. A. Filipe
Instituto Universitário de Lisboa BRU-IUL, Av. das Forças Armadas,
1649-026 Lisbon, Portugal
e-mail: jose.filipe@iscte.pt

© Springer Nature Switzerland AG 2019
A. Artal-Tur et al. (eds.), *Trends in Tourist Behavior*,
Tourism, Hospitality & Event Management,
https://doi.org/10.1007/978-3-030-11160-1_8

characteristics of Portugal internationally, progressively assuming its place as a competitive choice comparing to other touristic destinies.

In addition, the relevant external aspect associated to security is nowadays crucial when agents make a decision on touristic destinies in a world facing many uncertainties.

Data published by *Banco de Portugal* (BP) and *Instituto Nacional de Estatística* (INE) confirm a new maximum concerning overnight stays and visits in 2016 in Portugal.

Sport tourism is essentially associated to the convergence of two factors: the travel destination and the type of activity. When analysing destination region it is possible to see that there has been a change to the initial demand for sun and sea due to behavioural shifts leading to new realities and interest concerning other type of activities.

This type of tourism (sport) as we know it today appeared in mid-20th century and is associated to the Winter sports in Alps. According to Pigeassou, Bui-Xuan, and Gleyse (2003), the concept of sport tourism itself doesn't appear before the seventies of last century.

According to Gibson (1998), "the concept of Sports and Tourism is leisure based on the travel that takes individuals temporarily out of their origin communities to engage in physical activities, to watch physical activities or to worship attractions related to physical activities".

This author subdivides the topic of Sport Tourism into three major areas: Nostalgia Sport Tourism (as for example, the travel related to sporting attractions like a stadium, museums, etc.), Active Sport Tourism (the tourists want to participate in sport events, either being active if they travel to take part in a competition, or being hobbyists if they practice a sport as a way of leisure), and Sport Tourism Events (striking sport events like Olympic Games).

From this division, the second group—Active Sport Tourism—was the starting point for this research. According to Robinson and Gammon's (2011) characterization, tourists' motivations are divided in "hard" and "soft", depending on whether they are competitive or recreational sports, within sport tourism, thus contributing to describe motivations and experiences of sports tourists. For these authors a "soft definition" considers that tourists "would be someone who specifically travels (staying in places outside their usual environment) and who is primarily involved in active recreational participation of a sporting/leisure interest; for example, skiing and walking holidays. The active recreational aspects are the distinguishing factors here".

They stated clearly, however, that at this point it is still necessary a wider and more in-depth study of their respective interactions: "research now needs to focus more on these categories to further examine motives of the sport tourist and to assess in more general terms the utility of the framework".

At this point of the study, another theoretical contribution came from Aspas (2000) with a classification through a catalogue of active tourism activities and ordered by physical environment (air, water and land). According to this author, active tourism is definable as a type of recreation, an engagement in physical activities in a natural environment such as water, land, and air.

According to Hinch and Higham (2011), the sport tourism sector will demand a more in-depth study in the future. To these authors, all the following factors—issues surrounding socio-demographic characteristics, tourist's behaviour while traveling and its impact in each of these sports tourist groups—can play a fundamental role in the creation of strategies according to the chosen target group.

To Weed and Bull (2004), findings suggest that much of the sport tourism motivation research already undertaken has focused on sport events or sport spectators and not on the sport tourist as a participant. Therefore, once defined the type of tourist of the study, the need fell on the experience the tourist is supposed to enjoy during sport events.

In their work, these authors mentioned the impossibility to establish an absolute definition of the sports tourist profile considering the existing heterogeneity, although there are similarities in the motivations and behaviours among sports tourists surrounded by diverse activities they might help to build a "typology" for tourism sports.

According to Theodorakis, Kaplanidou, and Karabaxoglou (2015) "the consumption of sport events through direct participation can influence participants' perception of happiness with that experiential purchase given the time and resources invested in that experience".

Following the bibliographical review concerning Sport Tourism Events and Motivation areas, we shall now further assess the gap which will be particularly targeted in this work. "Not only the growing number of participants but also the increased economic relevance of sports may explain the latest research interests" (Hallmann, Feiler, Müller, & Breuer, 2012).

A study by Haughey (2015) on sport and active recreation allowed to conclude that the three most common reasons for taking part in sport and recreation are health and fitness, enjoyment, and social motives. These motives are common to both genders and include all ages, ethnicities, social-economical ranges, experiences, and location. However, the relevance of these motives varies according to the participants, namely within the gender group.

Our research study is intended to define a conceptual model to understand the experience perceived by the participants, considering Weed and Bull (2004) classification "Activity", "People" and "Place". Having this objective in mind, we therefore have two study targets:

- First, the analysis of the active sport tourism events, their framework, characterization, and evolution;
- Secondly, this tourist's profile type, his motivations, interactions, and possible segmentations.

8.2 Recreational Sport Tourism Events in Portugal

This research focuses on the study of recreational sport tourism events in Portugal, where this subject's history is very short but became essential to understand the path travelled in this work and to achieve a reflection on its evolution in this country. It has also provided a study run on three specific events concerning the participants' thoughts through an extensive inquiry with qualitative questions. According to the World Tourism Organization (UNWTO, 2003), the events market is becoming a highly specialized and relevant segment for tourism.

Every weekend, throughout Portugal, at least one sport tourism event takes place. It is important and adequate to study not only tourism but also sport, which is beginning to develop in this country, both socially and in terms of infrastructures.

Portugal managed to gather some sports ambassadors such as Cristiano Ronaldo in football, or McNamara in surf who has marked Portugal as the most required destination for surfers in Europe, thereby turning this country into the most recent European country to present all World Surf League competitions. As an example of an activity promoted by the government we can point out golf in Algarve, which allowed to slightly upset the seasonality of tourism. Until now this region was sought for its beaches and warm weather. Golf, a worldwide growing dynamic activity with increasingly larger number of tourists, was adequately developed and marketed, thereby becoming a successful profitable tourism product (Hinch & Higham, 2004).

Frequently sport events are set against regions different from the usual tourism regions, thereby allowing to develop other destinations. "[...] destinations use sport events to attract participants and spectators, who then hold perceptions of both the sport event and destination" (Kaplanidou & Vogt, 2010).

8.2.1 Characterization of Chosen Events

8.2.1.1 Land Event—All Nations Race

If initially land sports activities were mainly associated to trekking and BTT, especially due to clubs and societies initiative, recently it is noticeable that other outdoor experiences are being held, following new market trends. For instance, there is hiking, trekking, BTT-TT, guidance, paintball, birdwatching among others. Land activities can be held in different types of structures, and most take advantage from the conditions offered by the place, thereby pre-empting the activities according to the type of ground and existing structure.

Athletics is the oldest organized competition. Athletics was born in Greece's Ancient Games.

Racing is, in a way, the purest athletic expression developed by man. Although there is a bit of strategy and implicit technique, racing basically involves the athlete's fitness.

It was pointed out before that racing is a sport that anyone can practice without prior mandatory training or equipment and consequently it is the fastest growing discipline in number of events, in recreational terms. In Lisbon itself in 2005 over than 60 events were accounted, although in 2017 this number would have been probably largely exceeded. Any recreational participant can join the competition

Table 8.1 Number of participants in the event All Nations Race (2016/2017)

All Nations Race	2016	2017
Number of participants per race	2000	3000
Number of countries	5	21

Source Own elaboration

with a top-level athlete, but an amateur runner will hardly ever join a Formula 1 competition.

The event chosen for grading the physical environment land, geographically located in the centre of Portugal, was a race in Lisbon, the "All Nations Race".

A contact was initiated with Paulo Calisto from the company "Survivors Run", to request authorization to distribute the inquiries to the competitors. SURVIVORS RUN is an authentic and unforgettable life experience, exclusive for its participants.

This event took place in 2016 for the first time, during the month of October. The Organization intends to make this event a race where the five continents should be represented. The concept behind this event is to run or walk holding the colours of each one's country to portray a human framework reflecting the colours of the united world. The organization intends to promote healthy lifestyles through a message of union, interdependency and emotional sharing between peoples and cultures.

The event took place at Parque das Nações, where a 10-km night race and a 5-km hike are staged.

Also, this event was solidarity-related: The All Nations Race joined UNICEF Portugal, to which 1€ for every enrolment was delivered. The sum raised was allocated to these organization's aid programs for the most vulnerable children in the world.

The enrolment fee was different for hiking (5€) or racing (10€). There was no minimum age for hiking, and participants under 14 years did not pay. This fee included a technical t-shirt, chip, timing, prizes and participation certificate, race number bib, water, fruit, gifts, shower spots and a safe place to leave car keys (Table 8.1).

This event took place again in September 2017 following its huge success in the previous year, which allowed the organization more time to care about other aspects such as creation of new partnerships that add value to the competition in the participants opinion (Hospital CUF, Comboios de Portugal, Águas do Vimeiro, among others), and get Femédica's safe event quality label. This year, the chosen association was Navegar.

It gathered 21 nationalities, 4 of which were represented by their countries' embassies (Australia, South Africa, Finland and Colombia); therefore the event's slogan was "The race that unites the nations".

The qualitative jump in this specific example shows the sponsors' availability to invest in races and the participants' availability, which would have grown more if, for safety reasons, wouldn't have been limited to 1000 the number of new enrolments. Besides this race, the company added other sport events, such as wanderlust, a new concept in Portugal which mixes racing, yoga and meditation.

8.2.1.2   Water Event- Up and Down the Guadiana River Sail Regatta

Nautical tourism's main motivation lies in travelling with activities in contact with water (nautical), in this case of recreational nature. However, on account of its long coastline, with open sea zones and extremely sheltered waters, Portugal is increasingly sought for holding international competitions.

This country's potentials as regards to natural resources allow to explore this type of tourism. The whole maritime coast, all the beaches, rivers, dams and weather conditions are factors that promote development and raise interest in this type of products, although the most demanded disciplines are sailing, surf, windsurf, diving, rowing and cruises, besides a wide range of less requested activities.

This studied activity—sailing—requires a large quantity of material more than the boat itself. Usually the participant is not alone, because he/she needs support to prepare the boat, and this can also be a team sport, requiring access to a marina to be able to lower the boat to the water (access ramp). It is also important to have basic swimming skills and to hold a license as Day Skipper. It also depends on the weather conditions, such as wind and sea state. It should be stressed that this is a high maintenance sport and requires a considerable amount of time to practice (taking the boat to the open sea in order to be able to sail is time consuming and later it is also necessary to take time to take the boat out from the water).

This specific event was chosen because it takes place in Vila Real de Santo António, in the south of the country, and because Spain also takes part in it tourists are required to move so that they can participate. The responsible for this event, Edgar Pádua, from the Guadiana Naval Association, was interviewed.

Its first edition was in 1983 (in Algarve). It is the 3rd oldest regatta in the Iberian Peninsula, being organized with Spain, since the Guadiana River crosses both countries. The competition is organized by the Guadiana Naval Association, from Portugal side, and, on the Spanish side, by the Isla Canela Nautical Club, with the support of Alcoutim, Ayamonte and Vila Real de Santo António municipalities.

Its route happens in the course of two days, going up on a Saturday and coming back down to Vila Real de Santo António on Sunday.

It takes place during the month of August. The enrolment fee is 10€ per crew member and includes taking part in the competition, Saturday dinner and admittance in the music and entertainment party (foam party) (Table 8.2).

The competition is a sporting moment for meeting people and interact among sailors of all ages and nationalities, aiming at promoting sport, as well as strengthen-

Table 8.2 Number of participants in the event Guadiana regatta (2012/2016)

Guadiana regatta	2012	2013	2014	2015	2016
Number of boats	140	130	120	130	90
Number of participants	275	240	250	250	120

Source Own elaboration

ing the municipality's touristic demand, benefiting from its natural beauty, especially from the Guadiana river.

Although this is a long-lived regatta, in this 2017 year the number of athletes grew again to approximately 260 participants competing in the regatta, which completed its 21st edition with many new features.

8.2.1.3 Air Event—The National Paragliding Festival

Air sports convey a truly indescribable sense of adventure and freedom. Those who engage in this type of activities discharge a large amount of adrenalin, forget stress and face the problems in a very positive way. From the three physical environments, in these activities there are the newest sports, including hang-gliding, skydiving, paragliding, ultralight, glider, hot-air balloon, bungee-jumping.

Paragliding was introduced in Portugal ca. 1987. From all the air activities this is the riskier one, although there is no age limit to this air sport. This is also the activity that is more dependent from the weather conditions, and it requires special conditions to its practice. Also, it is essential to have the necessary equipment to fly and a permit to fly, and technical, practical and tactical expertise (how to watch the sky and how to interpret the evolution of clouds, wind velocity, respect the priority rules during flight and keep from flying alone) which drives up the costs connected to this sport for those who take it just for fun. Paragliding is about to be approved as an Olympic discipline and dates from the late 70s of the last century. This sport requires calm and contemplation, and aims at gliding, which can provide hours of relaxing through magnificent scenarios. This subject differs from skydiving because the jump starts on the ground, thereby requiring running a little to open the paragliding before the jump, which requires also a drop. It is frequent to fly from cliffs, over beaches and mountains.

In Portugal, one of the most sought for spots for paragliding is Linhares da Beira, in Serra da Estrela region.

The event concerned to this study is the Linhares da Beira International Paragliding Festival, which is one of the best spots to fly in Portugal. It also met the requirements because it was in the North and favoured leisure pilots. This is sponsored by the Celorico da Beira Municipality to promote the historical village of Linhares da Beira, and also the Celorico da Beira Council and its huge heritage. This event's main goal is to attract to this area pilots engaging in the modality, thereby increasing the demand of tourists for this area.

The company Wind is responsible for the event organization since its first edition. In this company we interviewed José Cardoso as the person in charge for the paragliding activities, and he acted as our contact for the event and follow-up.

This event requires very specific arrangements, and besides taking place in a historic village in the north of Portugal, with very few inhabitants, and it must evolve considerably to host many tourists at once. This event starts at the top of a mountain devoid of the basic amenities to provide some sort of comfort to the athletes and escorts (a cup of coffee, a place to seat, a shadow, toilet facilities, among others).

Table 8.3 Number of participants in the event paragliding festival (2012/2016)

Paragliding festival	2012	2013	2014	2015	2016
Number of teams	16	13	12	26	
Number of participants (pilots)	85	65	67	210	100

Source Own elaboration

Thus, for the event attendance to grow, a set of basic infrastructures must be locally implemented to improve the event conditions. The festival takes place during a weekend with a total cost of 20 euro, including this fee the transportation to the take off point, the official event's dinner and an event's t-shirt.

Considered the paragliding capital, since it gathers unique requirements to the practice of the sport. During the festival days there will be various sporting activities, within the components of this sport. The village was covered by hundreds of paragliders flown by participating pilots from all over the world, who were dazzled by the rich landscape of this beautiful area.

This event began in 2005 and usually takes place during the month of August (Table 8.3).

8.3 Research Methods

8.3.1 In-depth Interviews

The methodology was developed in two phases considering the main objectives of this study. First, an in-depth interview was made to three responsible managers of sport events companies in the considered different areas: Land, Water and Air (Survivors Run, Associação Naval do Guadiana and Wind). From these interviews, an open and close answer questionnaire was applied to compile the variables of the constructs (activity, place and people) and work as the basis to define some hypotheses of the model as will be seen in this work. This will allow understanding what the most important variables in each construct are. These variables will, therefore, be fundamental to the motivational classification which is intended to be created when inquiring the participants. These data have been analysed through the software MAXQDA 12.

8.3.2 Survey Questionnaire

The second phase is composed by questionnaires made to participants in three specific events in Portugal: Corrida das Nações (Nations trail)—Lisboa (1st edition);

Regata à Vela subida e descida Rio Guadiana (Up and Down the Guadiana River Sail Regatta)—Vila Real de Santo António (30th edition); and Festival Nacional de Parapente (National Paragliding Festival)—Linhares da Beira (11th edition). The participants in these events are the population of the research. They will characterize the motivational profile of this type of tourist. In this quantitative analysis, SPSS software was used.

8.4   Analysis of the Results

The information collected through interviews was examined according to a content qualitative analysis (Bardin, 2009; Mayring, 2014), which allowed to draw specific deductions on the variables that characterize the dimensions "Activity", "Place" and "People" and that might thus measure the satisfaction obtained from the experience in recreational sport tourism events. Despite the study results are not intended to be extrapolated, there are theoretical assumptions that might be applied in terms of other circumstances.

From the software analysis it is possible to draw the following conclusions.

In José Guimarães' interview, (land event), 41 interview extracts were marked as relevant for processing and in a later stage draw and add the final conclusions to the conceptual framework; from José Cardoso's interview, (air event), only 37 extracts were marked; and Edgar Pádua (water event) provided 30 extracts, in a total of 108 observations, processed later (Table 8.4).

Subsequently, the 108 observations were divided by 3 codes, with the last one Experience subdivided in the three study dimensions, "Activity", "Place" and "People". The table shows the distribution of those observations (Table 8.5).

This distribution shows that the organizers also give greater relevance to the construct "Place", followed by "Activity", and finally "People", according to how many times they are mentioned.

As can be seen, the words marked in the interview for the construct "Activity" by the software MAXQDA are listed (Table 8.6).

As can be seen, there are many references in this construct connected to the pleasure to engage in a sport.

Table 8.4 Number of interview extracts considered relevant

Interviews	Code system
José Guimarães	41
José Cardoso	37
Edgar Pádua	30
Total	108

Source Own elaboration

Table 8.5 Observation distribution by analysis codes

Code system	Constructs	Total obs.
Tourism events		42
Participant's motivations		25
Experience		10
	Activity	10
	People	8
	Place	13

Source Own elaboration

Table 8.6 Words marked in the interview for the construct "Activity"

Preview	Area
The pleasure of physical outdoor activities	80
Overcoming	9
Appreciation	11
Fear	4
Pleasure	6
Adventure	8
Unknown	12
Challenge	7
Try harder	25

Source Own elaboration

Table 8.7 shows the expressions that insert in the construct "Place" and already represented by the existing variables.

In the final table, and despite there were fewer observations for the construct "People", some of them did not fit in the existing variables and two new variables came up and were integrated in the conceptual model (Table 8.8).

To conclude, it is noticeable that the observations to qualify the "Activity" and "Place" fit within the existing variables, already included in the conceptual model. Only two more variables were added, both in the construct "People", which can be referred to as "Team spirit" and "Audience support". However, this construct is still the one with more variables.

The variable "Team spirit" was mentioned out of the necessity, in collective sports, of a motivation within the structure itself to improve the experience in recreational sport tourism events. According to the events' organizers, the group cohesion leads to a better experience as compared to its absence. As regards to the variable "Audience support", it is also mentioned the importance of the public support to improve motivation and comprehensiveness in the experience, and this is largely studied in competition sport events, although it was frequently forgotten until now.

The enquiry forms were distributed during the days of the events by a previously selected and prepared team.

Table 8.7 Words marked in the interview for the construct "Place"

Preview	Area
Every country has two or three paragliding sites	117
Another well-known place is Serra da Estrela	49
Flight conditions	16
Weather conditions	22
Historic village as a picture	37
Unknown	12
Beauty	6
Landscapes	9
Our winter for many tourists is like summer	56
Change routes	17
Site	5
Landscape	8
The secret is a way of combining several things in the organization with the site	71
Linhares da Beira is indeed contemplated as a sanctuary of paragliding	64

Source Own elaboration

Table 8.8 Words marked in the interview for the construct "People"

Preview	Area
People need recognition	37
Competition, a sexual topic	30
Team spirit	18
Making friends	16
Creating bonds	11
Event supporters	29
Audience doesn't work, it's a cultural issue	45
Paragliding groups, usually called crazy people	67

Source Own elaboration

The first survey (air) was carried out during the paragliding event in Linhares da Beira, *The National Paragliding Festival*, between 13th and 14th of August 2016. Forty-six enquiries were distributed among one hundred participants.

The second event (water) took place during the following weekend, between 20th and 21st August 2016, in Vila Real de Santo António, Algarve, and it was the *Up and Down the Guadiana River Sail Regatta*. Thirty-nine enquiries were completed among a total of one hundred twenty participants.

Finally, the event (land) urban trail was expected to happen at 17th September 2016 and was cancelled just a few days before that date. In view of that it was replaced by the *All Nations Race*, in 8th of October. Ninety-one participants, among a total of hundred fifty recreational participants completed the enquiries. Besides these recreational participants there were also professional athletes, which increased the number of competitors to two thousand.

It was not easy to fill the enquiries in the same day of the competition, while the participants need to prepare the gear. However, the minimum completion rate of 50% was achieved thanks to the investigators' persistence, who made themselves available to accompany the participant during his/her preparation for the competition.

The enquiry form totals 27 questions divided in three parts, the first concerning demographic data that allows to draw the event's participants profile; the second part concerns recreational sport tourism events in general; and finally, some questions about the event itself.

The participants in these events are the population of the research. They will provide the characterization of the motivational profile of this type of participants.

Besides drawing the event participants' profile, this first enquiry aimed at furthering knowledge and collecting information on the events in Portugal, their organization and logistics, and the participants' perspective, as up to now there are virtually no studies on this subject.

The results might be characterized according to participants for each event, considering there is a different physical environment for each one, but this is not significant because only one event for each physical environment was researched. In this context, it was decided to interpret all the results. However, whenever deemed useful, individual references were made by event, and for future studies it will be interesting to draw the participants profile for each physical environment.

The participants who completed the enquiries for the chosen events are distributed not only by physical environment (air, water, land) but also by geographical area (north, centre and south). However, the values provided reflect only the answers of the recreational participants. One might declare that in the sample as regards to gender, there is a relevant majority of male participants (68.2%), and concerning to the age, the most representative age ranges are 40–49 years old (29.5%) and 30–39 years old (29%). Additionally, of all the participants, 89.8% exercise regularly or engage in some sort of sport activity quite often. Over 50% exercise two or three times a week just because they enjoy it, although 83% considered themselves amateurs.

As regards to the country of residence, we find a vast majority of Portuguese people (86.4%) and Spanish people (7.4%), naturally associated with the fact that the event *Up and Down the Guadiana River* takes place between both countries.

Another significant aspect is concerned to the fact that 77.3% of the participants are accompanied. From them, 22.5% came with only one person, 17.5% with two; 15.3% with more than 5 persons. These numbers might reveal the effects in local economic potentization and the need to provide for accommodation infrastructures considering that 36.4% of people of this sample remained on-site until after the event. On the other hand, when asked whether they had ever replied to a survey in a sport event, 76.1% replied negatively, thereby revealing that somehow the necessary data to adjust the infrastructures to the needs of this type of events is lacking. Besides, considering the raise in this type of events in the last few years, it is urgent to conduct more satisfaction surveys, as the customer loyalty is paramount when one strives to make the event a regular one.

Briefly, the first part of the inquiries and considering the participants' profile, the results were in line with the findings of other studies on participants in sport events, although the results expose a smaller margin in gender and expansion of age ranges, now covering the limits. These athletes continue traveling with company and, during the stay, 50% of them either shop or visit cultural and touristic spots, what validates the idea that these events are essential to promote a touristic destination and the development of local economy.

When asked, ca. 80% mentioned that they usually take part in sport events regularly and the wide majority (98.3%) states that Portugal is an attractive country to engage in this type of events due to its climate and landscapes. They further state that there is a growing number of participants in this type of events (87.5%), according to their experience. One might consider that there are still huge opportunities to better use participants and their escorts as regards tourism opportunities.

For the participants in these events, the most important reason to enrol is firstly associated with the "Activity" offered by the event (28.6%), and its place (17.9) and itinerary (17.5%). Aspects such as safety (14.1%) and price (11.1%) are also put forward. Least relevant are "organizing", "authority" and "complementary offers".

As regards to the study events, more than one half participated for the first time (59.1%), thereby showing the need to improve the communication of these events, both nationwide and abroad, despite the information is largely transmitted word of mouth, considering that over 40.9% replied to have heard of the event from friends and, as secondary channel of communication, through the event page and social networks.

Open-ended questions address the issue of the benefits obtained with engaging into a sporting activity and most answers noted down some adjectives, such as freedom, happiness, well-being, and conviviality. For all these motives, 93.8% considered that the price was affordable and 73.9% would be willing to pay more if necessary to keep the event going on, and 44.3% of the respondents declared the organization needed no improvement. The remaining answers reflect the need for an improvement in catering, diversification of the route, more participants, and also more information on the event. Differentiating factors for each event: the race took place during night time, i.e. the schedule; the regatta participants appreciated the route and the landscape and for the paragliders the spot selected for the event was considered one of the best for this discipline.

When asked whether they intended to participate again in the same event, 60.3% replied they would for sure and 57% will recommend the event.

As for the key issue of this study, and while trying to perceive whether the participants value the three major constructs for their final experience, 98.3% mentioned that the element "Activity" was important for the experience obtained in the recreational sport tourism events, 96.6% answered to the same question but with the element "Place", and finally 94.3% point out the element "People" as relevant for the experience obtained in the recreational sport tourism events, as can be seen (Fig. 8.1).

Fig. 8.1 Relevance in %
attributed by the participants
to the elements "Activity",
"Place" and "People".
Source Own elaboration

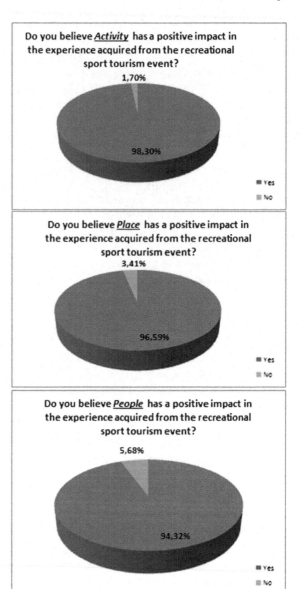

Fig. 8.2 Percentage of relevance in the experience for elements "Activity", "Place" and "People". *Source* Own elaboration

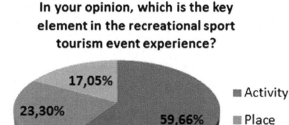

In your opinion, which is the key element in the recreational sport tourism event experience?

Although the three elements were considered of extreme importance in the experience obtained, when questioned about which was the most important the participants clearly chose the element "Activity" (59.7%), followed by "Place" (23.3%), and finally "People" (17%). These results can be explained in light of the intention of the participants to engage in their favourite sporting activity, choosing therefore the suitable place for it, and considering of lesser importance the people involved in this process.

There is a peculiarity on these study events: paragliding, sailing, racing; pursued in the perfect place allow a unique and ever-changing experience.

By way of example of what was previously said, for instance, the paragliding event can be pointed out, for the constantly changing wind direction affects the jump and the whole dynamic alters, but providing the experience is positive, the participant will always wish to return. Also, with sailing, climate conditions, and once more the wind direction, affect the competition performance, although other factors may also be at work. As for racing, there are not many climate factors interfering with the experience. Because of that it is important to invest more in the routes the participants will cross (Fig. 8.2).

8.5 Conclusion and Implications

The study of sport tourism events might give answers on what makes the experience in this type of events unique from the participants' perspective.

From the sport events touristic literature in Portugal, the existing studies are still insufficient to understand and apply the several on-the-ground review methodologies.

This country lacks a record of accomplishment of sport events large enough to allow to compare and perceive whether there is or not an evolution, although the conditions are now starting to be created for the development of these recreational events within tourism, thereby allowing the promotion of several tourism destinations. The work presented aimed at helping in this path.

After the in-depth interviews conducted with sport tourism events' managers, a conceptual framework was defined, with variables associated to the constructs "Activity", "Place" and "People" which can influence the participants' experience in recreational sport tourism events, as shown in Fig. 8.3.

In the interviews to the events' organizers, they were asked if there was some type of support from a public authority that recognized the relevance of this type of events to raise tourism in the area during the events. The interviewed mentioned the growing importance given to this type of events and the potentialities these events have in the area from a tourism perspective, during the event.

From the answers collected on the events' inquiries, it is possible to reach the following conclusions.

It is possible to perceive that there are discrepancies concerning the number of participants in different activities. These differences are originated by: accessibility to this activity, the investment required to practice, as well as trend factors.

Although the number of participants is not much large in recreational sport events, it is noticeable that participants like to help to improve not only the organization of the events in which they participate, but all the other ones that might generally promote outdoor sports activities.

Also, the place where it is practiced might affect the number of participants and the organized events. Not all the regions can manage the organization of such events, which required not only infrastructures for the event itself, but also physical, human and economic resources to promote this type of event and enjoy a certain level of success concerning adherence and the purpose of taking the region to other destinations.

Lisbon keeps being the preferred place to organize this type of events, and when comparing the number of participants by region, it is largely higher than any other place, even if one takes into account events that supposedly should not be taking place in the capital of the country.

In their open answers, responders added, in general, some improvements required, such as support during the event to participants by providing more information; logistics support as accommodation and catering served during the sojourn; more accurate schedules and support infrastructures at the venue (toilet facilities, shadows, extra activities for escorts), and especially the conditions to attract a larger audience during the whole route.

Another aspect noted which may give rise to some considerations is associated with events' fees. Contrary to entertainment events that rely entirely on the tickets value paid by the attendants, these events are paid by the enrolment fee charged to the participants. When questioned about this issue, respondents said the price per participant was accessible and only 10% thought otherwise. However, and considering that prices are usually the same regardless the promoting organization (10€ for a 10-km race event), if a participant enrols in more than one competition every month, he/she may find it difficult to manage financially to take part in more events.

It is important for organizers to ponder on the strategy intended for the future to tackle this issue, if they intend to raise the number of participations and, in that

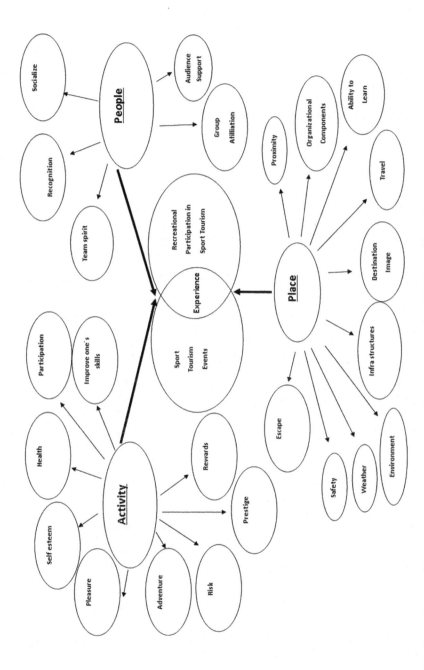

Fig. 8.3 Recreational participation in sport tourism events' experience conceptual model. *Source* Own elaboration

case, the amount should be analysed, or if they intend to increase the revenues by attracting new participants who can purchase more expensive tickets.

It would be interesting in the future to have a deeper study on the construct "People" to analyse its relevance in recreational sport tourism events and analyse if it is effectively less important than "Activity" and "Place" in the experience perception.

This study is limited to the national context applied to Portugal and the gathered data have been based only upon three events with a reduced number of investigations but provides the general analysis guidelines that enable it to be applied to other contexts and regions of similar characteristics.

References

Aspas, J. (2000). *Los deportes de aventura: consideraciones jurídicas sobre el turismo activo*. Zaragoza: Editora Prames.

Bardin, L. (2009). Análise de conteúdo. *Lisboa: Edições*, 70.

Gammon, S., & Robinson, T. (2003). Sport and tourism: A conceptual framework. *Journal of Sport & Tourism, 8*(1), 21–26.

Getz, D. (1998). Trends, strategies, and issues in sport-event tourism. *Sport Marketing Quarterly, 7*(2), 8–13.

Gibson, H. J. (1998). Sport tourism: A critical analysis of research. *Sport Management Review, 1*, 95–102.

Hallmann, K., Feiler, S., Müller, S., & Breuer, C. (2012). The interrelationship between sport activities and the perceived winter sport experience. *Journal of Sport & Tourism, 17*(2), 145–163.

Haughey, K. (2015). *Sport and active recreation in the lives of New Zealand adults 2013/14 active New Zealand survey results*. Wellington: Sport New Zealand.

Hinch, T. D., & Higham, J. E. S. (2004). *Sport tourism development*. Clevedon: Channel View Publications.

Hinch, T. D., & Higham, J. (2011). *Sport tourism development* (2nd ed.). Clevedon: Channel View Publications.

Kaplanidou, K., & Vogt, C. (2010). The meaning and measurement of a sport event experience among active sport tourists. *Journal of Sport Management, 22*, 544–566.

Mayring, P. (2014). Qualitative content analysis: theoretical foundation, basic procedures and software solution (Klagenfurt).

Pigeassou, C., Bui-Xuan, G., & Gleyse, J. (2003). Epistemological issues on sport tourism: Challenge for a new scientific field. *Journal of Sport Tourism, 8*(1), 27–42.

Robinson, T., & Gammon, S. (2011). A question of primary and secondary motives: Revisiting and applying the sport tourism framework. *1*(1), 58–71. Online Version, March.

Theodorakis, N. D., Kaplanidou, K., & Karabaxoglou, I. (2015). Effect of event service quality and satisfaction on happiness among runners of a recurring sport event. *Leisure Sciences, 37*(1), 87–107.

Weed, M., & Bull, C. (2004). *Sport tourism: Participants, policy and providers*. Oxford: Butterworth-Heinemann.

Websites

Associação Naval do Guadiana. Retrieved September 10, 2016, from https://www.anguadiana.com/.

Banco de Portugal. Retrieved March 8, 2016, from https://www.bportugal.pt/sites/default/files/anexos/A.pdf.

Corrida das Nações (Survivors Run). Retrieved May 8, 2016, from http://www.corridadasnacoes.com/.

Evasões. Retrieved May 10, 2016, from http://www.evasoes.pt/comer/estrelas-michelin-2017-estamos-em-festa-e-estamos-no-mapa/.

Instituto Nacional de Estatística. Retrieved January 10, 2016, from https://www.ine.pt.

Isla Canela. Retrieved September 5, 2016, from https://www.islacanela.es/en/xxxii-ascenso-descenso-vela-rio-guadiana-20-21-agosto/.

Urban Trail. Retrieved September 9, 2016, from http://urbantrail.pt/lang/1/portugues/. https://www.facebook.com/urbantrailrun/?ref=hl.

Word Tourism Organization (UNWTO). Retrieved January 10, 2016, from http://www2.unwto.org/press-release/2017-01-17/sustained-growth-international-tourism-despite-challenges.

Chapter 9
Impact of Superior Destination Experience on Recommendation

Gurel Cetin, Ismail Kizilirmak, Mehtap Balik and Sema Kucukali

9.1 Introduction

As destinations became increasingly accessible, the competition intensified and offering a desirable experience becomes a major competitive advantage for destinations (Crouch & Ritchie, 2005). Various studies discussed the positive relationship between tourist experiences and behaviors such as loyalty and recommendation (e.g. Gursoy, Chen, & Chi, 2014; Hosany & Gilbert, 2010). Tourist experiences are memorable activities, perceptions and events in a destination that positively affect tourist behavior. According to Huang and Hsu (2009), the tourism experience is influenced by tourists' multiple interactions with the physical and human environment, the nature of this participation being essential to the way the experience is lived. Hosany and Gilbert (2010) found that love, joy, positive surprise are emotions that can relate to experiences in the destinations. Sensory, affective, behavioral and intellectual experiences have also been discussed as major sources of tourists experiences.

Destinations would be more successful in creating loyalty and recommendation if they would be able to understand the experiential components of their offerings (Hosany & Gilbert, 2010). Hence identifying and understanding the components of visitor experiences is critical for destinations' success (Kim & Brown, 2012). A stream of research has already explored experiences in different settings (hotels,

G. Cetin (✉) · I. Kizilirmak · M. Balik · S. Kucukali
Faculty of Economics, Istanbul University, Istanbul, Turkey
e-mail: gurelc@istanbul.edu.tr

I. Kizilirmak
e-mail: ikizilirmak@yahoo.com

M. Balik
e-mail: mehtap.balk@gmail.com

S. Kucukali
e-mail: semaakucukali@gmail.com

© Springer Nature Switzerland AG 2019
A. Artal-Tur et al. (eds.), *Trends in Tourist Behavior*,
Tourism, Hospitality & Event Management,
https://doi.org/10.1007/978-3-030-11160-1_9

attractions, theme parks, cruises, restaurants) (e.g. Ali, Kim, Li, & Jeon, 2016; Arnould & Price, 1993; Cetin & Walls, 2016) however the overall tourist experiences in destinations have been neglected or analyzed from psychological, social or affective perspectives and usually tried to describe tourists' experiences without clearly identifying the supply side objective measures. The data required for these scales (e.g. novelty, intellectual cultivation, relaxation, pleasure) are not easily available without a sophisticated system for collecting data on visitors' experiences.

Exploring the features of travelers' supra-experiential destinations would be considered as a more holistic and practical approach rather than merely concentrating on one destination. Instead of describing experiences from a demand perspective this paper also sets out to look at experiences from a broader and more holistic perspective including characteristics of superior destinations and their impact on positive tourist behaviors from the supply side. While doing so it also aims to provide managerial implications for DMOs and other stakeholders in the destination. The main purpose of this study therefore is to identify the environmental features of destinations defined as the best experience scape ever by tourists and how these affect their recommendation behaviors. Such an understanding might offer a better understanding for tourist experiences in destinations and suggest implications for tourism industry and other stakeholders in creating, managing and marketing better experiences for tourists.

9.2   Tourism Destinations

Destinations are defined geographical areas with political and legislative boundaries and places that facilitate creation of tourism experiences (Barnes, Mattson, & Sorensen, 2014). Hence tourist destinations in this study have been operationally defined as spatial brands and geographical locations that reflect a combination of services, products, infrastructure and environment that form an overall vacation experience for travelers. Destination "is the combination of goods, services and holiday experiences offered on a local scale" (Buhalis, 2000: 98). Similarly, Coltman (1989: 4) defined destination as "places that contain different natural charms and characteristics that would be considered attractive to tourists". Yavuz (2007) argued that destination is the main element in providing an integrated presentation of the sources, activities and other products for tourism. Generally, destinations are defined as confined geographic areas such as a country, an island or a city (Hall, 2000; Davidson & Maitland, 1997). However, it is widely acknowledged that consumers should have a subjective interpretive perceptual destination concept based on their travel plans, cultural backgrounds, visiting purposes, educational levels and past experiences. For example; Istanbul may be considered as a destination for a business traveler who is visiting the city for two days and return whilst Europe can be a destination for a Japanese tourist who visit six European countries in two weeks (Buhalis, 2000).

Despite various studies have looked into tourist experiences in different settings (e.g. hotels; attractions, restaurants), components of a holistic destination experience are neglected. Experiences created through the interaction of the tourist with the tourism system (hotels, attractions, transportation, attractions etc.) are only a part of the overall experience. Thus the concept of destination including tourism industry and external factors (e.g. resources, infra-structure, local culture, climate etc.) can be regarded as the outer sphere of tourist experiences. Understanding tourist experience in destinations is more complex than measuring it for individual services also because the vacation extends for a period of time and involves a simultaneous and synergistic interaction and consumption of integrated and independent products and services (Burns & Holden, 1995). Therefore, destination is an integral part of tourist decision-making, however it is much more than the attractions, products and services in it. It is more complex than these components because it includes the interaction of these elements as well. The architecture, the hotel, local hospitality, activities, landmarks, nature, the taxi driver even the airport can affect the quality of overall vacation experience at the destination. Therefore, rather than experiences with individual tourism service providers this study focuses on the holistic experience produced in the destinations including exogenous factors besides the tourism industry.

Tourism is a complex human experience integrating various personal characteristics with clues acquired in a destination (Gunn, 1988). Traveler experience is also an amalgam of services and products consumed at the destination and interactions with the host community (Cetin & Yarcan, 2017). Hence, destination experiences can be framed based on different stakeholders in the destination including tourism resources, and the industry, residents, public bodies and tourist themselves (Oz, Demirkol, & Ozkoç, 2012). Ozdemir (2007) defines tourism as a complex product consisting of various tourism resources that a tourism destination possesses and services that are directly or indirectly provided by many institutions and organizations that attract and host the tourists.

Destinations provide the environment for tourists to fulfil their needs related to their travel experiences (Prebensen, Woo, Chen, & Uysal, 2012). On the other hand, each destination can match and satisfy certain types of demand. Therefore, tourism marketers need to evaluate travel motivations to develop offerings and brand their destinations appropriate for the right target markets. In order to determine the suitable target segments in destination marketing, it is necessary to understand different types of destinations first. Buhalis (2000) summarizes destination categories as follows:

- Urban: Urban destinations have been in tourism since the first years of civilization. Urban destinations attracted visitors who participated in meetings, conferences and business-related events and exhibitions. Many urban destinations are well equipped in terms of transportation and accommodation infrastructure, conference and exhibition halls that will facilitate major events. Urban destinations are also well supplied with educational institutions and hospitals. Thus they are usually attractive for education and health tourism as well.
- Seaside: Seaside destinations offer leisure vacations for tourists. While typical European leisure travelers spend their annual vacation on the Mediterranean coast, North Americans visit southern areas such as Florida, California and the Caribbean.

Beaches, climate and entertainment options are developed in such sun-lust destinations.

- Mountain: Mountain destinations are attracting tourists who come for winter sports
  such as skiing, as well as those who participate nature based tourism activities in
  all seasons. Mountain destinations also attract mountain bikers, hikers, trekkers,
  campers, adventure tourists and so on. Because of mountain destinations are usually close to the city centre, they are easily accessible by private car, many of which
  are still undiscovered and offer authentic experiences to visitors. Lakes and scenic
  areas add to the attractiveness of mountain destinations.
- Rural: Rural tourism is developing rapidly. Tourism is seen as an alternative tool
  for economic development of many rural areas where agriculture is loosing its.
  Rural areas usually attracting day trippers offer; natural and cultural resources, but
  still trying to adopt to the needs of holiday-makers on a daily basis.
- Authentic 3rd World: Authentic destinations are often described as unfooted third
  world countries. Tourists like to experience places where tourism develops is under
  developed in volume. Emerging destinations in Asia, South America and Africa
  are attracting a larger numbers of adventurous tourists who are ready to forgo their
  comforts for interaction with pristine regions and local communities.
- Unique-Exotic: Certain destinations are marked as "asexual" destinations because
  they offer unique and valuable experiences. Such destinations focus on maximizing
  revenue per visitor and offer luxury customized services.

Therefore, destinations have diverse resources and characteristics that offer different experiences to their visitors. Although there are numerous papers on experiences
from individual services (e.g., hotels, airlines, restaurants) in the destination, literature on creation of holistic destination experience that might be applicable for all
destinations has been overlooked (Karayilan & Cetin, 2016).

9.3 Tourist Experiences in Destinations

Traditional tourist theories are no longer sufficient in explaining changing tourist
needs and motivations (Mossberg, 2007). From mid-80s the tourism product has
transformed into more experiential and informative features. The common characteristics of these travel types (e.g., adventure tourism, cultural tourism) are that they
are more enriching, engaging, creative, adventuresome and informative than traditional mass tourism (Karayilan & Cetin, 2016). Mass tourism destinations are being
replaced by alternative experience intensive tourism destinations (Butler, 1990) and
many established superior quality sun-lust destinations in the tourism history are
suffering today. The choice of a destination is heavily dependent on the potential
quality and quantity of experiences available at the region. Tourists actively search
for experiences during their holidays; they seek "experience rich" destinations. Hence
experiential dimensions are becoming main antecedents of destinations' sustainable

competitive advantage success (Pine & Gilmore, 1998) and there is a need to redefine experiential attributes of destinations.

Tourist experiences were initially explored under four realms of customer experiences offered by Pine and Gilmore (1998). According to them education, entertainment, escape and esthetic features of a product or a service create an additional value for consumers. Various other studies have also integrated these concepts into tourism (e.g. Binkhorst & Dekker, 2009; Sundbo, 2009; Williams, 2006). The entertainment realm is related to events that create enjoyment, this is the most basic experience (e.g., jokes). Educational experiences are concerned with tourists' need for intellectual development (e.g., museums). Esthetic experiences are related to travelers' needs to appreciate beauty and harmony (e.g., nature). Escapist dimension of experiences calls for people's desire for novelty (e.g., adventure). Although these four realms have not been used in a holistic destination setting, they have the potential to explain the destination experience as well.

Tourism is more of a hedonic activity involving a distinctive physical, emotional and spiritual engagement rather than a rational consumption (Jansson, 2002). Hosany and Gilbert (2010) discuss love, joy and positive surprise as emotional outcomes of an experience. Sensory, affective, behavioral and intellectual factors were listed as components of tourist experiences by Barnes et al. (2014). Involvement, hedonism, happiness, pleasure, relaxation, stimulation, refreshment, social interaction, spontaneity, meaningfulness, knowledge, challenge, sense of separation, timelessness, adventure, personal relevance, novelty, escaping pressure, and intellectual cultivation were also considered as dimensions of tourist experience (Kim, Ritchie, & McCormick, 2012). Thus tourist experience is a multidimensional outcome formed by different factors and it is challenging to determine which are the key components. Although tourist experiences at destinations lacks a shared definition there are common characteristics mentioned in the literature that can be utilized to create a holistic factor pool of experiences.

The desire to visit destination is at the core of tourism flows (Swarbrooke & Horner, 2007). Larsen (2007) defines tourist experience as a strong personal travel related event that is memorized. Various destination attributes (i.e. pull) and personal factors (i.e. push) might have an impact on quality of experiences in destinations (Gunn, 1988). Notwithstanding the crucial role of all destination features and the 'sensescapes' they provide (Agapito, Mendes, & Valle, 2013), visitors play, an active role in producing their own experiences (Kastenholz, Carneiro, & Eusébio, 2015). Involvement emerges as an antecedent of experiences and can be defined as the identification and interest of the tourist in the destination characterized by enjoyment and self achievement (Selin & Howard, 1988). Thus interacting with different elements in the destination tourists co-create their subjective experiences and destinations can be considered as the pull factor for tourists. When deciding on a destination, travelers evaluate different attributes of the destination which might also be referred to as the pull factors. Mill and Morrison (1985) list attractions, facilities, infrastructure, transportation and hospitality as basic pull components of a destination.

According to Arnould and Price (1993) the peak experience emerges when experiencing something unique, unexpected and has a surprise dimension into it. Quan and Wang (2004) however argues a positive experience is only possible if the peak experience is accompanied by supporting experiences. They discuss service related destination qualities as supporting experiences. Thus accommodation facilities, service staff, physical comfort, safety, cleanliness, landscaping, public transportation in the destination might also be regarded as a part of tourists' experience (Cetin & Bilgihan, 2016). Hence the total experience quality in a destination depends both on peak and supporting experiences.

Infra-structure, value for money spent and costs, accessibility, local culture, physiography and climate, entertainment, environmental management (e.g. crowd, noise, cleanliness), landscapes, quality of service, variety of activities, signage, availability of information, local food, traffic, safety and security, special events and hospitality are also listed as experiential factors in a destination (Cetin, Alrawadieh, Dinçer, Dinçer, & Ioannides, 2017; Cetin & Okumus, 2018; Kim 2014; Okumus & Cetin, 2018). Weather, hotel standards, cleanliness and upkeep, geographical setting and scenic beauty, safety, ease of reach, friendliness and helpfulness of locals, artistic and cultural amenities, ease of getting around, crowding and congestion, nightlife and entertainment, quality restaurants, shopping alternatives, attractiveness of prices and adequacy of public services were identified by Haywood and Muller (1988). Authentic and novel perceptions of the destination also result in positive tourist experiences (Urry, 1990). Other research focusing on destination experience discuss social interactions with locals, servicescape, public services, knowledge enhancement, feeling comfortable, and welcome, having challenges and active participation as salient attributes of destination experience of tourists. These attributes are also widely covered in destination competiveness literature (e.g. Crouch & Ritchie, 2005).

Experiences during a trip might either be positive or negative. According to Ozdemir, Aksu, Ehtiyar, Çizel, Çizel, and İçigen (2012) attributes of the destination play an important role in determining satisfaction and positive future behaviors of visitors such as loyalty and recommendation. These experiences might be so powerful that the tourist might become emotionally attached to the destination and become loyal visitors visiting the same destination several times (Hidalgo & Hernandez, 2001) and recommend the experience to others (Cetin & Dincer, 2014a). If a tourist is not satisfied with his experience in a destination it is unlikely that he/she will return or recommend the destination which affects the future number of visitors to the destination. Despite valuable contributions on destination experiences no study so far attempted to analyze the relative importance of these items and their impact on tourist behaviors in destinations identified as superior by tourists.

9.4 Tourist Recommendation Behaviors

Majority of products and services such as automobiles, financial services and tourism attracts high involvement from customers' perspective as they relate to high risk and a larger amount of finances. Tourism is an intangible service, with limited pre-established standards and is consumed less frequently. Therefore, it is harder to evaluate it prior to actual experience (Cetin & Dincer, 2014a, b). In order to minimize the risk, tourists spend a great amount of time, effort and share of valet for a positive vaca-tion experience without unpleasant surprises. In order to minimize this risk, tourists depend on word of mouth of others (Dinçer & Alrawadieh, 2017). Various research identified tourist find C2C (Customer to Customer) interactions and online reviews more credible than traditional advertising. Particularly importance of E-Wom and social media in tourism is well-covered in tourism (Cetin, Akova, Gursoy, & Kaya, 2016a). Tourists' favourable experiences in a destination may lead to revisit inten-tion and more importantly they influence friends and relatives around them through positive word of mouth (Opperman, 2000). Recommendation about a destination for potential tourists is considered the most reliable source of information (Yoon & Uysal, 2005). Recommendations both from relatives or friends and social media, affects touristic buying decisions (Cetin et al., 2016b; Song, Yi, & Huang, 2017).

9.5 Methodology

Tourism is an experience intensive service and have been used as an ideal domain to study customer experiences. Vacation as a leisure experience is hedonic by motiva-tion and the impact of rational evaluations are limited compared to a manufactured product. This paper explores the experiential characteristics of travelers' supra desti-nations through existing knowledge and an empirical study. Based on various expe-riential destination characteristics mentioned in the literature, a pool of experiential items was identified and a survey was designed. Travelers were asked to rate these destination features based on their best leisure destination experience. The survey was based on extant literature on customer experience, tourist behavior, and desti-nation management. Participants' tendency to recommend the destination was also enquired in order to identify which attributes had a greater impact on word of mouth. Tendency to recommend is also suggested an important feature of positive customer experiences.

The first version of the survey included 34 items identified in the literature. These items were then refined during an expert panel of three tourism scholar. For exam-ple, scenery was considered under natural attractions and prices were merged with value for money. Information provision was also merged with quality of tourist ser-vices; night-life with entertainment; peacefulness with relaxation during the peer discussion. The survey included some demographic queries as well. This instrument was then pilot tested on 30 respondents to improve validity of items used. Based on respondents' feedback the questionnaire was modified to ensure a better under-standing. The data was also checked for reliability and loadings of the items. Some items had a large inter-correlation; these were merged others and items with weak loadings were removed. Three attributes were further removed or merged based on their loadings during this stage. For example, crowdedness received a lower rating with a large standard deviation, meaning this item is perceived both positive and negative by the respondents. Transportation network and public transportation were also perceived under accessibility and created confusion. Thus removed from the item pool. The final version of the questionnaire included 22 items that describe various characteristics of the destinations.

Data collection took seven weeks in May-June 2016 in Istanbul, domestic tourists were approached at well known attractions of the city as well as domestic departure terminals of two international airports. A total of 500 surveys were collected. 29 surveys were eliminated because of missing data and "ja" saying bias and a total of 472 surveys were included in data analysis. Respondents were requested to rate their best leisure destinations based on their experiences on a five point Likert scale. Some demographic (e.g. gender, age, marital status) and tripographic (e.g. frequency of travel) information were also requested. The screening criteria used for the surveys were being older than 18 years and to have traveled at least twice within the past year. Various descriptive statistics were utilized in order to identify the attributes that have higher loadings. In order to determine the impact of these experiential items on loyalty and recommendation, a stepwise regression was also utilized. These are discussed in the findings section.

9.6   Results

Concerning the demographic profile of respondents; among 472 respondents, 258 were male, 391 were between 20 and 40 years of age. 228 were married and 441 had university education. Descriptive statistics revealed that among 22 attributes; *being a well known destination, availability of detailed destination information, natural attractions, climate* and *value for money* were the highest rated items while the rest of the attributes also scored higher than three on a five point Likert Scale. Therefore, destinations' marketing communications (branding, information provision), the inherent features (natural attractions and climate) and value for money were rated as most important items. But all other items were also rated above average. Table 9.1 displays mean values of superior destination attributes.

In order to identify the impact of these experiential items on recommendation a stepwise regression was run. As presented in Table 9.2, seven items out of 22 were found to explain 0.52 of the variance in recommendation ($R^2 = 0.52$). These are; value for money ($\beta = 0.49$), climate ($\beta = 0.12$), service staff ($\beta = 0.1$), local hospitality ($\beta = 0.1$), tourist services ($\beta = 0.09$), entertainment ($\beta = 0.08$), and authenticity ($\beta = 0.09$).

9.7   Conclusion and Implications

The holiday is a risky purchase, often costs a lot of finances and a dedication of personal paid vacation time which is also limited. Therefore, includes a prior planning and usually a long process of decision making. It is also often loaded with emotions, day dreams and expectations (Goossens, 2000). Tourists' actually start experiencing the destination long before they travel to destination at home. Hence

Table 9.1 Relative importance of superior destination features

Destination attributes	Mean	Std. dev.
This is a well known destination	4.59	1.51
Tourism infrastructure is sufficient	4.3	0.9
I received good value for money	4.4	0.83
Tourism services are of high quality	4.26	0.83
Daily spending is affordable	3.65	1.03
Service staff are of high quality	4.02	0.89
Natural attractions are sufficient	4.45	0.8
Cultural attractions are sufficient	4.17	0.88
This destination is safe	4.32	0.84
This destination is geographically close	3.69	1.47
Detailed information about the destination is available	4.50	0.75
Entertainment services are sufficient	4.17	0.98
Diverse activities are available at the destination	4.11	0.95
The locals are welcoming	3.92	1.04
The climate is nice	4.43	0.74
Shopping alternatives are adequate	4.00	0.94
This destination is calm and quite	4.18	0.96
This destination is lively and exciting	4.12	1.01
This destination is clean	4.37	0.77
Local food is attractive	3.94	0.99
This destination is authentic	3.74	1.12
This destination is cheap	3.25	1.22

destination experience is a process, and includes a number of challenges during the travel from information search to departure for the vacation (Neuhofer, Buhalis, & Ladkin, 2012). Once in the destination tourists also interact with various actors and destination features depending on their motivations, environmental factors and availability of activities. Thus, tourist experiences do not occur in a vacuum and requires a great deal of planning at destination level and within the individual services in the destination. Travelers in way create their own experiences by interacting with these different elements and actors at the destination. Therefore, a number of factors have the possibility to affect the experience of tourists during this actual travel process (Karayilan & Cetin, 2016). Without a unified identity in the destination that is supported by individual elements, a positive overall tourist experience is at risk. Converting experiences into encounters and creating them in the destination is still a challenge. But identifying the dimensions of an overall destination experience is the first step. This paper offered 22 items that relate to these factors that affect over-

Table 9.2 Results of regression explaining the impacts of destination attributes on recommendation

Independent variables	B	SE	β	t	Sig.
Constant	0.44	0.20		2.17	0.03[a]
Value for money	0.46	0.04	0.49	2.79	0.01[b]
Climate	0.13	0.04	0.12	4.24	0.00[b]
Service staff	0.09	0.04	0.1	2.48	0.01[b]
Tourist services	0.08	0.03	0.09	2.42	0.03[b]
Hospitality of locals	0.08	0.03	0.1	2.86	0.05[a]
Entertainment	0.06	0.03	0.08	2.1	0.04[a]
Authenticity	0.06	0.02	0.09	2.49	0.01[b]

Note B: Coefficient; SE: Standard Error; β: Standardized Coefficient; t: t-Value; Sig.: Significance, Dependent Variable: Recommendation; $R = 0.72$; $R^2 = 0.52$; Adjusted $R^2 = 0.52$; Standard Error $= 0.54$. Insignificant items were excluded in this table
[a] Significant at $p < 0.05$ level
[b] Significant at $p < 0.01$ level

all destination experience. Understanding these attributes might be paramount for designing and enhancing positive visitor experiences in destinations.

By identifying the experiential characteristics of superior destinations this paper offers valuable empirical findings. The findings might be used by destination planners, and industry professionals to rate destinations based on the items identified in this study and benchmark competing destinations. This way various gaps might be identified and emphasis would be stressed on the experiential factors that differentiate destinations. Destination planers and all stakeholders should strive for producing or creating the facilitating environment for positive tourist experiences to emerge. These distinct experiences should also be used in the promotional materials of destinations. For example, *being a well-known destination* and *availability of destination information* might be improved through marketing communications. *Value for money* was also rated higher by respondents, while describing their superior destinations while *being cheap* and *affordable* were rated the lowest. This might refer to the fact that tourists are willing to pay more for experiential services that they value. Literature also confirms that tourists are willing to travel far and pay more for desirable experiences (e.g. Hidalgo & Hernandez, 2001). Thus destinations have the opportunity to increase per tourist spending as long as additional cost is supported with the experiential value offered.

Concerning recommendation *value for money* has the largest effect on tendency to recommend. While *climate, quality tourist services and service staff*, *hospitality of hosts, entertainment* and *authenticity* have also significant impacts on recommendation. These items were also discussed as important in tourism literature. All of these items except *climate* might be enhanced through a better destination management. The climate factor on the other hand is and inherent characteristic, yet is also valuable considering its subjective nature. For example, a sunny and hot destination climate might be attractive for sun-lust tourists yet the cultural tourists on the go might prefer a milder climate (e.g. Demiroglu, Turp, Ozturk, & Kurnaz, 2016). Thus the climate also emerges as an important factor for positioning the destination and targeting suitable segments. Experiential resources of a destination can also be used as a competitive advantage and a tool for differentiation and positioning. Segmentation and targeting strategies are also important. Based on the potential resources, experiences and desirable markets, destination should position themselves among competition and focus on specific target markets that it can satisfy better and create positive experiences and offer additional value.

Pine and Gilmore (1998) suggested five key principles to design memorable experiences. These are theming the experience, harmonizing impressions with positive clues, eliminating negative clues, mixing the experience with memorabilia, and engaging all five senses. Morgan (2006) discuss six principles as abundant choices, moments of amazement, shared experiences, fringes at the heart, local distinctiveness and positive values. Aho (2001) distinguishes among four essential core elements of the touristic experience: emotional experiences; learning experiences; practical experiences; and transformational experiences. Yet, because of the subjective nature of tourism destination experience, DMOs and tourism industry alone can not provide the experience to tourists. Rather they can only create the facilitating environment for tourists to create their own experiences. Different than its most previous studies focusing on meanings, emotions, this paper offers operational items that might affect the environment of destination experience and offer practical implications for destination stakeholders. Yet some of these stakeholders have competing interests. The real challenge for destinations is to arrange these relationships in such a way they also cooperate for the overall experience rather than compete on creating different individual experiences.

Scholars might also use the experiential items offered in this study for future research on destination competitiveness and tourist experience. The findings might also be used in positioning and design of marketing communications for destinations as well as measuring success of DMO related planning, management and marketing activities. Satisfaction acts as a processor of sensory and affective destination experience, governing the relationship between experience and visitor loyalty. In addition, current satisfaction is a strong predictor of future satisfaction (Verhoef, Lemon, Parasuraman, Roggeveen, Tsiros, & Schlesinger, 2009). Tourism providers should therefore take every opportunity to plan for and ensure consistent visitor relationship management throughout all touch-points with a visitor and to measure and monitor the level of satisfaction with the services delivered to visitors.

There are various limitations to this study. Tourists with different motivations and personal backgrounds might perceive the qualities of a destination different. Travelers from various cultural backgrounds and personal characteristics might interpret their experience differently from the same destination. Even for the same people, their moods at the particular moment might affect their interpretation of the environment. Previous travel experiences might also play a role in perception of destination qualities. Experiences are subjective and depend very much on personal interpretations and perceptions. A sun-lust tourist might desire passive elements of destination experience such as relaxation, esthetics and entertainment themes however a heritage tour might require more active engagement and education. Hence destination experiences are both subjective and context specific. Thus both pull (e.g. destination characteristics) and push (e.g. target markets) factors should be considered when trying to create experiences in destinations. According to Volo (2009) subjective nature of experiences and difficulties with standardizing environmental factors makes it challenging to create same level of experiences for everyone at each time. Commodification of experiences is also another challenge. If it is standardized and charged, its experiential value and authenticity decreases. Moreover, Larsen (2007) also indicate that tourists' experiences are based on their expectations and will influence their expectations from the next visit, creating a cycle.

Yet a general diagnostic tool like the items used in this study might still be utilized to measure the experiential potential of a destination. Thus we encourage future studies, explore a scale of destination features that might measure an experiential potential in a destination. Moreover, the study is focused on domestic tourists. Various political and security concerns have affected the international arrivals to Turkey during recent years mostly stemming from the political instability in Middle East. The international demand to the country decreased rapidly from 35 million to 25 million arrivals. Hence domestic market became an important market. Yet, concentrated on international European tourists for years, destinations in Turkey lack the knowledge on how to satisfy the needs of citizens. Hence, although the study is limited with domestic tourists, it also fills an important gap in the literature on destination choices of Turkish domestic tourists.

Acknowledgements This study was initially supported by Istanbul University Research Council (53528) and presented at ATMC Conference, 2017.

References

Agapito, D., Mendes, J., & Valle, P. (2013). Exploring the conceptualization of the sensory dimension of tourist experiences. *Journal of Destination Marketing & Management, 2*(2), 62–73.

Aho, S. K. (2001). Towards a general theory of touristic experiences: Modelling experience process in tourism. *Tourism Review, 56*(3/4), 33–37.

Ali, F., Kim, W. G., Li, J., Jeon, H. (2016). Make it delightful: Customers' experience, satisfaction and loyalty in Malaysian theme parks. *Journal of Destination Marketing & Management*. https://doi.org/10.1016/j.jdmm.2016.05.003.

Arnould, E. J., & Price, L. L. (1993). River magic: Extraordinary experience and the extended service encounter. *Journal of Consumer Research, 20*(1), 24–45.

Barnes, S. J., Mattsson, J., & Sørensen, F. (2014). Destination brand experience and visitor behavior: Testing a scale in the tourism context. *Annals of Tourism Research, 48*, 121–139.

Binkhorst, E., & Dekker, T. D. (2009). Agenda for co-creation tourism experience research. *Journal of Hospitality Marketing & Management, 18*(2–3), 311–327.

Buhalis, D. (2000). Marketing the competitive destination of the future. *Tourism Management, 21*, 97–116.

Burns, P. M., & Holden, A. (1995). *Tourism: A new perspective*. Prenticehall.

Butler, R. W. (1990). Alternative tourism: Pious hope or trojan horse? *Journal of Travel Research, 28*(3), 40–45.

Cetin, G., Akova, O., Gursoy, D., Kaya, F. (2016a). Impact of direct flights on tourist volume: Case of Turkish Airlines. *Journal of Tourismology, 2*(2), 36–50.

Cetin, G., Alrawadieh, Z., Dincer, M. Z., Dincer, F., & Ioannides, D. (2017). Willingness to pay for tourist tax in destinations: Empirical evidence from Istanbul. *Economies, 5*(2), 21–36.

Cetin, G., & Bilgihan, A. (2016). Components of cultural tourists' experiences in destinations. *Current Issues in Tourism, 19*(2), 137–154.

Cetin, G., Cifci, M., Dincer, F., & Fuchs, M. (2016b). Coping with reintermediation: The case of SMHEs. *Information Technology & Tourism, 16*(4), 375–392.

Cetin, G., & Dincer, İ. F. (2014a). Electronic word of mouth among hotel guests: Demographic and tripographic factors. *Bilgi Ekonomisi ve Yönetimi Dergisi, 9*(2), 35–41.

Cetin, G., & Dincer, İ. F. (2014b). Influence of customer experience on loyalty and word-of-mouth in hospitality operations. *Anatolia, 25*(2), 181–194.

Cetin, G., & Okumus, F. (2018). Experiencing local Turkish hospitality in Istanbul, Turkey. *International Journal of Culture, Tourism and Hospitality Research (Early cite)*.

Cetin, G., & Walls, A. (2016). Understanding the customer experiences from the perspective of guests and hotel managers: Empirical findings from luxury hotels in Istanbul, Turkey. *Journal of Hospitality Marketing & Management, 25*(4), 395–424.

Cetin, G., & Yarcan, Ş. (2017). The professional relationship between tour guides and tour operators. *Scandinavian Journal of Hospitality and Tourism, 17*(4), 345–357.

Crouch, G. I., & Ritchie, J. B. (2005). Application of the analytic hierarchy process to tourism choice and decision making: A review and illustration applied to destination competitiveness. *Tourism Analysis, 10*(1), 17–25.

Coltman, M. (1989). *Introduction to travel and tourism: An international approach*. New Jersey: Wiley.

Davidson, R., & Maitland, R. (1997). *Tourism destinations*. London: Hodder & Stoughton.

Demiroglu, O. C., Turp, M. T., Ozturk, T., & Kurnaz, M. L. (2016). Impact of climate change on natural snow reliability, snowmaking capacities, and wind conditions of ski resorts in Northeast Turkey: A dynamical downscaling approach. *Atmosphere, 7*(4), 52.

Dinçer, M. Z., & Alrawadieh, Z. (2017). Negative word of mouse in the hotel industry: A content analysis of online reviews on luxury hotels in Jordan. *Journal of Hospitality Marketing & Management, 26*(8), 785–804.

Goossens, C. (2000). Tourism information and pleasure motivation. *Annals of Tourism Research, 27*(2), 301–321.

Gunn, C. A. (1988). *Tourism planning* (2nd ed.). New York: Taylor and Francis.

Gursoy, D., Chen, J. S., & Chi, J. G. (2014). Theoretical examination of destination loyalty formation. *International Journal of Contemporary Hospitality Management., 26*(5), 809–827.

Hall, C. M. (2000). *Tourism planning: Policies, processes, relationships*. UK: Pretice Hall.

Haywood, K. M., & Muller, T. E. (1988). The urban tourist experience: Evaluating satisfaction. *Hospitality Education and Research Journal, 12*(2), 453–459.

Hidalgo, M. C., & Hernandez, B. (2001). Place attachment: Conceptual and empirical questions. *Journal of Environmental Psychology, 21*(3), 273–281.

Hosany, S., & Gilbert, D. (2010). Measuring tourists' emotional experience towards hedonic holiday destinations. *Journal of Travel Research, 49*(4), 513–526.

Huang, S., & Hsu, H.C. (2009). Travel motivation: linking theory to practice. *International Journal of Culture, Tourism and Hospitality Research, 3*(4), 287–295 (2009). https://doi.org/10.1108/17506180910994505.

Jansson, A. (2002). Spatial phantasmagoria: The mediatization of tourism experience. *European Journal of Communication, 17*(4), 429–443.

Karayilan, E., & Cetin, G. (2016). Tourism destination: Design of experiences. In M. Sotiriadis & D. Gursoy (Eds.), *The handbook of managing and marketing tourism experiences* (pp. 65–83). Emerald Group Publishing Limited.

Kastenholz, E., Carneiro, M. J., & Eusébio, C. (2015). Diverse socializing patterns in rural tourist experiences–a segmentation analysis. *Current Issues in Tourism*, 1–21.

Kim, J. H. (2014). The antecedents of memorable tourism experiences: The development of a scale to measure the destination attributes associated with memorable experiences. *Tourism Management, 44,* 34–45.

Kim, A. K., & Brown, G. (2012). Understanding the relationships between perceived travel experiences, overall satisfaction, and destination loyalty. *Anatolia, 23*(3), 328–347.

Kim, J. H., Ritchie, J. B., & McCormick, B. (2012). Development of a scale to measure memorable tourism experiences. *Journal of Travel Research, 51*(1), 12–25.

Larsen, S. (2007). Aspects of a psychology of the tourist experience. *Scandinavian Journal of Hospitality and Tourism, 7*(1), 7–18.

Mill, R. C., & Morrison, A. M. (1985). *The tourism system.* New Jersey: Prentice Hall.

Morgan, M. (2006). Making space for experiences. *Journal of Retail and Leisure Property, 5*(4), 305–313.

Mossberg, L. (2007). A marketing approach to tourist experience. *Scandinavian Journal of Hospitality and Tourism, 7*(1), 59–74.

Neuhofer, B., Buhalis, D., & Ladkin, A. (2012). Conceptualizing technology enhanced destination experiences. *Journal of Destination Marketing & Management, 1*(1–2), 36–46.

Okumus, B., & Cetin, G. (2018). Marketing Istanbul as a Culinary Destination. *Journal of Destination Marketing & Management* (In print).

Oppermann, M. (2000). Tourism destination loyalty. *Journal of Travel Research, 39,* 78–84.

Oz, M., Demirkol, Ş., Özkoç, A. G. (2012). İl Kültür Turizm Müdürlüklerinin Web Tabanlı Destinasyon Pazarlamasında Rolü: İl Kültür ve Turizm Müdürlükleri Web Siteleri Üzerinde bir Uygulama. I. Doğu Akdeniz Turizm Sempozyumu Bölgesel Destinasyon Yönetimi.

Ozdemir, B., Aksu, A., Ehtiyar, R., Çizel, B., Çizel, R. B., & İçigen, E. T. (2012). Relationships among tourist profile, satisfaction and destination loyalty: Examining empirical evidences in Antalya region of Turkey. *Journal of Hospitality Marketing & Management, 21*(5), 506–540.

Ozdemir, G. (2007). *Destinasyon yönetimi ve pazarlama temelleri: İzmir ili için bir destinasyon model önerisi (Yaynlanmamış Doktora Tezi).* İzmir: Dokuz Eylül University.

Prebensen, N. K., Chen, J. S., & Uysal, M. (2012). Motivation and involvement as antecedents of the perceived value of the destination experience. *Journal of Travel Research, 52*(2), 253–264.

Pine, B. J., & Gilmore, J. H. (1998). Welcome to the experience economy. *Harvard Business Review,* 97–107.

Quan, S., & Wang, N. (2004). Towards a structural model of the tourist experience: An illustration from food experiences in tourism. *Tourism Management, 25*(3), 297–305.

Selin, S. W., & Howard, D. R. (1988). Ego involvement and leisure behavior: A conceptual specification. *Journal of Leisure Research, 20*(3), 237–244.

Song, T., Yi, C., & Huang, J. (2017). Whose recommendations do you follow? An investigation of tie strength, shopping stage, and deal scarcity. *Information & Management, 54*(8), 1072–1083.

Sundbo, J. (2009). Innovation in the experience economy: A taxonomy of innovation organizations. *The Service Industries Journal, 29*(4), 431–455.

Swarbrooke, J., & Horner, S. (2007). *Consumer behaviour in tourism* (2nd ed.). Oxford: Butterworth Heinemann.

Urry, J. (1990). The 'consumption' of tourism. *Sociology, 24*(1), 23–35.

Verhoef, P. C., Lemon, K. N., Parasuraman, A., Roggeveen, A., Tsiros, M., & Schlesinger, L. A. (2009). Customer experience creation: Determinants, dynamics and management strategies. *Journal of Retailing, 85*(1), 31–41.

Volo, S. (2009). Conceptualizing experience: A tourist based approach. *Journal of Hospitality Marketing & Management, 18*(2–3), 111–126.

Williams, A. (2006). Tourism and hospitality marketing: Fantasy, feeling and fun. *International Journal of Contemporary Hospitality Management, 18*(6), 482–495.

Yoon, Y., & Uysal, M. (2005). An examination of the effects of motivation and satisfaction on destination loyalty: A structural model. *Tourism Management, 26*(1), 45–56.

Yavuz, M. C. (2007). *Identity building process in international destination branding: A case for the city of Adana.* Ph.D. thesis, Çukurova University, Adana, Turkey.

Chapter 10
What Percentage of Travelers Are Writing Hotel Reviews?

Juan Pedro Mellinas

10.1 Introduction

A new phenomenon called Web 2.0 has emerged in recent years (O'reilly, 2005). It has grown into a truly meaningful size thanks to the popularisation of social media and websites used for exchanging opinions about products and services. The concept of Web 2.0 describes the phenomenon whereby the users stop being mere spectators who just read information but instead become participants in the web. The user provides content, writes reviews, shares ideas, images and videos with the whole web. The success of this new dimension of Internet usage has given rise to immensely structured or semi-structured databases with millions of reviews and comments about various topics, products and services.

The tourism sector has been significantly affected by the development of information technologies, which have led to the emergence of both structural and organizational innovations (Stamboulis & Skayannis, 2003). These new technologies, especially the irruption of internet, have modified businesses strategies and structures in the tourist industry (Buhalis & Law, 2008). Millions of travellers write reviews about their travel experiences, seemingly receiving nothing in return. This altruistic phenomenon is considered as online reproduction of similar phenomena of friendliness and collaboration that exist in the offline or "real world" (Resnick & Zeckhauser, 2002).

This phenomenon has not been unnoticed in the academic world, resulting in becoming a source of information that certain disciplines have been taking advantage of. In order to obtain data on specific subjects one resorts to surveys that include significant financial costs and have some limitations, in terms of the number of surveys, therefore also entailing a statistically significant impact on the obtained results. The existence of hundreds, thousands or millions of reviews on some particular topics

J. P. Mellinas (✉)
International University of La Rioja, Av. de la Paz, 137, 26006 Logroño, La Rioja, Spain
e-mail: losmellinas@yahoo.es

© Springer Nature Switzerland AG 2019
A. Artal-Tur et al. (eds.), *Trends in Tourist Behavior*,
Tourism, Hospitality & Event Management,
https://doi.org/10.1007/978-3-030-11160-1_10

161

that have been submitted by internet users enables researchers to obtain information without any financial costs and from a number of individuals who in such a manner have interviewed themselves, something that would be hard to do using traditional methods (Hine, 2000; Kozinets, 2002). In this manner the studies can cover much larger geographical areas (all countries with a certain amount of connections to the Internet) and data can be gathered in any place at any time (Mann & Stewart, 2000).

Whenever applicable, researchers are replacing the data sets collected through questionnaires and interviews by those collected from specialized websites, with Booking.com and TripAdvisor being the most relevant sources (Stanisic, 2016). The increased use of big data collected from online review websites for research purposes is supported by automatically controlled systems, which acquire information about millions of reviews from thousands of hotels (Radojevic, Stanisic, & Stanic, 2015) quickly, cheaply and conveniently. Once these huge databases are obtained, researchers have attempted to process and analyze online traveler reviews using sophisticated technologies (Govers & Go, 2004; Ye, Law, & Gu, 2009a; Ye, Zhang, & Law, 2009b).

During the last years, hotel reviews databases have gained great importance, generating a large number of publications on this topic (Cantallops & Salvi, 2014; Kwok, Xie, & Richards, 2017). Although TripAdvisor seems to be the most used website, Booking.com has also been widely used in recent years (Mellinas, Mártinez María-Dolores, & Bernal García, 2015), especially in Europe because of the large number of reviews it collects (Murphy, 2017).

In these cases we are talking about a sample of customers (those who fill out the survey) from a universe of guests, but there is no information about the percentage that those samples represent. Information provided by TripAdvisor and Booking.com is very similar, but there is an important difference in terms of the process of collecting reviews.

The procedure for collecting information in Booking.com is quite clear and known by all. A few days after the stay, the traveler receives an email inviting to participate in the survey. In this case we could talk about "response rate", as every customer receives an invitation and some of them fill out the survey.

However, there is no procedure of how to collect hotel reviews on TripAdvisor, as this website does not have information about who is visiting hotels and cannot sent emails like Booking.com. In this context, the level of participation will depend on the percentage of registered active users on TripAdvisor among hotel visitors and actions implemented in order to promote participation between customers. In this case it is not appropriate to talk about "response rate" and we should talk about "participation rate". This level of participation could also increase due to the existence of fake reviews generated or promoted by hotels, using different strategies (Mayzlin, Dover, & Chevalier, 2014; Mellinas et al., 2015; Simonson, 2016).

Hundreds of papers have been published during the last decade using data from TripAdvisor, Booking.com and similar websites, but none of them provide information about the percentage that those samples represent. The purpose of this research is to make reliable estimates about "participation rates" or "response rates" in these surveys, both on TripAdvisor and on Booking.com. Additionally, a series of factors that can determine variations in this rates are studied.

10.2 Literature Review

10.2.1 User Generated Content and eWOM

The Web 2.0 ethos focuses on the user, by providing easy-to-use websites and facilitating editing, publication and information exchange. Smartphones connected to Internet and applications (Apps) adapted to this devices have increased the number of users and content shared in this way. Therefore, Web 2.0 refers to the ideological and technological foundations that allow the creation and exchange of User Generated Content (UGC), which may take the form of text, photos and/or videos… (Kaplan & Haenlein, 2010). New concepts, like "Tourism 2.0" and "Travel 2.0" have been introduced to describe how the Web 2.0 have influenced the way travelers search, evaluate, purchase and consume touristic services (Christou, Sigala, & Gretzel, 2012).

A fundamental principle of consumer behavior refers to the fact that users have the ability to significantly influence on each other (Dichter, 1966), something that has been called "word of mouth" (WOM). Recommendations between users in tourism sector is a widely discussed topic, even before the existence of Internet (Butler, 1980; Cohen, 1972). Electronic Word of Mouth (eWOM) is a non-formal online communication about products, services or their sellers, the digital equivalent of WOM (Litvin, Goldsmith, & Pan, 2008). eWOM is more influential than traditional WOM due to its speed, convenience, ability to reach many and the lack of human pressure which influences face to face communication (Sun, Youn, Wu, & Kuntaraporn, 2006).

Travel online reviews are perceived as similar to the recommendations provided by friends and relatives, and as a more trusted source of information than the official one provided by companies (Browning, So, & Sparks, 2013; Ricci & Wietsma, 2006; Wang, Yu, & Fesenmaier, 2002; Yoo, Lee, Gretzel, & Fesenmaier, 2009). Such is the significance of UGC that has forced hoteliers to design organizational strategies of continual vigilance and monitor UGC (Baka, 2016). Hotel reviews can identify errors in aspects that are considered important by customers and that cause most of their complaints (Levy, Duan, & Boo, 2013; Cunningham, Smyth, Wu, & Greene, 2010).

Academic researchers have been focusing on online distribution as alternative to increase reservations, revenue and profit (Pal & Mishra, 2017; Talluri & Van Ryzin, 2006). Hotel reviews are essential in the decision-making process when booking online: 77% of travelers usually or always consult reviews before choosing a hotel,

53% will not commit to booking until they read reviews and 80% read at least 6–12 reviews before booking a hotel (TripAdvisor, 2014). Several studies have revealed the impact of reviews when making decisions about hotels (Dellarocas, 2003; Gretzel & Yoo, 2008; Schuckert, Liu, & Law, 2015; Vermeulen & Seegers, 2009).

10.2.2 Motivations to Write and Read Reviews

Incentive hierarchies have been created in an attempt to motivate users to contribute writing reviews in websites or Apps. For instance, TripAdvisor incentivizes users by awarding them increasingly higher status on the platform after fulfilling a certain threshold, e.g. if they generate certain number of reviews (Liu, Schuckert, & Law, 2016). However, sharing content online is usually an altruistic behaviour, and entails no economic compensation. This phenomenon can be considered equivalent to that one that takes place offline, where consumers also share information about products and services with the only desire to help them making better decisions (Resnick & Zeckhauser, 2002).

Motivations behind writing and sharing online reviews have discussed in the academic literature (Hennig-Thurau, Gwinner, Walsh, & Gremler, 2004; Schuckert et al., 2015). The motivation for posting negative reviews ranges from taking revenge to warning others (Wetzer, Zeelenberg, & Pieters, 2007). However, some authors argue that contributors are mostly driven by intrinsic and positive motives such as enjoyment, concerns for other consumers or wanting to help rather than revenge (Yoo & Gretzel, 2008).

Complaining online to the company may reduce both economic and psychological complaint cost for customers (Hong & Lee, 2008). Products and services reviews on the Internet show the best and the worst of people (Whitty & Joinson, 2008). Anonymity favors users to give more honest opinions, but also encourages some users to lie more than they would in real life and show complaints after an unsatisfactory hotel experience (Chiappa & Dall'Aglio, 2012).

Consumers seek the opinions of others online for a variety of reasons, ranging from basic utilitarian to more hedonic motives. Furthermore, it is evident that some of the factors seem more deliberate and planned, while other motivations are more spontaneous in nature. Previous research identified 8 main factors that motivate consumers for seeking opinions online: *Perceived risk, influence of others, price consciousness, ease to use, accidentally, it's cool, saw on TV and to get information* (Goldsmith & Horowitz, 2006). Consumers can be motivated by one or more of these factors, even by others additional factors not registered in this list. Nonetheless, the main point is that they seek for opinions, they trust them and their behavior is influenced by the content.

10.2.3   The Importance of the Number of Reviews

According to the existing literature, it confirms that there is a positive relationship between the number of reviews (also called volume) and the purchase intention or the increase on sales in different products or services (Dellarocas, Zhang, & Awad, 2007; Duan, Gu, & Whinston, 2008; Godes & Mayzlin, 2004; Liu, 2006; Park, Lee, & Han, 2007; Sparks & Browning, 2011; Vermeulen & Seegers, 2009). It may be seen as a sign of popularity (Zhang, Zhang, Wang, Law, & Li, 2013; Zhu & Zhang, 2010). In the hospitality industry, a large number of reviews allows the hotel to have more visibility could reflect better the reality of hotel quality, and can lead the idea that more reviews, more guests, so more popular (Xie, Zhang, & Zhang, 2014).

When travelers search for touristic services in the Internet, search engines usually provide results with a list, based in some sort of ranking. Information placed in the top of the list is considered very relevant, but the relevance of the information decreases exponentially when presented in lower positions (Spoerri, 2008). Online ranking lists are very important and useful in the hospitality sector (Filieri & McLeay, 2014) and more credible when published by well-known online travel communities like TripAdvisor (Casalo, Flavian, Guinaliu, & Ekinci, 2015). TripAdvisor says that its popularity Index algorithm is based on three key ingredients: the quality (average rating), quantity (number of reviews) and recency of reviews (TripAdvisor, 2013). In 2016 TripAdvisor enhanced its popularity ranking algorithm focusing in the quantity and consistency of reviews (TripAdvisor, 2016), which means that the review volume is now even more important for rankings.

TripAdvisor also provides a review collection tool called "review express" to send professional-looking emails that encourage guests to write reviews (TripAdvisor, 2014). This kind of strategies to collect more reviews seems to work, as reported by Shangri-La Hotels (PATA, 2014). They obtained relevant results in terms of quantity and recency of reviews: *"Prior to the review collection partnership with TripAdvisor, Shangri-La properties were averaging six reviews each month. Since the partnership began in July 2013, that average has increased 250% to 21 reviews per property per month. Altogether, the review collection partnership has driven an average of 534 out of 1930 reviews per month"*. Moreover, the use of other tools to collect reviews gets satisfactory results with an average of 409% increase on the TripAdvisor review volume (Revinate, 2014). Nonetheless, hotels can only send emails to those customers who have provided it, which is only a percentage of total guests.

Despite a period of tension and the lawsuits filed by hotels against review websites regarding the publication of fake and misleading reviews in 2011 (Hunter, 2012), the relationship between these parties has improved since 2012 (McEvilly, 2015). Wyndham and Accor encourage guests to write reviews on TripAdvisor after their stay; the total number of reviews, average ratings, and recent review content on this website is then displayed on each property page.

Previous studies demonstrated that *"as the number of reviews of a hotel increases, the ratings in these reviews are more positive"* (Melián, Bulchand-Gidumal, & González López-Valcárcel, 2013). But results are not so convincing when research is about direct effect of volume of online reviews on RevPAR growth and sales. A recent study demonstrated that the volume of reviews has no effect on RevPAR growth for branded chain hotels and a positive effect on RevPAR growth for not-branded chain hotels (Raguseo & Vitari, 2017).

10.3 Methodology

We used a selection of 200 hotels (3 and 4 stars), located in five major urban destinations in Spain (Madrid, Barcelona, Valencia, Sevilla, Granada). We choose the 40 hotels closest to the city centre in each city. This way we avoided possible biases that could occur with coastal hotels, because of the temporary closure during the low season in most of them.

We identify the number of rooms in each hotel, number of reviews during 2016 (TripAdvisor and Booking.com), total number of reviews, number of reviews written in English and hotel ratings. We also check if the hotel usually responds to customer reviews in TripAdvisor, by checking the last 30 reviews. The use of "Review Express" is also identified for each hotel, also checking the last 30 reviews.

> Reviews collected using "Review Express" show messages like: *"Review collected in partnership with Ibis Hotels"* and additional information: *"This business uses tools provided by TripAdvisor (or one of its official Review Collection Partners) to encourage and collect guest reviews, including this one"*.

TripAdvisor: Using data from the Spanish statistics national institute (INE, 2017), we identify occupancy rates and the average stay in each city, for 3 and 4 stars hotels. This information allows us to estimate the number of guests per hotel room in a year (118–158) and therefore the total number of customers per year in each hotel (category/city). We consider this figure as the "universe" for each hotel and the number of reviews as the "sample", so we can estimate participation rates using the 200 hotels data set.

Booking.com: The share of online travel agencies (OTAs) in hotel room Booking.coms is 22.3% (62% comes from Booking.com) in Europe and 27.6% in Spain (54.9% comes from Booking.com) (Schegg, 2016). It means that about 15% of hotel room reservations are made through Booking.com in Spain, but we do not have information about this percentage for each hotel, neither for urban hotels. Therefore, we cannot estimate the real "universe", since it would be the number of users who reserved that hotel with Booking.com, something that varies for each hotel. Accordingly to this limitation, we calculate the ratios for Booking.com using the total customers as "universe", but it only would be real in the case of a hotel that sells everything through Booking.com. If we knew the real percentage of sales using Booking.com, we should multiply that ratios by a corrective number, which would be 6.66 for 15%, 4 for 25% or 2 for 50%.

10.4   Results

Results show average participation percentages of about 2% (mean: 2.33; median: 1.95) on TripAdvisor, with more than 60% of hotels with percentages between 1% and 3% (Table 10.1). Only 10% of hotels exceed 4% rate and a single hotel exceeds 10% (El Rey Moro hotel boutique in Sevilla: 16 rooms and 13.88 participation rate).

We observe how the percentage of reviews registered in English has an important influence on participation rates (Table 10.2). The data range from 1.48% of hotels with less than 25% of reviews in English, to 3.77% of those with more than 60%.

This data could be explained by TripAdvisor popularity in English speaking countries (Paris, 2013). Contributions are not only related with population, but with popularity of this website.

Ratios by cities do not show significant differences, with percentages ranging from 1.88% in Valencia to 2.95% in Barcelona, probably related to the higher levels of English-speaking users in this cities (Table 10.3).

We observe that there are no significant differences by hotel category (3 or 4 stars). Nevertheless, we noticed that hotels that are active in their relationship with

Table 10.1 Participation rate and average score in TripAdvisor

Participation rate (%)	Number of hotels	Average score
0–1	28 (14%)	3.59
1–2	75 (37.5%)	3.89
2–3	48 (24%)	4.07
3–4	29 (14.5%)	4.26
4–14	20 (10%)	4.41

Table 10.2 Participation rate in TripAdvisor (reviews in English)

% Reviews in English	Number of hotels	Participation rate (%)
0–25	49	1.48
25–40	54	2.08
40–60	67	2.53
60–100	30	3.77

Table 10.3 Percentage of reviews in English

City	% Reviews in English
Barcelona	60
Madrid	40
Sevilla	40
Granada	32
Valencia	27

Source Own elaboration

TripAdvisor tend to accumulate more reviews. Besides, we observed that not active hotels show average participation rates of 1.88%, while those who respond to reviews and use "Review Express" reach 2.89% (Table 10.4).

We analyzed the relationship between participation rate for each hotel and the average rating obtained in TripAdvisor, observing a clear relationship between both values. When dividing the sample into five groups, we observe how the scores range from 3.59 to 4.41 (Table 10.1). A graphical representation is designed using results for each hotel, reflecting "participation rate" on the x-axis and "hotel score" on the y-axis (Fig. 10.1). As shown in Table 10.1 and Fig. 10.1, there is a much more pronounced relationship than between the number of reviews and scores (Melián et al., 2013). Its scores range from 3.51 to 3.98 in the six groups in which the sample was divided, based on the total number of reviews of each hotel. When they analyze the evolution of average ratings of reviews as number of reviews, the sample is divided into five groups and the scores range from 3.73 to 3.81.

Table 10.4 Participation rate and active hotels

	Number of hotels	Participation rate (%)
Not active hotels	57	1.88
Answer reviews	72	2.28
Use "Review Express"	18	2.36
Answer reviews and use "Review Express"	53	2.89

Source Own elaboration

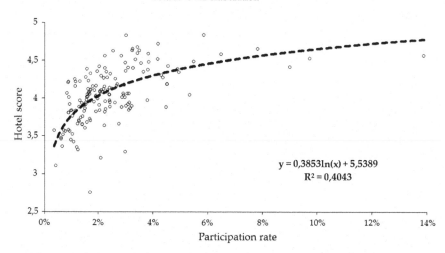

Fig. 10.1 Logarithmic regression for participation rate and hotel scores in TripAdvisor. *Source* Own elaboration

Table 10.5 Participation rate in Booking.com

Participation rate (%)	Number of hotels
0–5	39
5–10	69
10–15	57
15–20	17
20–30	15

Source Own elaboration

In the case of Booking.com the average response rate is close to 10%, without major variations by city or hotel category in terms of average value. However, we observe important differences between hotels, that range from 1 to 30% (Table 10.5). If we assume that only 15% of hotel room reservations are made through Booking.com in Spanish hotels (Schegg, 2016), real response rates in Booking.com would be around 66%. Probably the percentage of sales through Booking.com for urban hotels in big Spanish cities is higher than the Spanish hotels average. But, even assuming that it could be doubled (30%), we would be facing 33% response rates for Booking.com surveys.

10.5 Conclusion and Implications

Although TripAdvisor claims a huge database of 500 million reviews (most of them about hotels) it only represents a small percentage of total hotel stays. Data show that studies conducted using TripAdvisor hotel reviews have been using samples, which represents around 2% of customers who visit hotels. This percentage can vary for each hotel or geographical area, depending on TripAdvisor popularity and actions taken by the hotels in order to help in increasing the number of reviews.

This issue is relevant in determining the reliability of results and conclusions by using this valuable source of information, but none of previous researches pay attention at this figure. This lack of information should be assumed by academics and recognized as a limitation in every research using hotel reviews databases. Researchers should provide information on the sample design, similar to how it is done when conducting conventional surveys.

Hotels should encourage their customers to write reviews on TripAdvisor, since the website itself indicates that it improves their rankings. Increasing the number of reviews will also provide more complete and reliable information on the actual hotel perception by customers. Moreover, it has been shown that increasing the number of reviews is associated with a higher average score. However, take the total number of hotel reviews as the only indicator as proposed by Melián et al. (2013) is not the best way to measure this phenomenon. As shown in our study, it is more appropriate to take into account the number of rooms and determine the percentage of clients who write reviews. We cannot equally compare a 50-rooms hotel that generates 50 reviews in a year to one of 500 rooms that also generates 50 reviews; the first has a much higher participation rate. That is why the relationship between participation rate for each hotel and the average rating obtained in TripAdvisor is much stronger than that between the number of reviews and the average rating obtained in TripAdvisor.

Hoteliers should set their targets on participation ratios based on the number of customers they receive. In this regard, it is important to be realistic and set rational objectives, achievable by the staff in charge of this task. Once observed the data obtained in the present study, it seems very difficult to reach figures close to 5% and almost impossible to reach 10%. Despite the efforts that some hotels seem to make, even compiling emails from customers, to invite them to participate on TripAdvisor, results indicate that it is unusual to exceed 4% of participation rate, while the percentages in Booking.com usually exceed that figure. The high rates detected in Booking.com could be due to the fact that these travelers are active users of the Internet or the fact that they have provided a valid email in which they receive an invitation to write a review. Conversely, a percentage of total hotel visitors are not even active users of Internet or they do not receive any email inviting them to review the hotel in TripAdvisor. Furthermore, even if they are invited to participate in TripAdvisor, the user must register in this website, something that is not necessary in Booking.com, since the user has done it previously.

These data shown for Booking.com indicate that participation figures on TripAdvisor could increase substantially if clients were actively invited to participate. It requires an effort by hotels, which necessarily implies the collection of emails, among other possible strategies. However, it seems very complicated to reach the participation levels that Booking.com obtains for the reasons explained above.

Global data in Spain indicate that about 15% of sales are made through Booking.com (Schegg, 2016), while we observe in our sample an amount of reviews equivalent to 10% of estimated stays, suggesting a 66% response rate for Booking.com surveys, which seems too high. We observe that there is a group of 15 hotels (7.5% of the sample) that have 20–30% participation rates in relation to the total hotel customers. Even considering that these hotels could funnel almost all their sales through this intermediary, the data indicate that we could be facing response rates above 20% for Booking.com surveys.

Limitations and Suggestions for Future Research

Conclusions of this study are limited to urban hotels in 5 major Spanish urban destinations, therefore it would be advisable to use different samples around the world to check if the results are similar or significant variations are observed. It could show differences in participation rates for TripAdvisor by countries or hotel profiles, as suggest our results regarding reviews in English. We could also test our hypothesis on the greater market share of Booking.com in the urban hotels of large Spanish cities compared to the rest of the hotel profiles.

We assume that all hotels in each city have the same occupancy levels and average stay. We also do not know if any of them has been closed during 2016 for a while. This means that the data obtained is not totally accurate and some of the extreme data found could be due to some of these figures showing anomalous values.

Future studies should attempt to collect individualized hotel information on the exact number of guests received and number of reservations through Booking.com over a period. These data would allow to determine more accurate participation ratios than the estimated in this initial approach. However, it is very difficult to obtain this information from hotels, which are usually reluctant to share this information.

References

Baka, V. (2016). The becoming of user-generated reviews: Looking at the past to understand the future of managing reputation in the travel sector. *Tourism Management, 53,* 148–162.

Browning, V., So, K. K. F., & Sparks, B. (2013). The influence of online reviews on consumers' attributions of service quality and control for service standards in hotels. *Journal of Travel & Tourism Marketing, 30*(1–2), 23–40.

Buhalis, D., & Law, R. (2008). Progress in information technology and tourism management: 20 years on and 10 years after the Internet—The state of eTourism research. *Tourism Management, 29*(4), 609–623.

Butler, R. W. (1980). The concept of a tourist area cycle of evolution: Implications for management of resources. *The Canadian Geographer/Le Géographe canadien, 24*(1), 5–12.

Cantallops, A. S., & Salvi, F. (2014). New consumer behavior: A review of research on eWOM and hotels. *International Journal of Hospitality Management, 36,* 41–51.

Casalo, L. V., Flavian, C., Guinaliu, M., & Ekinci, Y. (2015). Do online hotel rating schemes influence booking behaviors? *International Journal of Hospitality Management, 49,* 28–36.

Chiappa, G. D., & Dall'Aglio, S. (2012). Factors influencing Travellers' e-Ratings and e-Complaints about hotel services: Insights from an Italian tourism destination. In *Information and Communication Technologies in Tourism 2012* (pp. 448–459). Springer: Vienna. https://doi.org/10.1007/978-3-7091-1142-0_39.

Christou, E., Sigala, M., & Gretzel, U. (2012). *Social media in travel, tourism and hospitality: Theory, practice and cases* (Edición: 1.). Farnham, Surrey, Burlington, VT: Routledge.

Cohen, E. (1972). Toward a sociology of international tourism. *Social Research,* 164–182.

Cunningham, P., Smyth, B., Wu, G., & Greene, D. (2010). Does tripadvisor makes hotels better. *School of Computer Science & Informatics, University College Dublin, Technical Report UCD-CSI-2010-06*, pp. 1–11.

Dellarocas, C. (2003). The digitization of word of mouth: Promise and challenges of online feedback mechanisms. *Management Science, 49*(10), 1407–1424.

Dellarocas, C., Zhang, X. M., & Awad, N. F. (2007). Exploring the value of online product reviews in forecasting sales: The case of motion pictures. *Journal of Interactive Marketing, 21*(4), 23–45.

Dichter, E. (1966). How word-of-mouth advertising works. *Harvard Business Review, 44*(6), 147–160.

Duan, W., Gu, B., & Whinston, A. B. (2008). The dynamics of online word-of-mouth and product sales—An empirical investigation of the movie industry. *Journal of Retailing, 84*(2), 233–242.

Filieri, R., & McLeay, F. (2014). E-WOM and accommodation: An analysis of the factors that influence travelers' adoption of information from online reviews. *Journal of Travel Research, 53*(1), 44–57.

Godes, D., & Mayzlin, D. (2004). Using online conversations to study word-of-mouth communication. *Marketing Science, 23*(4), 545–560. https://doi.org/10.1287/mksc.1040.0071.

Goldsmith, R. E., & Horowitz, D. (2006). Measuring motivations for online opinion seeking. *Journal of Interactive Advertising, 6*(2), 2–14. https://doi.org/10.1080/15252019.2006.10722114.

Govers, R., & Go, F. M. (2004). Projected destination image online: Website content analysis of pictures and text. *Information Technology & Tourism, 7*(2), 73–89. https://doi.org/10.3727/1098305054517327.

Gretzel, U., & Yoo, K. H. (2008). Use and impact of online travel reviews. *Information and Communication Technologies in Tourism, 2008,* 35–46.

Hennig-Thurau, T., Gwinner, K. P., Walsh, G., & Gremler, D. D. (2004). Electronic word-of-mouth via consumer-opinion platforms: What motivates consumers to articulate themselves on the internet? *Journal of Interactive Marketing, 18*(1), 38–52.

Hine, C. (2000). *Virtual ethnography.* Sage.

Hong, J.-Y., & Lee, W.-N. (2008). Consumer complaint behavior in the online environment. In *Web Systems Design and Online Consumer Behaviour* (Gao, Y., pp. 1607–1619). New Jersey: Idea Group Inc (IGI).

Hunter, M. (2012). TripAdvisor scolded by UK ad regulator for 'trust' claims. In *CNN Travel.* https://edition.cnn.com/travel/article/tripadvisor-advertising-uk/index.html. Accessed 19 Feb 2018.

INE. (2017). *Hotel Occupancy Survey.* Instituto Nacional de Estadística of Spain. http://www.ine.es/dynt3/inebase/en/index.htm?padre=238&dh=1. Accessed 18 January 2018.

Kaplan, A. M., & Haenlein, M. (2010). Users of the world, unite! The challenges and opportunities of social media. *Business Horizons, 53*(1), 59–68. https://doi.org/10.1016/j.bushor.2009.09.003.

Kozinets, R. V. (2002). The field behind the screen: Using netnography for marketing research in online communities. *Journal of Marketing Research, 39*(1), 61–72.

Kwok, L., Xie, K. L., & Richards, T. (2017). Thematic framework of online review research: A systematic analysis of contemporary literature on seven major hospitality and tourism journals. *International Journal of Contemporary Hospitality Management, 29*(1), 307–354.

Levy, S. E., Duan, W., & Boo, S. (2013). An analysis of one-star online reviews and responses in the Washington, DC, lodging market. *Cornell Hospitality Quarterly, 54*(1), 49–63.

Litvin, S. W., Goldsmith, R. E., & Pan, B. (2008). Electronic word-of-mouth in hospitality and tourism management. *Tourism Management, 29*(3), 458–468.

Liu, Y. (2006). Word of mouth for movies: Its dynamics and impact on box office revenue. *Journal of Marketing, 70*(3), 74–89.

Liu, X., Schuckert, M., & Law, R. (2016). Online incentive hierarchies, review extremity, and review quality: Empirical evidence from the hotel sector. *Journal of Travel & Tourism Marketing, 33*(3), 279–292.

Mann, C., & Stewart, F. (2000). *Internet communication and qualitative research: A handbook for research online.* JSTOR. http://www.jstor.org/stable/pdf/42858229.pdf. Accessed 19 July 2017.

Mayzlin, D., Dover, Y., & Chevalier, J. (2014). Promotional reviews: An empirical investigation of online review manipulation. *The American Economic Review, 104*(8), 2421–2455.

McEvilly, B. (2015). How online review sites are affecting your hotel. In *Hospitality Net.* https://www.hospitalitynet.org/opinion/4070901.html. Accessed 19 Feb 2018.

Melián-González, S., Bulchand-Gidumal, J., & González López-Valcárcel, B. (2013). Online customer reviews of hotels: As participation increases, better evaluation is obtained. *Cornell Hospitality Quarterly, 54*(3), 274–283.

Mellinas, J. P., Martínez María-Dolores, S. M., & Bernal García, J. J. (2015a). El control de irregularidades y TripAdvisor. *TURyDES, 8*(18).

Mellinas, J. P., Mártinez María-Dolores, S.-M., & Bernal García, J. J. (2015b). Booking. com: The unexpected scoring system. *Tourism Management, 49,* 72–74.

Murphy, C. (2017). Report: 78% of all online hotel reviews come from the top four sites. In *Revinate.* https://learn.revinate.com/blog/report-78-of-all-online-hotel-reviews-come-from-the-top-four-sites. Accessed 19 Feb 2018.

O'reilly, T. (2005). *What is web 2.0.* https://books.google.es/books?hl=es&lr=&id=DDI_XTmXI3MC&oi=fnd&pg=PA225&dq=web+2.0&ots=3Gv3Sue7n9&sig=3yDVmupP51H4EiormcyrnrD2kBQ. Accessed 19 July 2017.

Pal, S. K., & Mishra, P. (2017). Portfolio of online distribution channels across mid-market hotels: An evaluative review. *Enlightening Tourism, 7*(1), 19–35.

Paris, N. (2013). London is TripAdvisor's most reviewed city. In *The Telegraph*. http://www.telegraph.co.uk/travel/destinations/europe/united-kingdom/england/london/articles/London-is-TripAdvisors-most-reviewed-city/. Accessed 19 Feb 2018.

Park, D.-H., Lee, J., & Han, I. (2007). The effect of on-line consumer reviews on consumer purchasing intention: The moderating role of involvement. *International Journal of Electronic Commerce, 11*(4), 125–148.

PATA. (2014). *Shangri-La Hotels and resorts study shows review collection partnership with TripAdvisor leads to more reviews and higher ratings*. Pacific Asia Travel Association. https://www.pata.org/shangri-la-hotels-and-resorts-study-shows-review-collection-partnership-with-tripadvisor-leads-to-more-reviews-and-higher-ratings/. Accessed 18 January 2018.

Radojevic, T., Stanisic, N., & Stanic, N. (2015). Solo travellers assign higher ratings than families: Examining customer satisfaction by demographic group. *Tourism Management Perspectives, 16*, 247–258. https://doi.org/10.1016/j.tmp.2015.08.004.

Raguseo, E., & Vitari, C. (2017). The effect of brand on the impact of e-WOM on hotels' financial performance. *International Journal of Electronic Commerce, 21*(2), 249–269.

Resnick, P., & Zeckhauser, R. (2002). Trust among strangers in Internet transactions: Empirical analysis of eBay's reputation system. In *The Economics of the Internet and E-commerce* (pp. 127–157). Emerald Group Publishing Limited.

Revinate. (2014). Revinate announces results of TripAdvisor review collection partnership. In *Revinate*. https://www.revinate.com/es/blog/2014/10/revinate-announces-results-tripadvisor-review-collection-partnership/. Accessed 19 Feb 2018.

Ricci, F., & Wietsma, R. T. (2006). Product reviews in travel decision making. *Information and Communication Technologies in Tourism, 2006*, 296–307.

Schegg, R. (2016). European hotel distribution study. Results for the reference year 2015. In *OEHV.AT*. https://www.oehv.at/Lobbying/Tourismusmarkt-Osterreich/Hotrec-Umfrage-Hoteldistribution/final_public_schegg_2016_european_hotel_distributi.aspx. Accessed 19 July 2017.

Schuckert, M., Liu, X., & Law, R. (2015). Hospitality and tourism online reviews: Recent trends and future directions. *Journal of Travel & Tourism Marketing, 32*(5), 608–621.

Simonson, I. (2016). Imperfect progress: An objective quality assessment of the role of user reviews in consumer decision making, a commentary on de Langhe, Fernbach, and Lichtenstein. *Journal of Consumer Research, 42*(6), 840–845. https://doi.org/10.1093/jcr/ucv091.

Sparks, B. A., & Browning, V. (2011). The impact of online reviews on hotel booking intentions and perception of trust. *Tourism Management, 32*(6), 1310–1323.

Spoerri, A. (2008). Authority and ranking effects in data fusion. *Journal of the American Society for Information Science and Technology, 59*(3), 450–460. https://doi.org/10.1002/asi.20760.

Stamboulis, Y., & Skayannis, P. (2003). Innovation strategies and technology for experience-based tourism. *Tourism Management, 24*(1), 35–43.

Stanisic, N. (2016). *Recent trends in quantitative research in the field of tourism and hospitality* (SSRN Scholarly Paper No. ID 2875849). Rochester, NY: Social Science Research Network.

Sun, T., Youn, S., Wu, G., & Kuntaraporn, M. (2006). Online word-of-mouth (or mouse): An exploration of its antecedents and consequences. *Journal of Computer-Mediated Communication, 11*(4), 1104–1127.

Talluri, K. T., & Van Ryzin, G. J. (2006). *The theory and practice of revenue management* (Vol. 68). Springer.

TripAdvisor (2013). TripAdvisor popularity ranking: Key factors and how to improve. In *TripAdvisor Insights*. https://www.tripadvisor.com/TripAdvisorInsights/w722 Accessed 19 Feb 2018.

TripAdvisor (2014). 24 insights to shape your TripAdvisor strategy. In *TripAdvisor Insights*. https://www.tripadvisor.co.uk/TripAdvisorInsights/n2120/24-insights-shape-your-tripadvisor-strategy?language=en-GB. Accessed 19 Feb 2018.

TripAdvisor (2016). Everything you need to know about the TripAdvisor popularity ranking algorithm. In *TripAdvisor Insights*. https://www.tripadvisor.com/TripAdvisorInsights/w765. Accessed 19 Feb 2018.

Vermeulen, I. E., & Seegers, D. (2009). Tried and tested: The impact of online hotel reviews on consumer consideration. *Tourism Management, 30*(1), 123–127.

Wang, Y., Yu, Q., & Fesenmaier, D. R. (2002). Defining the virtual tourist community: Implications for tourism marketing. *Tourism Management, 23*(4), 407–417.

Wetzer, I. M., Zeelenberg, M., & Pieters, R. (2007). "Never eat in that restaurant, I did!": Exploring why people engage in negative word-of-mouth communication. *Psychology & Marketing, 24*(8), 661–680.

Whitty, M. T., & Joinson, A. (2008). *Truth, lies and trust on the Internet* (1 ed.). London, New York: Routledge.

Xie, K. L., Zhang, Z., & Zhang, Z. (2014). The business value of online consumer reviews and management response to hotel performance. *International Journal of Hospitality Management, 43*, 1–12.

Ye, Q., Law, R., & Gu, B. (2009a). The impact of online user reviews on hotel room sales. *International Journal of Hospitality Management, 28*(1), 180–182. https://doi.org/10.1016/j.ijhm.2008.06.011.

Ye, Q., Zhang, Z., & Law, R. (2009b). Sentiment classification of online reviews to travel destinations by supervised machine learning approaches. *Expert Systems with Applications, 36*(3), 6527–6535. https://doi.org/10.1016/j.eswa.2008.07.035.

Yoo, K. H., & Gretzel, U. (2008). The influence of involvement on use and impact of online travel reviews. In *Hospitality Information Technology Association (HITA) Conference* (pp. 15–16).

Yoo, K.-H., Lee, Y., Gretzel, U., & Fesenmaier, D. R. (2009). Trust in travel-related consumer generated media. *Information and Communication Technologies in Tourism, 2009*, 49–59.

Zhang, Z., Zhang, Z., Wang, F., Law, R., & Li, D. (2013). Factors influencing the effectiveness of online group buying in the restaurant industry. *International Journal of Hospitality Management, 35*, 237–245.

Zhu, F., & Zhang, X. (2010). Impact of online consumer reviews on sales: The moderating role of product and consumer characteristics. *Journal of Marketing, 74*(2), 133–148.

Chapter 11
Destination Choice, Repeating Behaviour and the Tourist-Destination Life Cycle Hypothesis

Andrés Artal-Tur, Antónia Correia, Jaime Serra and María Isabel Osorio-Caballero

11.1 Introduction

Repeat visitation is a desired target when managing a destination, which remarks the consolidation of a place as a tourist location and its capacity of attraction. Repeating visitors ensure a stable flow of income, spreading the word on the place advantages, what in turn helps to reduce marketing costs (Choo & Petrick, 2014; Schofield & Fallon, 2012). Some studies reflect that repeater tourists usually show less sensitivity to price and a focus on quality when buying tourism services (Assaker & Hallak, 2012). They can also raise total expenditure and stay duration, given that this type of tourists explore more extensively the destination (Jarvis, Stoeckl, & Liu, 2016; Alegre, Mateo, & Pou, 2011). Repeating behaviour also allow visitors to become familiar with the destination, resulting in higher levels of satisfaction with the vacational experience (Lau & McKercher, 2004).

A. Artal-Tur (✉)
Technical University of Cartagena, C\Real 3, 30201 Cartagena, Spain
e-mail: Andres.artal@upct.es

A. Correia
CEFAGE, Universidade do Algarve, Universidade Europeia,
Rua Antonio Henrique Balte, lote 78, 8005-328 Faro, Portugal
e-mail: ahcorreia@gmail.com

J. Serra
Universidade de Évora, CIDEHUS - Centro Interdisciplinar de História,
Culturas e Sociedades, Palácio do Vimioso, Largo do Marquês de Marialva, n.º 8,
Apartado 94, 7000-809 Évora, Portugal
e-mail: jserra@uevora.pt

M. I. Osorio-Caballero
Universidad Nacional Autónoma de México, Circuito interior s/n,
Ciudad Universitaria, 04510 Ciudad de México, Mexico
e-mail: isabelosorio@economia.unam.mx

© Springer Nature Switzerland AG 2019
A. Artal-Tur et al. (eds.), *Trends in Tourist Behavior*,
Tourism, Hospitality & Event Management,
https://doi.org/10.1007/978-3-030-11160-1_11

According to literature, several reasons underlie repeating behaviour of tourists, including the formation of habits, development of ties with local population, or risk reduction in a comfortable social environment (Fuchs & Reichel, 2011; Crompton, 1992). Periodical visits could also be rooted on a good accessibility of the place, its capacity to offer particular activities to the visitor, like sports or annual events, or because of its special beauty and other advantages based on existing natural resources (Hailu, Boxall, & McFarlane, 2005; Williams & Vaske, 2003). More generally, a range of destination characteristics usually explain the repeating behaviour of visitors, including the tourist experience, destination image and scenery, accessibility, and the capacity of fulfil expectations and needs of visitors (Tan, 2017; Sun, Chi, & Xu, 2013; Goldsmith & Tsiotsou, 2012). Leisure and time constrains could also explain why some visitors choose the same destination every year (Alexandris, Funk, & Pritchard, 2011; Albayrak, Caber, & Crawford, 2007).

After a number of visits, tourists develop a sense of attachment towards the destination (Alegre & Garau, 2010). In fact, emotional attachment explains the positive influence of previous experience on the intention to return (Campo-Martinez, Garau-Vadell, & Martínez-Ruiz, 2010). Building on such attachment feelings, tourists develop important ties with particular destinations along their lives. Deeper experiences with the destination help to build profound relationships with the place of visit. Periodical returns to the same place could lead to a more careful behaviour of tourists regarding the environment, while people start to get involved with local culture and discover the authenticity of the place. In this way, emotional ties of visitors appear to be important for the sustainability of destinations from an economic, social and environmental dimension (Artal-Tur & Kozak, 2015; Hall, Gössling & Scott, 2015). In summary, both tourists and destinations benefit from a lasting relationship, making the visit a more enjoyable and profound experience (Alegre, Mateo, & Pou, 2011; Vaske & Kobrin, 2001; Vorknin & Riese, 2001). As a result, a deeper understanding of factors explaining repeating behaviour is pivotal for destination managers (Correia, Zins, & Silva, 2015).

With this aim we introduce the tourist-destination life cycle (TDLC) hypothesis, namely, that tourist behaviour, choices and vacational experiences evolve along a life cycle built between repeating tourists and destinations. Of course, in this framework life cycle of tourists and those of destinations become mixed. While destinations evolve towards maturity and rejuvenation stages, tourists accommodate their vacational experience through their life cycle. In this way, both features mix to offer a changing experience. As a result, there are many dimensions to be analysed in this framework. In this chapter we start by focusing on repeating tourists, the influence of factors driving their revisiting behaviour, and changes taking place along the TDLC. In this respect our modelling strategy combines components of the repeating choice behaviour theory, like attachment feelings, with other features of the tourists' life cycle theory, like time and income restrictions. Empirical testing includes the use of OLS and quantile regression models, which help us to ascertain how TDLC affects factors driving repetition behaviour of tourists. The rest of the paper follows the next structure: After this introduction, Sect. 11.2 includes the literature review on the topic and research hypotheses. Section 11.3 describes the methodology for the empirical modelling exercise. Finally, Sects. 11.4 and 11.5 present the results and conclusions of the research, respectively.

11.2 Literature Review and Research Hypotheses

The literature on the product life cycle, and its application to tourism, is quite developed (Doyle, 1976; Vernon, 1966; Wagner, 1999). The concept of the life cycle has been applied to destinations by relevant authors, showing that at every stage of development different profiles of tourists could be attracted (Butler, 1980; Getz, 1992). In this context, as circumstances in life change with time, tourists' behaviour could also vary along their life cycle. Oppermann (1995) associates this phenomenon to changes in the family structure. Pearce (1993) highlights changes in age of tourists and family career. More generally, recent studies have focused on the tourists' life-cycle (TLC) theory (Alén, Nicolau, Losada, & Domínguez, 2014; Cooper, Fletcher, Fyall, Gilbert, & Wanhill, 2007). This theory states how the age dimension of an individual could strongly influence the type of tourist experience chosen. Pivotal variables in this setting are those of time and income restrictions faced by tourists. For example, a relationship has been discerned between the life cycle stage of the subject, and trip duration (Grigolon, Borgers, Kemperman, & Timmermans, 2014; Lawson, 1991; Seaton & Palmer, 1997). Starting to consider the relationship built between tourists and destinations is the main objective of the present study. In particular, we are interested in better understanding how aspects of tourist life cycle and attachment feelings influence repeating behaviour, and how these driving factors modulate their influence along the TDLC hypothesis. In this sense, our study borrows some characteristics of the tourist life cycle theory, but in the context of the revisiting behaviour analysis, based on sentiments of personal attachment of visitors with destinations. To start exploring this framework, we formulate a number of hypotheses for empirical testing.

Hypothesis 1 "The influence of time and income restrictions on repeating choice changes along the TDLC". A number of variables could shape the behaviour of tourists through the TDLC. In order to identify those related to the TLC theory, we focus on time and income restrictions. Following the literature, our selected variables for the modelling exercise will be those of age of the visitor, company while in vacations (family, friends, alone or with couple), professional status, duration of the trip, travel frequency, and use of a package travel. Age, company and professional status would help to determine the stage of the life cycle characterising the visitor. Duration of the trip is a variable previously pointed out by literature on TLC framework, while travel frequency and package travels also would report some hints on the TDLC hypothesis.

Additionally, as explained in the introduction, attachment feelings emerge and consolidate along the TDLC (Williams & Vaske, 2003). Our second hypothesis investigates how aspects of attachment to destinations affect the repetition behaviour along the TDLC.

Hypothesis 2 "The influence of attachment variables on repeating choice changes along the TDLC". Several variables of interest emerge in this context. First, we will test for the role of specialisation of destinations. We are interested in understanding if some specific type of vacational products, for example sun-and-sand holidays, promote repetition patterns, inducing higher loyalty of visitors and attachment. In testing for such an issue, we include two main products, sun-and-sand and cultural vacational motives. As shown by literature, tourists use to develop important attachment and repeating behaviour with seaside destinations (Aguiló, Alegre, & Sard, 2005). By the contrary, urban and cultural destinations need to constantly renovate their offer in order to maintain repetition behaviour. As a result cultural-urban destinations show lower repetition behaviour (Artal-Tur, Briones-Peñalver, & Villena-Navarro, 2018; Artal-Tur, Villena-Navarro, & Alamá-Sabater, 2018).

Secondly, it is observed that different destinations shape the relationship between tourist and destinations in a different way (Assaker & Hallak, 2012). In this paper we will test for the single effect of particular destinations in the sample, including three main destinations in Spain like Valencia, Barcelona and Mallorca. As specialisation differs for those three destinations, we expect to find different effects in driving repeating choices through the TDLC. For example, Valencia is a typical beach destination for domestic tourism and family trips, Mallorca is an international seaside destination, while Barcelona has become the main urban destination in Spain with 8 million visits per year, mainly focused on culture (Artal-Tur et al., 2018). In this way, we can test how features of destinations shape the repeating behaviour through the years, according to the TDLC hypothesis. Other variables in this attachment set are those of trip purpose, type of accommodation, with special emphasis on family-and-relatives' houses and second-home stays, and attachment feelings developed by tourists according to their country of origin. Trip purpose allow us to test for the difference effects on repeating behaviour of VFR (visiting family and relatives) trips versus more general leisure trips (Seaton & Palmer, 1997). As expected, family visits should create a tie between tourists and destinations, but we are also interested in increase our understanding on ties developed by leisure travellers along the TDLC. Second-home choices are also important signs of attachment feelings to destinations (Aguiló et al., 2005; Baloglu, 2001). Tourists employing relatives and friends houses in a repeating pattern denote important ties to destinations as well. Moreover, destinations also show particular lasting relationships with some source countries of visitors. Ties could be explained because of proximity issues in terms of geographical distance, or cultural, historical and other type of ties with the destination. Both sets of variables, accommodation type and country of origin will help us to test for the specific attachment argument and how it evolves along the TDLC.

The role of satisfaction on revisiting behaviour could also change along the TDLC hypothesis. Trip satisfaction usually conforms the perception of tourists on destinations, with great influence on revisiting intention, especially in the case of mature destinations (Aguiló et al., 2005). In fact, high levels of satisfaction are expected to be present in the initial visits to a destination in order to ensure revisiting behaviour and further attachment feelings (Assaker & Hallak, 2012). Behavioural intentions could also become influenced by attributes of the destination, purpose of the visit, and activities while in vacations (Kozak, 2001). In this way, overall satisfaction help to explain the positive influence of previous experience on the intention to return (Campo-Martinez et al., 2010). Correia, Kozak, & Ferradeira (2013) showed the different approaches, views and theories on these issues, including the disconfirmation paradigm, showing a link between expectations and the level of performance held by a product (Oliver, 1980; Spreng, MacKenzie, & Olshavsky, 1996). Repeating behaviour reduces uncertainty and reinforces overall satisfaction once the tourist has established a lasting relationship with the destination (Jang & Feng, 2007). Visitor knows in advance what and whom is going to find at this well-known destination, despite continue seeking for new experiences and vacational activities not discovered in previous visits. New dimensions and opportunities of the destination emerge along the TDLC, adding to the positive perception of the visitor for that particular place, and creating a virtuous cycle regarding vacational experience (Pizam & Milman, 1993). This process clearly underlies the TDLC hypothesis. All these issues lead to the third hypothesis of the study.

Hypothesis 3 "The influence of overall trip satisfaction on destination choice changes along the TDLC".

Finally, we add a fourth hypothesis in order to control for individual profile of visitors on repeating destination behaviour, and how it evolves along the TDLC. We particularly focus on educational profile of visitors, this being an interesting feature of the visitor. On the one hand, we can argue that more educated visitors will tend to better perceive all features of the destination, enjoying more profoundly the experience along the TDLC. However, it is also possible that more educated visitors have a greater propensity to choose new destinations in order to discover new places, given higher intellectual needs in spending their leisure time. This is the case, for example, of cultural visitors, who exhibit lower repetition patterns (Artal-Tur et al., 2018). In any case, we are interested here in understanding how educational profile of the visitor affects his/her repeating vacational choice along the TDLC, what lead us to propose the following hypothesis.

Hypothesis 4 "The influence of educational profile of the tourist on destination choice changes along the TDLC". After stating the hypotheses of the present investigation, in the following section we describe the empirical methods to test for them.

11.3   Empirical Methods for Estimation and Data Issues

In this investigation, we are interested in better understanding how factors driving repeating choice behaviour of tourists evolve along the TDLC. In measuring the length of the tourist relationship with a destination we employ data on "the number of years a tourist declares to have been coming to the destination along his/her life". As we afford for the possibility that in some particular years the tourist did not visit the destination, the variable under study resemble to follow a typical count data process. In fact, we are interested in analysing only those tourists revisiting at least one year the destination, so, by definition of the experiment, data is truncated at value 1, and accordingly we employ Truncated Count Data (TCD) procedure in estimation (see, i.e. Wooldridge, 2002; Cameron & Trivedi, 2005, for details on this type of models and related estimation issues).

In a second stage of the estimation process, we employ OLS regressions in search for a more parsimonious approach as recommended by the literature (Thrane, 2012). Thirdly, we apply quantile regressions (QREG) to see how the TDLC hypothesis shapes the influence of factors driving repeating choices of tourists. The use of quantile regressions is recently rising in the tourism literature, proving to be helpful when we seek for different point estimates along the distribution of the dependent variable, as it is our case (see, i.e., Thrane, 2015).

The data sample we employ includes questionnaire responses by international tourists visiting Spain along the year 2013. Data is collected through interviews at the departing point when the tourist is leaving the country after the vacational period. The Institute of Tourism Studies (IET) of the Ministry of Tourism of Spain is in charge of collecting data, and details on the features of the gathering process and on the design of the survey can be consulted in the Appendix. After depuration, leaving aside daily-visitors, business tourists, and people arriving for the first time, we count on around 72,000 questionnaires for the investigation. A first look at data in Fig. 11.1 shows that tourists in the sample present a very steady relation with Spain, with a number of years coming that spread from 27 times on average for those with the longer relationship starting 38 years ago, to 3 times for the most recent tourists coming since 5 years ago. Regarding the tourist-destination relationship, data also shows that around the 55% of the sample made their first visit in years 1975–1988, 18% of the sample arrived in 1989–1998, 14% in 1999–2003, 8% in 2004–2008, and the remaining 5% in 2009–2013. In this regard an important share of the sample has yet developed an attachment feeling to the destination and the bulk of them count on a TDLC hypothesis to be tested.

Table 11.1 also shows that tourists come predominantly from the European Union (EU) countries, with middle and old age, mostly secondary and tertiary studies, travelling for leisure purposes, with high degree of satisfaction, travelling alone or in couple, to a hotel or family-and-friends house, enjoying the beach and cultural activities, and visiting some well-known destinations in the Mediterranean coast of Spain. Their last visit to Spain took 6.6 nights of mean stay, suggesting that despite the number of their visits, they still feel attached to this particular destination. In the next section we present the main findings of the analysis.

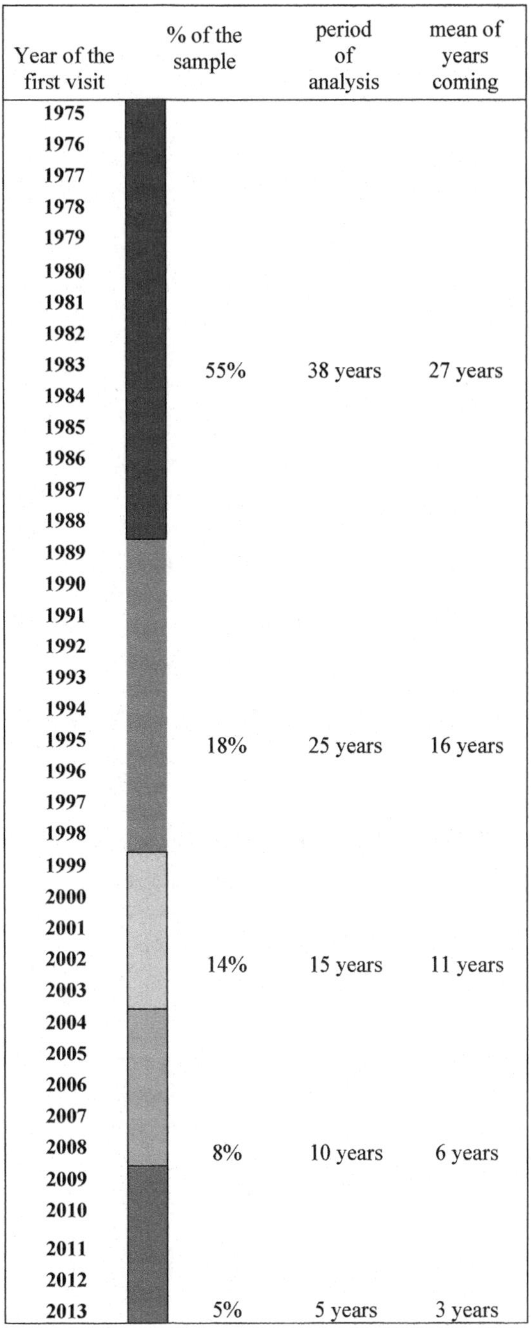

Fig. 11.1 Revisiting behaviour of international tourists coming to Spain in 2013. *Source* Own elaboration from Egatur (2013)

Year of the first visit	% of the sample	period of analysis	mean of years coming
1975			
1976			
1977			
1978			
1979			
1980			
1981			
1982			
1983	55%	38 years	27 years
1984			
1985			
1986			
1987			
1988			
1989			
1990			
1991			
1992			
1993			
1994			
1995	18%	25 years	16 years
1996			
1997			
1998			
1999			
2000			
2001			
2002	14%	15 years	11 years
2003			
2004			
2005			
2006			
2007			
2008	8%	10 years	6 years
2009			
2010			
2011			
2012			
2013	5%	5 years	3 years

Table 11.1 Descriptive statistics of sample data

Variable	% of the sample
Nationalities	
Germany	13.7
United Kingdom	20.4
Ireland	2.9
France	10.7
Sweden	3.5
Finland	1.4
USA	0.3
Rest of the world	47.4
Age	
<30 years old	3.4
31–50 years old	48.5
>50 years old	48.1
Education	
Elementary	3
Secondary	29.9
Tertiary	67.1
Trip purpose	
Leisure	79.7
VFR	20.3
Overall trip satisfaction	
Unsatisfied	13.6
Satisfied	60.6
Very Satisfied	25.8
Professional state	
Entrepreneur	16.7
Manager/director	61
Intermediate position	5
Blue-collar worker	17.3
Travel companion	
Couple	39.5
Family	18
Friends	8.2
Alone	39.4
Package travel	19.7

Table 11.1 (continued)

Variable	% of the sample
Type of accommodation	
Hotel	54.6
Second-home	10.3
Friends-house	26.7
Rent-house	8.4
Pull motives	
Beaches	44.7
Culture	42.8
Destinations	
Valencia	16.9
Mallorca	22.3
Barcelona	25.4
N observ.	72346

Source Own elaboration from Egatur (2013)

11.4 Results

The estimates of the empirical model are presented in Table 11.2. The table includes results for TCD, OLS and QREG models. Table 11.2 only includes coefficients of the covariates in the model and their corresponding level of significance for sake of simplicity. To make results comparable between the econometric output of these three modelling approaches, the TCD model shows the estimated IRR values (Incidence Rate Ratios) in percentage of change, while OLS and QRE results are reported according to the percentage of change for the estimated coefficients (Cameron & Trivedi, 2005).[1] First estimates regarding TCD model shows the role of the explanatory variables in influencing the repeating behaviour of tourists visiting different destinations in Spain. General results show that all hypotheses in the model cannot be rejected, with nearly all coefficients in the model being significant. OLS results appear to be very close to those of count data models, so we refer to those sets of estimation results indistinctly. The reference category in the model appears in parenthesis below each variable in Table 11.2. In general, the reference visitor is a young tourist, less than 30 years old, coming alone, low qualified worker, coming for leisure purpose, accommodated in a hotel, with low level of trip satisfaction and primary education. In this way, results of the model refer to changes in this reference profile.

Hypothesis H1 reflects the influence of variables related to tourist life cycle in such revisiting behaviour, as defined in Sect. 11.2. In particular, AGE of the visitor appears to be clearly correlated with the repeating behaviour shown by tourists. Older age increases the probability of higher number of visits, although both middle and older

---

[1]Full estimation results are available for interested readers under request to authors as usually.

Table 11.2 Factors determining revisiting behaviour of tourists visiting Spain along the tourist-destination life cycle

Hypotheses	Variables (category of reference)		TNB	OLS	QRE					F-test	
			% change (in IRR)	% change (in levels)	% change (in levels)						
					Q5	Q15	Q25	Q50	Q75		
H1	Age (up to 30 years old)	Between 31 and 50	0.121	0.124	0.072	0.136	0.163	0.170	0.190	F = 5.64	Prob > F = 0.00
		More than 5 0	0.271	0.299	0.186	0.393	0.389	0.383	0.386	F = 23.62	Prob > F = 0.000
	Travel companion (alone)	Family	0.053	0.057	0.038	0.093	0.086	0.090	0.081	F = 9.25	Prob > F = 0.000
		Couple	0.025	0.029	0.044	0.070	0.054	0.047	0.033	F = 9.75	Prob > F = 0.000
		Friends	−0.017	−0.010*	0.023	0.012*	−0.001*	−0.003*	−0.022	F = 4.42	Prob > F = 0.001
	Professional status (blue collar worker)	Entrepreneur	0.046	0.058	0.139	0.114	0.106	0.083	0.047	F = 9.03	Prob > F = 0
		Manager/director	−0.001*	0.001*	0.191	0.189	0.181	0.152	0.103	F = 8.29	Prob > F = 0
		Intermediate position	−0.057	−0.083	−0.157	−0.131	0.122	0.089	0.052	F = 11.82	Prob > F = 0
	Length of stay		0.002	0.003	0.004	0.004	0.004	0.004	0.003	F = 13.31	Prob > F = 0
	Travel frequency		−0.162	−0.202	−0.259	−0.259	−0.244	−0.222	−0.194	F = 251.38	Prob > F = 0
	Package travel		−0.050	−0.051	−0.036	−0.046	−0.049	−0.045	−0.051	F = 1.80	Prob > F = 0.125

(continued)

Table 11.2 (continued)

Hypotheses	Variables (category of reference)		TNB % change (in IRR)	OLS % change (in levels)	QRE % change (in levels)					F-test
					Q5	Q15	Q25	Q50	Q75	
H2	Tourism product	Beaches	0.063	0.073	0.045	0.109	0.090	0.102	0.098	F = 20.67 Prob > F = 0.000
		Culture	−0.066	−0.079	−0.052	−0.106	−0.091	−0.088	−0.084	F = 19.61 Prob > F = 0.000
	Destinations	Valencia	0.004*	0.004*	0.022	0.013	0.008	0.005	0.003	F = 10.09 Prob > F = 0.003
		Mallorca	0.016	0.019	0.002	0.013	0.003	0.001	0.003	F = 11.16 Prob > F = 0.025
		Barcelona	−0.062	−0.044	0.033	−0.025	−0.041	−0.074	−0.078	F = 20.26 Prob > F = 0.000
	Trip Purpose (leisure)	VFR	0.009	0.011	0.042	0.018	0.003	0.001	0.001	F = 11.39 Prob > F = 0.000
	Type of accommodation (hotel)	Second-home	0.041	0.066	0.336	0.096	0.043	0.024	0.001*	F = 84.82 Prob > F = 0.000
		Friends-house	0.069	0.072	0.060	0.125	0.112	0.105	0.096	F = 89.70 Prob > F = 0.000
		Rent-apartment	0.028	0.026	0.004*	0.020*	0.035	0.053	0.039	F = 86.90 Prob > F = 0.000
	Country of residence (Rest of the World)	United Kingdom	0.066	0.088	0.121	0.130	0.105	0.100	0.074	F = 29.56 Prob > F = 0.000
		Germany	0.048	0.062	0.107	0.120	0.082	0.085	0.054	F = 6.46 Prob > F = 0.000
		France	0.073	0.089	0.049	0.103	0.069	0.093	0.074	F = 8.58 Prob > F = 0.000

(continued)

Table 11.2 (continued)

Hypotheses	Variables (category of reference)	TNB	OLS	QRE					F-test	
		% change (in IRR)	% change (in levels)	% change (in levels)						
				Q5	Q15	Q25	Q50	Q75		
	Finland	−0.07	−0.069	−0.040	−0.080	−0.084	−0.089	−0.087	F = 1.84	Prob > F = 0.118
	USA	−0.199	−0.221	−0.159	−0.268	−0.361	−0.330	−0.318	F = 6.00	Prob > F = 0.000
H3	Satisfaction (unsatisfied) Satisfied	0.002*	0.001*	−0.014	−0.013*	−0.005*	0.002*	0.003*	F = 1.87	Prob > F = 0.113
	Very satisfied	0.025	0.021	−0.004*	0.011*	0.015	0.028	0.031	F = 11.40	Prob > F = 0.000
H4	Education (primary) Secondary	−0.040	−0.048	−0.052	−0.046	−0.058	−0.056	−0.052	F = 0.21	Prob > F = 0.935
	Tertiary	−0.074	−0.089	−0.083	−0.094	−0.102	−0.109	−0.099	F = 0.58	Prob > F = 0.673
	N	72346	N 72346	72346	72346	72346	72346	72346		
	Wald-test (Chi2)	29839.04	F-test 1480.01	0.2249	0.2498	0.2575	0.2521	0.2019		
	Prob > Chi2	0.0000	Prob > F 0.0000							
	Log likelihood	−172846.69	R-sq 0.3246							
	AIC	345755								
	BIC	346040								

The model includes a constant. (*) means not significant at p < 0.05

age show important coefficients regarding the rest of variables in the model, showing the relevance of these type of variables in our framework of analysis. In what regards TRAVEL COMPANION, those visitors coming with family or in couple show the highest revisiting pattern.

In fact, family visits seem to create the highest linkages with destinations, as shown for example by Aguiló et al. (2005), who proved that family tourists are the most steady market in the Balearic Islands. In contrast, those visitors coming with friends appear to create the lowest ties with a destination, what would be reflecting the different behaviour characterizing these two groups of tourists. Coefficients for those tourists coming alone stays below that of family and couple, but above those coming with friends. Variable of PROFESSIONAL STATUS reflects that visitors occupying positions of entrepreneurs usually increase their linkages with the destination, while intermediate workers reduce them regarding the reference category of less qualified workers.

A greater TRAVEL FREQUENCY, defined as four or more visits per year, seems to reduce the probability of revisiting all years the same destination, perhaps because of searching for other places. However, one or two visits per year appear to increase that linkages between tourists and destinations. This seems to be the behaviour of foreign visitors in Spain mainly coming once a year from closer European countries, and travelling to other places in other seasons. This behaviour could be responding to the type of specialization followed by sun and sand destinations in Spain, and the seasonality issues characterizing the summer time visit by foreign visitors. However, as results show, higher LENGTH OF STAY increases the ties between tourists and destinations, so larger stays reinforce the desire to revisit, showing that competitiveness of these destinations is still important. PACKAGE TRAVEL reduce the revisiting behaviour as expected, given the standardised visit that this type of vacations usually offers, not allowing for a deeper understanding of the qualities of the destination by package visitors. In general, variables reflecting tourist life cycle in H1 significantly influence the revisiting behaviour of tourists as we have seen. Most important appear to be those of age of the tourist, family and couple visits, for entrepreneurs, with longer stays per visit, not coming with packaged travel and making few visits per year to the same destination. In this way, it appears to be a traditional vacational experience lasting for many years before, where tourists seek for familiarity and well-known activities, and renovate the contact and personal linkages with the destination and other visitors.

Regarding hypothesis H2, we test for the role of variables reflecting personal attachment of tourists explaining their revisiting behaviour. TCD and OLS results show that tourism products such as BEACH VACATIONS increase the length of relationship with the destination, while cultural activities reduce them. Such a result confirms findings in previous literature, as seaside destinations usually show higher loyalty and repetition patterns, while CULTURAL VISITORS would seek for new destinations with new cultural offer. In this way, the renovation of cultural activities and events becomes a necessity for cultural destinations eager to maintain and enlarge the linkages with traditional visitors. The effects of particular DESTINATIONS reinforce the previous findings, with Mallorca, a seaside destination, showing positive effects on repetition, and Barcelona, mainly a cultural destination, showing negative ones. Results for Valencia appear not significant.

TRIP PURPOSE variable shows that VFR visitors increase the linkage tourists-destination, in comparison with leisure tourists, although with slight differences between these two groups of tourists, what shows the important revisiting behaviour of leisure tourists in general too. In terms of ACCOMMODATION types, having a second-home at destination or coming to a house provided by friends and relatives show the highest probability or effect on revisiting behaviour as one would expect. It is worth noting that coming to a house of friends and relatives enhances the ties with the destination even above the level shown by buying a second-home what is in fact a remarkable effect. Coming to a rent house also increases the number of years to be coming to the destination, all above the effects of visitors coming to a hotel that is acting as the category of reference in this point. Regarding the COUNTRY OF RESIDENCE, traditional EU visitors of Spain coming from the United Kingdom, Germany or France show positive and significant coefficients, what means a positive contribution to maintaining the linkage with the destination. Visitors coming from new sending countries like Finland show a negative coefficient, as well as more distant tourists coming from the USA, reducing the probability of revisiting behaviour given large distance and less ties with the destination.

Results regarding hypothesis H3 show that overall trip satisfaction level declared by the tourist clearly affects repetition behaviour, mainly increasing that in the case of very satisfied visitors. This result is in line with the literature, where trip overall satisfaction and fulfilment of expectations affects the evaluation of the destination made by visitors, influencing their perception on the capacity of a destination to provide quality products and services. This is important also for mature destinations, as seaside ones for example, as pointed out by previous research. Results reinforce in this way the link of high trip satisfaction as an underlying reason for revisiting behaviour of tourists.

Finally, H4 on the role of EDUCATIONAL LEVEL of tourist on his/her behaviour shows that this is another important matter in influencing the relationship with a destination. The higher the level of education, the lower revisiting expectancy seems to arise in our empirical results. Tertiary educated visitors indeed reduce the most these linkages with destination, confirming that this type of visitors seek to discover new destinations while travelling, in comparison with visitors with lower levels of education.

In general, we have seen that percentual changes shown by TCD and OLS models appear to be very close, in line with claims for simplicity of recent authors (Thrane, 2012). Moreover, and once reviewed the general results of these two models, we move now to results in the quantile regression analysis. These results really allow us to test for the full meaning of the working hypotheses in the study, showing how factors driving repetition behaviour of tourists evolve along the tourist-destination life cycle (TDLC). In testing for such hypothesis, we define five quantiles of our dependent variable, the length of relationship between a tourist and a particular destination, including the following quantiles: Q5 (tourist up to 5 years coming), Q15 (tourist up to 9 years coming), Q25 (tourist up to 15 years coming), Q50 (tourist up to 28 years coming), and Q75 (tourist up to 34 years coming). Then, we estimate our preferred specification for each of these quantiles, showing how coefficients in the model evolve along the TDLC. All results are included in Table 11.2 too.

Results show most of these effects to be significant and varying along the quantiles defined. We also run an F-test, for the null hypothesis (H0) of equality of coefficients across quantiles, for each explanatory factor. As seen in the table, in most cases H0 is rejected, with coefficients varying for explanatory variables when relationship with the destination increases along time, resulting in changing behaviour across the different sets of tourists in the sample, showing a support for our working hypotheses H1–H4. Main variables influencing revisiting behaviour in the first years of the TDLC appear to be those of professional status, travel frequency, age, tourism product, accommodation and origin of the tourist. However, when lasting ties are quite present between tourists and destinations some variables loose influence on destination choice behaviour, such as professional status, destination profile, purpose of the visit, accommodation type and country of origin of the tourist. On the contrary, other variables reinforce their role in pulling visitors to the same destination, including trip satisfaction perceptions, visiting friends' houses, older age, coming with the family, or going to the beach. In this way, aspects reinforcing the type of vacational experience searched by tourists, and strengthen the link with destinations, are clearly connected to the tourism product they seek, company they know at destination, and tourist experiences shared with family and friends since long time ago. The service quality and other resources provided by the place, including scenery and richness of natural landscapes are also important despite the well-known content of the stay. What is important here is that tourists appear to seek for a similar and familiar experience, so familiarity appears as a significant determinant. Cultural closeness also emerge as an important factor linking visitors and destinations in the first stages of the TDLC, with particular EU countries showing good connections with Spanish destinations. Buying a second home is also important in developing ties at the beginning of the relationship, then assimilating to other type of accommodations, such as hotels.

The effect of age is also quite appealing in this loyalty and revisiting framework. This being always a relevant variable with important explanatory power in the model, effects of middle and older aged groups in the last stages of the TDLC more than double those of the first years. Moreover, ties appear to rapidly develop for older visitors after only five years coming, showing a rapid capacity of the Spanish destinations to develop intense ties with the foreign visitor. This result would be confirming that highly revisiting tourists reinforce in fact the relationship with the place along time, with no exhaustion effects appearing even for mature seaside destinations. In the case of tourists between 31 and 50 years old, effects also increase when the relationship with the destination develops, although not so rapidly as for older tourists. Leisure purpose becomes similar in pulling effects when time develops such as visiting friends and relatives, another interesting result of the model. In general, tourist life cycle factors, attachment variables, trip satisfaction and level of education appear to be important factors in explaining the revisiting behaviour of tourists, leading to a non-rejection of H1–H4. In this sense, and as stated for the TDLC hypothesis in this study, we have also observed that some of these factors reinforce its pulling capacity with time, showing the preference of tourists for such dimensions along the TDLC relationship, while other loose explanatory power, becoming more neutral in leading the tourists choice. All these findings provide relevant policy recommendations for destinations managers.

11.5   Conclusion and Implications

The present chapter has focused on better understanding how ties between tourists and destinations evolve along time, and how this relationship could shape the behaviour of visitors and their repeating choice of destination. Main results have shown that certain variables lose capacity power in explaining revisiting behaviour of tourist along the TDLC, becoming of less relevance, while other reinforce its hierarchy in this framework. Along the TDLF, visitors seek for familiarity issues, repeating experiences with selected companions, as friends and relatives, with seaside destinations providing a perfect scenery for such an annual pleasant stay. Geographical and cultural closeness appear to be necessary conditions to develop such lasting ties. In this way, revisiting behaviour and all benefits associated with this vacational pattern appear to be related with characteristics of the destinations, such as scenery, tourism product, and accessibility conditions, but also with the required service quality level leading to high trip overall satisfaction that ensures future visits. In sum, in order to develop lasting ties with visitors, the destination has to ensure a recognising scenery for the revisiting visitors and capacity of recreating traditional activities that the visitor expects to experience on each visit. However, the destination would also have to enable a required level of service quality and innovate supplies, opening new opportunities and amusement to the repeating visitor in order to maintain the compromise with that particular place.

Technical details of the EGATUR Survey, IET, Spain:
Geographical scope
23 border crossings by road, 23 airports, 7 sea ports and 7 international railway lines.
Population scope
Non-Spanish-resident tourist and day-visitors by road, air, sea port or railway.
Reference period
Continuous annual statistical survey on a monthly basis.

Type of sampling
Randomized and stratified by reference country, access route and border crossing. The sample is divided into 19 strata: 5 road strata, 9 air strata, 3 port strata and 2 railway strata. Minimum monthly quotas are specified by country of residence.
Collection of information
Information is collected by personal interview using handheld computers allowing for data entry, validation, recording and telemetric transmission of information collected in the field, and ensure maximum quality of collected data and prompt reporting of information obtained.
Universe
Monthly entries of non-Spanish-residents crossing the Spanish border, itemized by: type of visitor (tourist and day-tripper); border crossing; country of residence; means of transport; reason for travel, and form of organization.
Egatur also provides tourist expenditure information on the basis of sociodemographic variables, activities engaged in, travel frequency, degree of satisfaction, use of the Internet in relation to travel, group composition (companions), and persons travelled with.

Acknowledgements Prof. Andres Artal-Tur acknowledges financial support by Groups of Excellence of the Region of Murcia, Fundación Séneca, Science and Technology Agency, project 19884/GERM/15, and FEMISE Association (Project ENPI/2014/354-494) Research Projects FEM 41-04 and FEM 41-13.
Prof. Jaime Serra thanks receipt of FEDER funds, under the new PT2020 partnership agreement and by national funds FCT/MEC—Foundation for Science and Technology under the UID/HIS/00057/2013—POCI-01-0145-FEDER-007702 project CIDEHUS.
Prof. Antonia Correia thanks financial support from Fundação para a Ciência e a Tecnologia (Grant UID/ECO/04007/2013) and FEDER/COMPETE (POCI-01-0145-FEDER-007659).

References

Aguiló, E., Alegre, J., & Sard, M. (2005). The persistence of the sun and sand tourism model. *Tourism Management, 26,* 219–231.
Albayrak, T., Caber, M., & Crawford, D. (2007). Leisure constrains and the pursuit of adventure activities in Turkey. *Anatolia, 18*(2), 243–254.
Alegre, J., & Garau, J. (2010). *Place attachment in sund and sand destinations.* Mimeo, Universitat de Ses Illes Balears (UIB).
Alegre, J., Mateo, S., & Pou, L. (2011). A latent class approach to tourists' length of stay. *Tourism Management, 32,* 555–563.
Alén, E., Nicolau, J. L., Losada, N., & Domínguez, T. (2014). Determinant factors of senior tourists' length. *Annals of Tourism Research, 49,* 19–32.
Alexandris, K., Funk, D. C., & Pritchard, M. P. (2011). The impact of constraints on motivation, activity attachment, and Skier intentions to continue. *Journal of Leisure Research, 43*(1), 56–79.

Artal-Tur, A., Briones-Peñalver, & Villena-Navarro (2018). Tourism, cultural activities and sustainability in the Spanish Mediterranean regions: A probit approach. *Tourism & Management Studies, 14*(1), 7–18.

Artal-Tur, A., Villena-Navarro & Alamá-Sabater, L. (2018). The relationship between cultural tourist behaviour and destination sustainability. *Anatolia: An international Journal of Tourism and Hospitality Research, 29*(2), 237–251.

Artal-Tur, A., & Kozak, M. (2015). *Destination competitiveness, the environment and sustainability: Challenges and cases.* Wallingford, Oxfordshire: CAB International Publisher.

Assaker, G., & Hallak, R. (2012). European travelers' return likelihood and satisfaction with Mediterranean sun-and-sand destinations: A chi-square automatic identification detector-based segmentation approach. *Journal of Vacation Marketing, 18*(2), 105–120.

Baloglu, S. (2001). An investigation of a loyalty typology and the multidimensional loyalty of international travelers. *Tourism Analysis, 6,* 41–52.

Butler, R. W. (1980). The concept of the tourist area life-cycle of evolution: Implications for management of resources. *Canadian Geographer, 24*(1), 5–12.

Cameron, A. C., & Trivedi, P. (2005). *Microeconometrics: Methods and applications.* Cambridge, Massachusetts: Cambridge University Press.

Campo-Martinez, S., Garau-Vadell, J. B., & Martinez-Ruiz, M. P. (2010). Factors influencing repeat visits to a destination: The influence of group composition. *Tourism Management, 31*(6), 862–870.

Choo, H., & Petrick, J. F. (2014). Social interactions and intentions to revisit for agritourism service encounters. *Tourism Management, 40,* 372–381.

Cooper, C., Fletcher, J., Fyall, A., Gilbert, D., & Wanhill, S. (2007). *Tourism. Principles and practice* (3rd ed.). United Kingdom: Prentice Hall.

Correia, A., Kozak, M., & Ferradeira, J. M. (2013). From tourist motivations to tourist satisfaction. *International Journal of Culture Tourism and Hospitality Research, 7*(4), 411–424.

Correia, A., Zins, A. H., & Silva, F. (2015). Why do tourists persist in visiting the same destination? *Tourism Economics, 21*(1), 205–221.

Crompton, J. (1992). Structure of vacation destination choice sets. *Annals of Tourism Research, 19*(3), 420–434.

Doyle, P. (1976). The realities of the product life cycle. *Quarterly Review of Marketing, 1,* 1–6.

Egatur, (2013). *Tourist expenditure survey for international tourism in Spain.* Institute of Tourism Studies (IET), Ministry of Tourism, Madrid: Spain.

Fuchs, G., & Reichel, A. (2011). An exploratory study into destination risk perceptions and risk reduction strategies of first time vs. repeat visitors to a highly volatile destination. *Tourism Management, 32,* 266–276.

Getz, D. (1992). Tourism planning and destination lifecycle. *Annals of Tourism Research, 19,* 752–770.

Grigolon, A. B., Borgers, A. W. J., Kemperman, A. D. A. M., & Timmermans, H. J. P. (2014). Vacation length choice: A dynamic mixed multinomial logit model. *Tourism Management, 41,* 158–167.

Goldsmith, R. E., & Tsiotsou, R. H. (2012). Introduction to experiential marketing. In R. H. Tsiotsou & R. E. Goldsmith (Eds.), *Strategic marketing in tourism services* (pp. 207–214). Bingle, UK: Emerald.

Hailu, G., Boxall, P. C., & McFarlane, B. L. (2005). The influence of place attachment on recreation demand. *Journal of Economic Psychology, 26,* 581–598.

Hall, C. M., Gössling, S., & Scott, D. (Eds.). (2015). *The Routledge Handbook of Tourism and Sustainability.* London: Routledge.

Jang, S., & Feng, R. (2007). Temporal destination revisit intention: The effects of novelty seeking and satisfaction. *Tourism Management, 28*(2), 580–590.

Jarvis, D., Stoeckl, N., & Liu, H.-B. (2016). The impact of economic, social and environmental factors on trip satisfaction and the likelihood of visitors returning. *Tourism Management, 52,* 1–18.

Kozak, M. (2001). Comparative assessment of tourist satisfaction with destinations across two nationalities. *Tourism Management, 22*(4), 391–401.

Lawson, R. (1991). Patterns of tourist expenditure and types of vacation across the family lifecycle. *Journal of Travel Research, 29*(4), 12–18.

Lau, A. L. S., & McKercher, B. (2004). Exploration versus acquisition: A comparison of first-time and repeat visitors. *Journal of Travel Research, 42,* 279–285.

Oliver, R. L. (1980). A cognitive model of the antecedents and consequences of satisfaction decisions. *Journal of Marketing Research, 17*(4), 460–469.

Oppermann, M. (1995). Family lifecycle and cohort effects: A study of travel patterns of German residents. *Journal of Travel and Tourism Marketing, 4*(1), 23–44.

Pearce, P. (1993). Fundamentals of tourist motivation. In D. Pearce & R. Butler (Eds.), *Tourism research: Critiques and challenges* (pp. 113–134). London: Routledge.

Pizam, A., & Milman, A. (1993). Predicting satisfaction among first time visitors to a destination by using the expectancy disconfirmation theory. *International Journal of Hospitality Management, 12*(2), 197–209.

Schofield, P., & Fallon, P. (2012). Assessing the viability of university alumni as a repeat visitor market. *Tourism Management, 33,* 1373–1384.

Seaton, A. V., & Palmer, C. (1997). Understanding VFR tourism behaviour: The first five years of the United Kingdom tourism survey. *Tourism Management, 18*(6), 345–355.

Spreng, R. A., MacKenzie, S. B., & Olshavsky, R. V. (1996). A reexamination of the determinants of consumer satisfaction. *Journal of Marketing, 60*(3), 15–32.

Sun, X., Chi, C. G. Q., & Xu, H. (2013). Developing destination loyalty: The case of Hainan Island. *Annals of Tourism Research, 43,* 547–577.

Tan, W.-K. (2017). Repeat visitation: A study from the perspective of leisure constraint, tourist experience, destination images, and experiential familiarity. *Journal of Destination Marketing & Management, 6,* 233–242.

Thrane, C. (2012). Analyzing tourists' length of stay at destinations with survival models: A constructive critique based on a case study. *Tourism Management, 33,* 126–132.

Thrane, C. (2015). Students' summer tourism: An econometric analysis of trip costs and trip expenditures. *Tourism Management Perspectives, 15,* 65–71.

Vaske, J. J., & Kobrin, K. (2001). Place attachment and environmentally responsible behaviour. *Journal of Environmental Education, 32*(4), 116–121.

Vernon, R. (1966). International investment and international trade in the product cycle. *Quarterly Journal of Economics, 80,* 190–207.

Vorknin, M., & Riese, H. (2001). Environmental concern in a local context: The significance of place attachment. *Enviromental Behaviour, 33*(2), 249–363.

Wagner, R. E. (1999). Austrian cycle theory: Saving the wheat while discarding the chaff. *Review of Austrian Economics, 12,* 65–80.

Williams, D. R., & Vaske, J. J. (2003). The measurement of place attachment: Validity and generalizability of a psychometric approach. *Forest Science, 49*(6), 830–840.

Wooldridge, J. F. (2002). *Econometric analysis of cross section and panel data.* Cambridge, Massachusetts: MIT Press.

Chapter 12
Back to the Same Place of Holidays. An Analysis of European Tourists' Preferences Towards Cultural Tourism

Rui Amaral and Jaime Serra

12.1 Introduction

Cultural tourism remains one of European tourists' main preference for travelling inside Europe (Kozak, 2002; Chaldler & Costello, 2012). The European Commission (EC) estimated that cultural tourism accounts for 40% of all European tourism; 4 out of 10 tourists choose their destination based on cultural attributes and attractions (EC, 2018). Furthermore, travel has long been associated with cultural standards and levels, because a visitor who is motivated to explore, discover and learn about the attractions of a country or region exerts an incalculable personal, social and professional investment.

Tourism demand and the study of tourists' preferences have had a profound effect on the tourist behaviour field of research. In this way, different perspectives can be broadly categorized, such as under a decision-making process of destination, regarding the point of view of tourism experience and the identification of the components of tourist behaviour (Suh & Gartner, 2004, among others). Particularly, revisit behaviour or repeat visitation is affected by several factors, such as reputation or quality of a particular destination (Alegre & Cladera, 2006; Barros & Assaf, 2012; Perales, 2002, among others). A controversial idea about motivations of cultural tourists was stated by Pulido-Fernández and Sánchez-Rivero (2010), who claimed that these individuals are motivated by novelty, because they are more complex, sophisticated and demand more experience about destinations, prices and availability, motivated by new and unique experiences in the destination. Although several studies have been conducted on revisit intentions to sun and sand destinations (among others, Correia & Zins,

R. Amaral (✉) · J. Serra
Interdisciplinary Centre for History, Cultures and Societies (CIDEHUS),
University of Évora, Évora, Portugal
e-mail: ramaral@uevora.pt

J. Serra
e-mail: jserra@uevora.pt

© Springer Nature Switzerland AG 2019
A. Artal-Tur et al. (eds.), *Trends in Tourist Behavior*,
Tourism, Hospitality & Event Management,
https://doi.org/10.1007/978-3-030-11160-1_12

2015), limited focus has been given to investigating return reasons based on cultural tourism preferences (Kastenholz, Eusébio, & Carneiro, 2013). Thereby, to the best of our knowledge, previous studies revealed that tourist preferences are associated with destination attributes, past visits and intention to revisit (Woodside & Lysonski, 1989; Decrop & Snelders, 2005; Li & Hudson, 2016).

Following the previous axioms, the study intends to identify the preferences of Europeans in their demand for cultural tourism in terms of revisiting the previous place of holidays. The attributes that explain the preferences of Europeans when intending to revisit the same place of holidays for cultural reasons will be also analysed. Findings are expected to provide European National Tourism Organisations and practitioners with a number of rich insights concerning the identification of return reasons arising from cultural tourism preferences.

This chapter is organized as follows: the next section discusses and summarizes the literature review based on revisiting cultural destinations and cultural tourist preferences; the third section presents the methodology and the data set considered in the present research. Estimated results and interpretations are provided in the fourth section. The fifth section summarizes and presents the conclusions, limitations and perspectives for future research.

12.2   Theoretical Considerations

12.2.1   Revisit Behaviour at Cultural Destination

According to Giltelson and Crompton (1984), there are five reasons for tourists revisiting a destination: risk reduction, socializing with those alike to them, fulfilling an emotional attachment, looking for new experiences and exposure of friends to the destination (Tiefenbacher, Day, & Wlaton, 2000). Familiarity draws tourists to a place, and as familiarity grows, thus the image of the place becomes more positive (Milman & Pizam, 2012; Echtner & Richie, 1991, 1993). As Milman and Pizam (2012) showed, the more familiar people are with an area, the more positive their images are of it and the likelihood that they will visit that area is higher than for other travellers who are merely aware of it. Cultural tourism has become more complex, not only because of its clear expansion, but tourists today are increasingly experienced, sophisticated and demanding (Pulido-Fernández & Sánchez-Rivero, 2010).

Polo-Peña, Frías-Jamilena, and Rodríguez-Molina (2013) stated that first-time visitors have a higher probability of visiting major tourist attractions in order to fulfil their motivations for novelty-seeking; repeat visitors, however, are more likely to engage in niche social and cultural activities. According to Sun, Chi and Xu (2013), the number of prior visits to a destination is a common indicator of familiarity with a destination, and this is a major influence on how destination image and appeal is formed. A paramount part of the cultural tourism topic still has a lack of consensus among researchers, as there is a lack of agreement about the exact meaning of "cultural tourism", because the term "culture" itself has many possible meanings (Kastenholz et al., 2013). Nevertheless, according to Chandler and Costello (2012), a relationship exists between heritage tourism and the cultural destination, or indeed attraction to a community, region or institution's history, lifestyle and heritage (Kastenholz et al., 2013). There is consensus that what tourists nowadays want cultural tourism to have significant forms, co-creation activities and varied and authentic, satisfying experiences. Many variables are important in the study of the cultural tourist's profile. A dimension of the demographic profile which includes age, gender, education level, marital, employment and family status, and the psychographic profile with items such as the lifestyle and activity level preferences needs to be analysed (Chandler & Costello, 2012). This former dimension takes on relevant importance in case of destinations with a considerable amount of revisit behaviour from visitors, such as European profiles (Kastenholz et al., 2013; Tiago, Couto, Tiago, & Faria, 2016). The tourist profile need also to be analysed through a market segmentation perspective because their behaviour occurs in a very competitive context and environment and within rapid technological transformation (Tiago et al., 2016). Woodside and Lysonski (1989) argue that repeat visits are related to psychographic characteristics and may be improved through pleasure with the attributes of a destination, because if a tourist is satisfied with the destination they tend to return (Decrop & Snelders, 2005; Li & Hudson, 2016).

12.2.2 Factors that Influence Tourists' Preferences for Revisiting Cultural Destinations

Tourist preferences is a concept related to consumer behaviour and has been studied by different social sciences (Slovic, 1995). Preferences are considered tourist strategies and have many factors to describe motivations and processes of choice of products, attractions, destinations and revisit intentions (Hsu, Tsai, & Wu, 2009; Merino-Castelló, 2003; Tosun, Debeoglu, & Fyall, 2015). These factors have the potential to influence the tourist's choices, which grants the supply stakeholders a better and more competitive position using a reformation of tourist information, via various statistical techniques for breaking them down (Li & Hudson, 2016). Many researchers agree that preferences appear before motivations, because when individuals intend to consume a product, they make a choice after evaluating internal and external factors (Crouch, 2011; Mak, Lumbers, Eves, & Chang, 2012). Other studies evidence tourist preferences as an individual mental construction (Hsu et al., 2009) to demonstrate that affective and cognitive factors are intrinsically and extrinsically present. Indeed, results provided by former studies have revealed that internal forces arise out of physical, psychological and social factors was well as destination exploration, while the tangible and intangible factors emerge from external forces. According to Woodside and Lysonski (1989) and Tosun et al. (2015), there are other important measures, such as destination image and revisit behaviour. According to these authors, this dimension is revealed as the prime factor in choice and the consumer's trip criteria. The image of cultural services, according to Strielkowski, Wang and Platt (2013), is based on the potential and priorities of "e-service tourism" in cultural tourists' preferences, since these products satisfy the needs of the baby boomer generation, which is of great interest from the demographic point of view. Other studies, such as Pulido-Fernández and Sánchez-Rivero (2010), state that cultural tourism is not homogenous nor non-monolithic, but includes all the touristic components of the destination, despite the different needs and expectations of visitors. Thus, it was possible to identify three types of segmentation related to cultural tourism: the *culturephiles*, who are a highly likely to be motivated to visit by events; the *culturally inactive*, for whom the destination's events present no cultural interest; and finally, the *roaming culturophiles*, who are the most attracted. The last segment choose the destination to celebrate life moments associated with events that are already happening. In this kind of cultural tourism, the age of the segment is high, as is their expenditure on hospitality and food, as well as their attraction to tourist entertainment, which leads to higher levels of investment by the visitors, as they are expecting positive, memorable and lasting experiences. Accordingly, there is evidence in the literature that revisit behaviour is affected by factors such as quality, comfortability, image, past experiences and preferences of a destination (among others, Hsu et al., 2009; Correia & Zins, 2015; Tosun et al., 2015). In addition, destination attributes (Yoon & Uysal, 2005; Huang & Hsu, 2009), destination facilities (Barros & Assaf, 2012) and tripographic variables, such as the level of prices of a particular destination (Tussyadiah & Pesonen, 2015; Park & Santos, 2017) are other factors that explain visitors' revisit behaviour. In the same stream of research, Kim and Fesenmaier (2017), state that the repeat visit is an intrinsic relationship between the experience and emotion lived at the destination and post trip evaluations.

Another factor that influence preference tourists for revisit cultural destinations is the destination loyalty they feel, built upon previous recommendations from family and friends (Chi, 2011; Prayag & Ryan, 2012). In the same stream of research, Meleddu, Paci and Pulina (2015) claim that tourists' loyalty to a particular destination is fundamental for tourism management due to the importance of the business opportunities that repeat tourists bring to tourism destinations (Oppermann, 2000). This has led to an analysis of the link between loyalty and repeat behaviour in various studies. Sun, Chi and Xu's (2013) comprehensive review of the literature on destination loyalty showed that the frequency of prior visits to a destination is a common indicator of familiarity with a destination. This in turn influences the image formation and appeal of the destination. The repeat visit segment is both cost-effective and desirable for organizations responsible for destination marketing. Further, for a tourism destination, it is important to understand which additional elements may influence revisit behaviour patterns. Following the model proposed by Kastenholz et al. (2013) (Fig. 12.1), this study intends to analyse the factors that explain the return to the same place of holidays for cultural reasons in a European geographic context. Based on this assumption the following model is proposed to be tested.

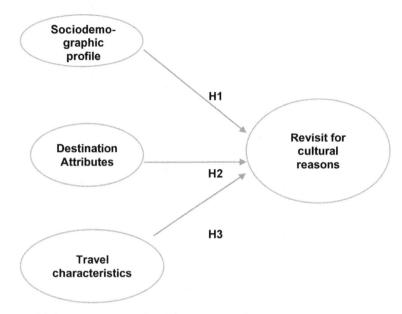

Fig. 12.1 Suggested model of factors influencing the return to the same place of holidays for cultural reasons. *Source* Own elaboration adapted from Kastenholz et al. (2013)

12.3   Methods and Hypotheses

According to the FLASH EUROBAROMETER 2014, based on "Preferences of Europeans towards tourism", the survey was designed to explore a range of aspects regarding European attitudes regarding the decision for going on holiday in 2014 and 2015, in particular: respondents' reasons for going on holiday in 2014; information sources used to organise their holidays; respondents' travel sociodemographic profiles, preferred destinations and type of holidays; degree of satisfaction with various aspects of their holidays in 2014; plans for the next holidays in 2015, including the impact of the current economic situation on their holiday plan.

The Eurobarometer database comprises more than 30,000 observations, covering the population from European Union Member States, aged over 15 years old. In order to answer the questionnaire, respondents were called both on fixed lines and mobile phones. The applied sample design for all EU member states was a multistage random (probability). In each household, the respondent was randomly drawn following *the last birthday rule* (EC, 2016).

One of the main questions of the survey was "*Which of the following would make you go back to the same place for holidays firstly?*". Specifically, respondents needed to answer what were the reasons for returning and repeating a visit to the same place for holidays. To answer, respondents had to choose 4 out of 9 options (**the natural features**—landscape; weather conditions); **the quality of accommodation;**

cultural and historical attractions; the general level of prices; the quality of activities available—transport, restaurants, leisure, activities; **how tourist are welcomed**—e.g. services for children, customer care, pets welcome policy; **accessibility facilities for people with special needs**—e.g. disabled elderly, children with prams; **I don't go back to the same place**—spontaneous; **other**—spontaneous; **don't know**).

Based on European tourists' preferences and in order to evaluate the likelihood of choosing the same place of holidays for cultural reasons, a logit regression (*Logit*) was adopted. This model specifies a relation in a mathematical formula in which the coefficients are statistically calculated and confirmed for a probability (Cameron & Trivedi, 2005; Morley, 2012). A logit model was selected because it allows an evaluation of the importance of the independent variables and the use of ordinary least squares (OLS) to estimate the regressive coefficients and is stochastic in the end because it includes an error. Thus, an econometric model is required that initiates the construction of a representation of the relation between variables, presented by the following expression:

$$Logit(\hat{\pi}) = Ln\left(\frac{\pi}{1-\pi}\right) \qquad (12.1)$$

In order to develop and test our logit model, the secondary data available from the Flash Eurobarometer 392—Preferences of Europeans Towards Tourism 2014 (EC, 2016) was adopted. The Eurobarometer database comprises 30,000 observations, from it a sample of 4460 observations was selected, which includes tourists from the following countries: Germany, Spain, France, Ireland, the Netherlands and the United Kingdom (Table 12.1).

From the database the following variables were extracted: sociodemographic variables (age (*K1_15–24 years old*), (*K2_25–39*); (*K3_40–54*), (*K4_55 or older*); education levels (*E1_until the age of 15*), (*E2_16–19*), (*E3_over 20*); subjective urbanization (*LR1_Rural Zone*), (*LR2_Other Town/Urban Centre*), (*LR3_Metropolitan Zone*) and Gender (D7); destination attributes (quality of accommodation (D1); natural features (D2)—(weather conditions, landscape etc.); how tourists are welcomed (D4)—(e.g. services for children, customer care, "pets-welcome" policy, etc.); quality of activities/services available (D5)—(transport, restaurants, leisure activities, etc.); and travel behaviour variables (shortness of trip (D6)—up to 3 consecutive nights away; general level of prices (D3)).

According to Wooldridge (2002), it is assumed a model that involve a latent or unobserved variable (y*), that is related to the observed independent variables by the structural equation (Long & Freese, 2006),

$$y_i^* = x^i\beta + \varepsilon_i \qquad (12.2)$$

where i indicates the observation and ε is a random error. For one independent variable, we can simplify the notation to,

Table 12.1 Characterization of the sample

			% (N = 4460)
Gender		*Country of Residence*	
Male	43%	Germany	18.3%
Female	57%	Spain	12.7%
Age		France	18.1%
15–24	5.7%	Ireland	17.3%
25–39	16.4%	The Netherlands	13.3%
40–54	30.9%	The United Kingdom	20.3%
55 (+)	47.0%	*Travel Behaviour*	
Education (end of)		Short-stay trip (<3 days)	43.6%
(–) 15	11.0%	Long-stay trip (>3 days)	56.4%
16–19	38.9%	*Destination attributes*	
20 (+)	45.4%	Natural surroundings	26.6%
Still studying	4.7%	Tourists are welcomed	17.7%
Live in…		Quality of accommodation	23.7%
Rural area or village	35%		
Small or middle-sized town	37%		
Large town	27.8%		

Source Own elaboration

$$\gamma_i^* = a + \beta x_i + \varepsilon_i \tag{12.3}$$

The observed binary y and the latent y^* is made with a simple measurement equation:

$$y_i = f(x) = \begin{cases} 1 & if \gamma_i^* > 0 \\ 0 & if \gamma_i^* \leq 0 \end{cases} \tag{12.4}$$

Since the main goal is to identify the probability of returning to the same place of holidays for cultural reasons, all independent variables were computed as dummies D_i, which verifies $D_i = 1$ if tourists go back to the same place of holidays for cultural reasons and $y_i = 0$ otherwise. The logit model has the following form:

$$Ln\left(\frac{P_i}{1 - P_i}\right) = \beta_0 + \beta_1 D_{1i} + \beta_2 D_{2i} + \beta_3 D_{3i} + \beta_4 D_{4i} + \beta_5 D_{5i} + \beta_6 D_{6i} + \beta_7 D_{7i}$$
$$+ \beta_8 E_{1i} + \beta_9 E_{2i} + \beta_{10} E_{3i} + \beta_{11} K_{1i} + \beta_{12} K_{2i} + \beta_{13} K_{3i} + \beta_{14} K_{4i}$$
$$+ \beta_{15} L R_{1i} + \beta_{16} L R_{2i} + \beta_{17} L R_{3i} + \mu_i \tag{12.5}$$

The impact of a combination of related independent variables—socio-demographic, destination attributes and travel behaviour—is analysed, as explained in the model specification below. After estimating the model, the results obtained from the independent variables that explain the dependent variable are as follows:

$$Ln\left(\frac{P_i}{1 - P_i}\right) = \beta_0 + \beta_1 D_{1i} + \beta_2 D_{2i} + \beta_4 D_{4i} + \beta_6 D_{6i} + \mu_i \qquad (12.5.1)$$

According to this assumption the following hypotheses was stated:

Hypothesis 1 (*socio-demographic characteristics*) *gender, age, education level and subjective urbanization* influence European tourists to return to the same place of holidays for cultural reasons. The present hypothesis is supported by Chaldler and Costello (2012) and Valek, Shaw and Bednarik (2014). In this line of thought, Pulido-Fernández and Sánchez-Rivero (2010) described a latent class approach to segmenting cultural tourism demand based on socio-demographic variables. In particular, age influences the predisposition of tourists toward the practice of cultural tourism. The term that will be used for the client of this type of product is the "culturophile tourist". Masiero and Nicolau (2012) show us that motivations have greater ability to segment the tourism market than socio-demographic characteristics.

Hypothesis 2 (*destination attributes*) destination attributes, such as *quality of accommodation, natural features, how tourists are welcomed and the quality of activities/services available*, influence European tourists to return to the same place of holidays for cultural reasons (Yoon & Uysal, 2005; Huang & Hsu, 2009).

Hypothesis 3 (*travel characteristics*) the shortness of the trip (not more than three nights) influences European tourists to return to the same place of holidays for cultural reasons (Tussyadiah & Pesonen, 2015; Park & Santos, 2017).

12.4 Findings

Data from 4460 valid responses were used for the analysis. As reported (Table 12.1), 57% of respondents are female and 43% male. Considering the age groups, 11% are less than 15 years old and 45.4% are more than 20 years old; 35% live in a rural area or village and 37% live in a small or medium town. Concerning destination attributes, Natural Surroundings (26.6%), Tourists are welcomed (17.7%) and Quality of Accommodation (23.7%) account for almost 70% of the total destination attributes of European tourists who return to the same place of holidays for cultural reasons. Regarding the travel behaviour dimension, expressed by length of stay from 4460 surveyed individuals, 56.4% assume a long stay trip (more than 3 nights) and 43.6% stay less then 3 nights (classified as a short stay).

Based on the results obtained, it was found that the explanatory variables are independent from each other. The model follows a normal distribution, with at least one independent variable related to the logit model. In this way, in order to identify the potential explaining variables which significantly influence the dependent one, the Wald test was adopted. The Wald test has an asymptotic Q-square distribution:

$$X^2 wald_i = \left(\frac{\hat{B}_i}{\widehat{SE}\left(\hat{B}_i\right)} \right)^2 \overset{a}{\sim} X^2_{(1)} \tag{12.6}$$

The binary logistic regression analysis shows the impact of the independent variables on the fact that tourists go back to the same place of holidays for cultural reasons or not. The results showed a high adjusted coefficient of determination, where the logit revealed the independent variables with explanatory power. Further, for the logistic regression analysis, the method *ENTER* was chosen, based on the Wald statistic for evaluating the contribution of each independent variable (Wooldridge, 2002). In order to evaluate the goodness-of-fit, classification tables are used and the X^2 statistics for the model was considered and the *Hosmer-Lemeshow* test was used. The same was done with the results (Table 12.2). The logistic regression revealed good values in terms of goodness-of-fit for the *Hosmer–Lemeshow* test (sig. = 0.499). In conclusion, the reasons for the probability of going to the same place of holidays for cultural reasons are reported in Table 12.2. The results of the Wald test, F-statistics and their significance level are also described.

H1 was rejected, as the socio-demographic characteristics of European tourists are not statistically significant. Considering this result, they were removed from Table 12.1. This result is not in line with several studies which focus on the relationship between destination choice and socio-demographic profile characteristics and its effects on the determinants of tourism return behaviour as stated by Oom do Valle, Correia and Rebelo (2008).

Table 12.2 Results of binary logistic regression analyses

		β	S.E.	Wald	df	Sig b		Exp(β)
Step 1a	D1_Quality of accommodation	0.339	0.086	15.354	1	0.00	(*)	1.403
	D2_Natural surroundings	0.333	0.085	15.438	1	0.00	(*)	1.395
	D4_Tourists are welcomed	0.216	0.097	4.935	1	0.026	(**)	1.241
	D6_Short stay trip	0.357	0.077	21.292	1	0.00	(*)	1.429
	Constant	−1.841	0.066	777.83	1	0.00	(*)	0.159
N		4460						
Hosmer and Lemeshow test		Chi-square = 5.356						
		Sig. = 0.499						

[a]Variable(s) entered on Step 1: D1_Quality of Accommodation, D2_Natural Surroundings, D4_Tourists are welcomed, D6_Short stay trip
[b]*significant at the 1% level; **significant at the 5% level

H2 was not rejected, as it evidenced different explanatory values as well as different increments, because the associated sign is statistically significant with positive effects, *ceteris paribus*, to $ln\left(\frac{P_i}{1-P_i}\right)$. This represents a clear association between the quality of destination facilities (in the case of this study—accommodation facilities) and returning to the same place of holidays for cultural reasons. In this way, the increment values are linked to the quality of accommodation, which means that better quality accommodation facilities increase by 1.403 times the probability of European visitors going back to the same place of holidays for cultural reasons. This result is in line with Tosun et al. (2015), who concluded that destination service quality affects image and intension to revisit, with the moderating role of past experience. Therefore, no significant difference was found if a tourist was a first-time visitor or a repeat visitor. Oom do Vale et al. (2008) also stated that accommodation is an important factor in the choice of destination (Oom do Valle et al. 2008). In the same line of thought, Tiago et al. (2016), suggest that homebody groups are more interesting in and concerned with quality of accommodation than other subgroups like explorers and vacationers in the European profiles. Tosun et al. (2015) also suggest that in the quality of accommodation, the perception of revising intentions is more powerful among the repeaters. According to Masiero and Nicolau (2012), value for money, which compares the amount spent on the quality of accommodation and service, is central in tourism and, as such, has been described as a critical indicator of competitiveness. Post travel experiences in terms of accommodation are very important to tourists because many described how much of their pre-trip memories were mostly around collecting their travel information and how they remembered the accommodation (Park & Santos, 2017). According to Tussyadiah and Pesonen, (2015, p. 1029), the "two factors suggest that the use of peer-to-peer accommodation among respondents was driven by (1) the social motivation to get to know, interact, and connect with local communities in a more meaningful way; to experience tourism destinations as a local; and to contribute to local residents, as well as (2) the motivation to get quality accommodation with lower cost". In the case of the natural surroundings, the probability of going back to the same destination for cultural purposes increases 1.305 times. Among others (Randriamboarison, Rosoamanajara & Solonandrasana, 2013; Tosun et al., 2015), natural surroundings are intrinsically related to the quality and beauty of destination, as well as the services provided there as an important attribute in the destination choice. However, this result does not match the literature. The study developed by Oom do Valle et al. (2008) stated that in Brazil the facilities and landscape features are not significant predictors of returning to the destination. In the same way, results provided in the study conducted by Kastenholz et al. (2013) pointed to attributes that were selected from cultural tourism such as natural features reflecting both the material and immaterial dimension of the tourism experience and are not determinant on visitors repeat visitation (Kastenholz et al., 2013). Masiero and Nicolau (2012) adopted market segmentation and the moderate price sensitivity as explanatory attributes to explain returning to the same place for holidays, which basically characterized tourists who evaluate "experiences below the average of nature and landscape". This result is justified by the authors due to the fact that tourists are looking for entertainment and fun. According to Oom do Valle et al. (2008) facilities and landscape features are not significant predictors to explain intention to return to the destination. Finally, the variable "how tourists are welcomed" increases the probability of return intention by 1241 times. This result is in line with the literature because, as stated by Tosun et al. (2015), it is excepted that hospitality will increase positive perceptions, affecting mostly the psychological components through host and guest interaction. 'Traditions and hospitality' are associated with the items 'regional gastronomy', 'customs and traditions' and 'hospitable local people', aspects which reflect the social and ethnographic, immaterial cultural heritage (Kastenholz et al., 2013). According to Tussyadiah and Pesonen (2015), social interactions with local hosts, as well as the authenticity of experiences outside of tourism places, allow tourists to engage in a plethora of activities typically accessible only to locals. Moreover, tourists are thought to value social interactions with locals and at the same time other tourists take risks in the search for authentic experiences, and are drawn to natural landscapes (Park & Santos, 2017).

H3 was not rejected as travel behaviour characteristics are positive and statistically significant. With regard to "short holiday/trip (less to 3 nights)", this result suggests that tourists value the shortness of the holiday, and due to the associated positive sign, this lead, *ceteris paribus*, to $ln\left(\frac{P_i}{1-P_i}\right)$, which means that short stays increase the probability of tourists going back to the same place of holidays for cultural reasons by 1.429 times. In a cultural experience context, the possibility of repeating a globally satisfactory, spontaneous short break should not be neglected (Kastenholz et al., 2013). Shortened travel distances could have been a sufficient incentive to make some individuals visit the sites for their own personal interests (Chaldler & Costello, 2012).

Previous results highlighted empirical evidence about European cultural tourists' behaviour and their destination loyalty patterns. Consequently, results evidence that those tourists who travel for cultural motivations are more likely to go back to the same place if destinations remain their physical and service standards (such as maintenance of an attractive natural landscape within quality of accommodation services combined with a social and commercial hospitality behaviour). Not least is the evidence of short trip patterns linked to European cultural tourists inside Europe, which is a feature granted by the accessible prices and routes inside Europe promoted by airline companies.

12.5   Conclusion and Implications

Repeat visitation patterns are reported in the literature associated with novel seeking behaviour patterns and engagement in niche social and cultural activities (Polo-Peña et al., 2013). As our results revealed, revisit patterns of European tourists for cultural reasons are explained by the quality of the services and the characteristics of the destinations, such the landscape and hospitality/welcoming characteristics. These last remarks might contribute to increasing the competitiveness of cultural destinations. In this sense, the influence of these attributes on the decision to go back to the same place of holidays for cultural reasons is engaged with the sense of familiarity in a particular destination (Milman & Pizam, 2012; Echtner & Richie, 1991, 1993). As stated by these authors, the more familiar an area becomes, the more positive is the image of a destination and thereby the probability of repeating the visit increases. As a consequence, destinations should continue to invest in the preservation of natural landscapes and maintain the authenticity of cultural attributes. Additionally, they should add value onto welcoming/hospitality characteristics because these are the most important and attractive points that influence a revisit intention for the next holiday season. These results may promote a number of benefits, for instance fostering more expenditures and reducing seasonality of holiday preferences, as was evidenced by a preference for a short holidays period (at least 3 nights). The results provided some insights into the body of knowledge in terms of explained variables of revisit behaviour. As described in the suggested model (Fig. 12.1) which tested three hypotheses, the influence of the quality of accommodation (Spasojevic & Bozic, 2016) and the natural and landscape characteristics (Tukamushaba, Xiao, & Ladkin, 2016) are confirmed as explanatory attributes in going back to the same place for holidays for cultural reasons (Kim & Fesenmaier, 2017; Park & Santos, 2017; Chandler & Costello, 2012). All research has limitations. Methodologically this research is based on secondary data. Moreover, this research did not cover all tourist preferences items in order to explain the context of return reasons. Other limitations refer to the nature of the sample. Data analysis only partially covers a few European countries, such as Germany, Spain, France, Ireland, and the Netherlands. Future research should extend the number of countries and nationalities from Europe. An attempt can also be made to explore possible differences between high and low seasons in terms of preferences for returning to the same place of holidays for cultural reasons.

Acknowledgements The authors disclosed receipt of the following financial support for the research, authorship, and/or publication of this article: This work is financed by FEDER funds, under the new PT2020 partnership agreement and by national funds FCT/MEC—Foundation for Science and Technology under the UID/HIS/00057/2013—POCI-01-0145-FEDER-007702 project —CIDEHUS.

References

Alegre, J., & Cladera, M. (2006). Repeat visitation in mature sun and sand holiday destinations. *Journal of Travel Research, 44*, 288–297.

Barros, C. P., & Assaf, A. G. (2012). Analysing tourism return intention to an urban destination. *Journal of Hospitality and Tourism Research, 36*(2), 216–231.

Cameron, A., & Trivedi, P. (2005). *Micro econometrics: Methods and applications*. London: Cambridge University Press.

Chi, C. G.-Q. (2011). Destination loyalty formation and travelers' demographic characteristics: A multiple group analysis approach. *Journal of Hospitality and Tourism Research, 35*(2), 191–212.

Chandler, J., & Costello, C. (2012). A profile of visitors at heritage tourism destination in east Tennessee according to Plog's lifestyle and activity level preferences model. *Journal of Travel Research, 41,* 161–166.

Correia, A., & Zins, A. (2015). Why do tourists persist in visiting the same destination? *Tourism Economics, 21*(1), 215–221.

Crouch, G. (2011). Destination competitiveness: An analysis of determinant attributes. *Journal of Travel Research, 50*(1), 27–45.

Decrop, A., & Snelders, D. (2005). A grounded typology of vacation decision-making. *Tourism Management, 26,* 121–132.

Echtner, C., & Ritchie, J. R. (1991). The meaning and measurement of destination image. *Journal of Tourism Studies, 2*(2), 2–12.

Echtner, C., & Ritchie, J. R. (1993). The measurement of destination image: An empirical assessment. *Journal of Travel Research, 31*(4), 3–13.

European Commission. (2016). *Preferences of Europeans towards Tourism—Flash Eurobarometer report.* European Commission, Madrid. Accessed https://ec.europa.eu/growth/tools-databases/vto/eurobarometer.

European Commission. (2018). http://ec.europa.eu/growth/sectors/tourism/offer/cultural_en. Accessed 13 May 2018.

Gitelson, R., & Crompton, J. (1984). Insights into to repeat vocation phenomenon. *Annals of Tourism Research, 11,* 199–217.

Huang, S., & Hsu, C. H. C. (2009). Effects of travel motivation, past experience, perceived constraint, and attitude on revisit intention. *Journal of Travel Research, 48*(1), 29–44.

Hsu, T.-K., Tsai, Y.-F., & Wu, H.-H. (2009). The preference analysis for tourist choice of destination: A case study of Taiwan. *Tourism Management, 30,* 288–297.

Kastenholz, E., Eusébio, C., & Carneiro, M. (2013). Studying factors influencing repeat visitation of cultural tourists. *Journal of Vocation Marketing, 19*(4), 343–358.

Kim, J., & Fesenmaier, D. (2017). Sharing tourism experiences: The post-trip experience. *Journal of Travel Research, 56*(1), 28–40.

Kozak, M. (2002). Comparative analysis of tourist motivation by nationality and destinations. *Tourism Management, 23,* 221–232.

Li, J. & Hudson, S. (2016). Conjoint analysis of consumer preferences to destination brand attributes. *Tourism, Travel and Research Association, 22.* http://scholarworks.umass.edu/ttra/2016/Academic_Papers_Visual/22. Retrieved 20 March 2017.

Long, J. S., & Freese, J. (2006). *Regression Models for Categorical Dependent Variables Using Stata* (2nd ed.). Texas: Stata Press.

Mak, A., Lumbers, M., Eves, A., & Chang, R. (2012). Factors influencing tourist food consumption. *International Journal of Hospitality Management, 31,* 928–936.

Masiero, L., & Nicolau, J. (2012). Tourism market segmentation based on price sensitivity: Finding similar prices preferences on tourism activities. *Journal of Travel Research, 51*(4), 426–435.

Meleddu, M., Paci, R., & Pulina, M. (2015). Repeated behaviour and destination loyalty. *Tourism Management, 50,* 159–171.

Merino-Castelló, A. (2003). Eliciting consumers' preferences using stated preference discrete choice models: Contingent ranking versus choice experiment. *Merck Company Foundation.* Ph.D. thesis, Chapter 3.

Milman, A., & Pizam, A. (2012). The role of awareness and familiarity with a destination: The central Florida case. *Journal of Travel Research, 33*(3), 21–27. https://doi.org/10.1177/004728759503300304.

Morley, C. (2012). Technique and theory in tourism analysis. *Tourism Economics, 18*(6), 1273–1286.

Oom do Valle, P., Correia, A. & Rebelo, E. (2008). Determinants of tourism return behaviour. *Tourism and Hospitality Research, 8*(3), 2005–2019.

Oppermann, M. (2000). Tourism destination loyalty. *Journal of Travel Research, 39*(1), 78–84.

Park, S., & Santos, C. (2017). Exploring the tourist experience: A sequential approach. *Journal of Travel Research, 56*(1), 16–27.

Perales, R. (2002). Rural tourism in Spain. *Annals of Tourism Research, 29*(4), 1101–1110.

Polo-Peña, A., Frías-Jamilena, D., & Rodríguez-Molina, C. (2013). Market orientation as a strategy for the rural tourism sector: Its effect on tourist behaviour and performance of enterprises. *Journal of Travel Research, 52*(2), 225–239.

Prayag, G., & Ryan, C. (2012). Antecedents of tourists' loyalty to Mauritius: The role and influence of destination image, place attachment, personal involvement, and satisfaction. *Journal of Travel Research, 51*(3), 342–356.

Pulido-Fernández, J., & Sánchez-Rivero, M. (2010). Attitudes of the cultural tourist: A latent segmentation approach. *Journal of Cultural Economics, 34,* 111–129.

Ramdriamboarison, R., Rasoamanajara, F., & Solanandrasana, B. (2013). Tourism return frequency demand in Madagascar. *Tourism Economics, 19*(4), 943–958.

Slovic, P. (1995). The construction of preference. *American Psychologist, 50*(5), 364–371.

Spasojevic, B., & Bozic, S. (2016). Senior tourists' preferences in the developing countries—measuring perceptions of Serbian potential senior market. *European Journal Tourism Hospitality Research, 7*(2), 74–83. https://doi.org/10.1515/ejthr-2016-0009.

Strielkwoski, W., Wang, J., & Platt, S. (2013). Consumer preferences for cultural heritage and tourism e-services: A case study of three European cities. *University of Zagreb, Faculty of Economics and Business, 25*(31), 161–176.

Suh, Y. K., & Gartner, W. C. (2004). Preferences and trip expenditures—a conjoint analysis of visitors to Seoul, Korea. *Tourism Management, 25,* 127–137.

Sun, X., Chi, G., & Xu, H. (2013). Developing destination loyalty: The case of Hainan Island. *Annals of Tourism Research, 43,* 547–577.

Tan, W. K. (2017). Repeat visitation: A study from the perspective of leisure constraint, tourist experience, destination images, and experiential familiarity. *Journal of Destination Marketing and Management, 6,* 233–242.

Tiago, M., Couto, J., Tiago, F., & Faria, S. (2016). Baby boomers turning grey: European profiles. *Tourism Management, 54,* 13–22.

Tiefenbacher, J. P., Day, F. A., & Walton, J. A. (2000). Attributes of repeat visitors to small tourist-oriented communities. *Social Science Journal, 37*(2), 299–308.

Tosun, C., Dedeoglu, B., & Fyall, A. (2015). Destination service quality, affective image and revisit intention: The moderating role of past experience. *Journal of Destination Marketing and Management, 4,* 222–234.

Tukamushaba, E., Xiao, H., & Ladkin, A. (2016). The effect of tourists' perceptions of a tourism product on memorable travel experience: Implication for destination branding. *European Journal Tourism Hospitality Research, 7*(1), 2–12.

Tussayadiah, P., & Pesonen, J. (2015). Impacts of peer-to-peer accommodation use on travel patterns. *Journal of Travel Research, 55*(8), 1022–1040.

Valek, N., Shaw, M., & Bednarik, J. (2014). Socio-demographic characteristics sport tourism choices. *Acta Gimnica, 44*(1), 57–65.

Wooldridge, J. (2002). *Econometric analysis of cross section and panel data.* Cambridge: Cambridge University Press.

Woodside, A., & Lysonski, S. (1989). A general model of traveller destination choice. *Journal of Travel Research, 27*(4), 8–14.

Yoon, Y., & Uysal, M. (2005). An examination of the effects of motivation and satisfaction on destination loyalty: A structural model. *Tourism Management, 26*(1), 45–56.

Chapter 13
Factors Influencing Tourism Expenditure on Accommodation in World Heritage Cities

Juan Ignacio Pulido-Fernández, Isabel Carrillo-Hidalgo and Ana Belén Mudarra-Fernández

13.1 Introduction

Expenditure is one of the economic variables that has been most profoundly analyzed in studies of tourism in recent decades, especially with respect to cultural destinations. Over time, the interest of researchers has become focused on the identification and understanding of the factors that condition tourism expenditure as a key variable to ensure the multiplier effect of tourism on the territory and, thereby, on the competitiveness of tourism destinations overall.

The analysis of the expenditure made by tourists in cultural destinations and, more specifically, in World Heritage Cities is based on the symbiosis of culture and tourism, have, which are currently linked in a joint and necessary cooperation for economic development of certain geographical areas. The need for economic resources has led to destinations putting the spotlight on tourism expenditure, generating a growing need to determine the components of that expenditure and to what extent it can be increased (Lara and Lopez-Guzman, 2004).

Authors including Brida, Monterubbianes, and Zapata-Aguirre (2013b), Disegna, Scuderi, and Brida (2012) and Pulido-Fernández, Cárdenas-García, and Carrillo-Hidalgo (2016) have studied expenditure in the cultural tourism sector. But there have been very few authors, who have specialized in the study of the factors that influence expenditure on accommodation by tourists in World Heritage Cities.

J. I. Pulido-Fernández · I. Carrillo-Hidalgo (✉)
Laboratory of Analysis and Innovation in Tourism (LAInnTUR), University of Jaén,
Campus Las Lagunillas, D3-273, 23071 Jaén, Spain
e-mail: ihidalgo@ujaen.es

J. I. Pulido-Fernández
e-mail: jipulido@ujaen.es

A. B. Mudarra-Fernández
University of Jaén, Campus Las Lagunillas, D3-273, 23071 Jaén, Spain
e-mail: abmf0003@ujaen.es

© Springer Nature Switzerland AG 2019
A. Artal-Tur et al. (eds.), *Trends in Tourist Behavior*,
Tourism, Hospitality & Event Management,
https://doi.org/10.1007/978-3-030-11160-1_13

209

Starting from the case of Úbeda and Baeza and by using a multivariate double-hurdle model, which allows analyzing the probability of making an expense and, subsequently, the quantification of the it, it has been possible to identify the factors that influence the tourist spending on accommodation made in this kind of destinations.

13.2 Literature Review

In order to carry out an analysis of the variables that influence the expenditure by tourists in World Heritage Sites, a comprehensive review of the scientific literature found in the Scopus and Web of Science databases was carried out, following the proposal of Webster and Watson (2002).

Table 13.1 shows the variables which, according to the authors analyzed, influence the spending of tourists in World Heritage Cities. The variables marked in the table with a tick, are those for which a relationship with tourism expenditure has been identified.

13.3 Methodology

13.3.1 Case Study

Úbeda and Baeza are two cities located in the province of Jaén whose main sources of revenue are tourism, agriculture and artisan workshops (Cárdenas-García, Pulido-Fernández, & Mudarra-Fernández, 2014). They have known tourism since the late 19th and early 20th century, but it was not until 2003, when UNESCO declared them a World Heritage Site under the title "Úbeda and Baeza: Urban Duality and Cultural Unity", that the development of tourism was promoted in the cities. Today, Úbeda and Baeza have very diverse resources which can meet the needs of cultural tourists, thanks to their rich heritage and the many festivals, fairs and events that are held.

As well as the tourism resources, these cities also have a large number of public and private services offering accommodation, restaurants, transport, information and interpretation services, which are revalorized by means of tourism products such as cultural routes, gastronomy related to the olive oil culture, artisan products, events, fairs, etc.

Both cities have belonged to the group of World Heritage Cities since 2014. Furthermore, they devote significant effort to their promotion so that potential tourists are aware of the different resources and activities offered and decide to make the visit.

All of these efforts have been rewarded by the increase in tourism expenditure in both cities since they were declared World Heritage Sites, rising from a mean daily spend in 2003 of €74.94 to €196.80 in 2012 (Cárdenas-García et al., 2014).

Table 13.1 Variables that influence the spending made by tourists in World Heritage Cities, according to the literature reviewed

		Andrade (2016)	Serra, Borges, and Marujo (2016)	Amir, Osman, Bachok, and Ibrahim (2015)	Brida, Pulina, Riaño, and Zapata (2013c)	Siebinga (2013)	Esteban, Mondejar, and Cordente (2009)	Molina, Martin-Consuegra, Esteban, and Diaz (2007)	Troitiño (1998)
Socio-economic variables	Age	✓		✓	✓		✓	✓	
	Level of education	✓						✓	
	Occupation	✓							
	Nationality		✓			✓			
Variables related to the characteristics of the trip	Duration of the stay		✓	✓	✓			✓	✓
	Type of accommodation	✓		✓			✓		
	Places visited				✓				
	Loyalty to the destination				✓	✓			
	How the trip was organized							✓	
	Means of transport	✓			✓				
	Type of tourist and accompanying persons	✓							
Variables related to the destination	Participation in activities in the destination	✓	✓	✓					
Psychological variables	Reasons for the trip								✓
	Satisfaction		✓				✓		

Source Own elaboration

These figures are explained by the consolidation of Úbeda and Baeza as cultural tourism destinations which have attracted tourists with a high disposable income, thereby increasing the mean expenditure in the destination. This has not only affected expenditure, but also the length of stay in the destination and the number of tourists, which have also risen, though to a lesser extent than the mean daily spent.

13.3.2 Questionnaire

In order to determine the factors that influence expenditure by tourists in these two cities, data from 2,126 survey questionnaires answered in the cities between June and September 2016 was analyzed. The technical details of the survey are shown in Table 13.2.

For this reason, given the impossibility of limiting the object of the study (all of the tourists who visit the cities during the months in which the survey was taken) and, therefore, being an infinite population, a simple random sample was taken, in which the only criterion for selection was to have spent at least one night in either of the two cities. The surveys were taken in the places in each city which received most visits, such as Plaza de Santa María in Úbeda and the old Antonio Machado University in Baeza.

The survey was structured in seven blocks, four relating to the different types of variables to be analyzed (socio-economic, variables related to the characteristics of the trip, variables related to the destination and the evaluation and opinions of the tourist), and three blocks which were more closely related to the tourist's travel budget and the expenditure incurred by the tourist at the point of origin and in the destination. Different types of questions were used: open, closed (dichotomous and multichotomous, with either a single or a multiple answer) and mixed. The scales used to measure the variables of the study were also of different types: firstly, a

Table 13.2 Technical details of the survey

Population	Spanish and foreign tourists who spend a night in one of the destination cities
Scope	Úbeda and Baeza
Type of survey	Structured questionnaire answered in a personal interview
Sample size	2,126 valid surveys
Sampling error	2.1%
Confidence interval	95% (p = q = 0.50)
Period of fieldwork	June, July, August and September 2016

Source Own elaboration

Likert-type measuring scale and, secondly, nominal non-metric scales to identify the categories or options with which the behavior of the interviewee is identified, in the case of qualitative variable analysis without quantitative significance.

13.3.3 Analytical Model

In order to determine the variables associated with the different groups of expenditure incurred by tourists, double-hurdle statistical models were applied, estimating expenditure on accommodation by means of a two-stage system involving the analysis of the probability of incurring expenditure on accommodation and the quantification of the expenditure on accommodation incurred (Blundell & Meghir, 1987; Brida et al., 2013b; Cragg, 1971; Deaton & Irish, 1984; McFadden, 1974; Tobin, 1958; Vuong, 1989). The model allows the different variables in the study to be associated with the probability and quantification of the expenditure. Multivariate models were constructed for each one of the four groups of expenditure considered (accommodation, transport, food, and visits and leisure). It was not possible to adjust a single multivariate model with the information available in the four blocks studied, due to problems of overestimation of the parameters and of co-linearity between some of the variables of the different blocks, as well as asymptotic problems in the adjustment of the model, due to the number of parameters estimated simultaneously.

For these reasons, the models presented are the result of multivariate models selected by the "backward" method of elimination of variables in each block of the survey analyzed. The measurement of the goodness of fit (Vuong, 1989) was checked and the R2 coefficient of each model is presented (McFadden, 1974). The results shown indicate the statistically significant variables associated with the expenditure variables analyzed.

The distribution of probability of the values observed and of the double-hurdle model is a mixed discrete-continuous distribution which assigns a probability mass function of $p(y = 0)$ for $y = 0$ and a density function of $f_+(y)$ for $y > 0$, where:

$$P(y = 0) + \int_0^\infty f_+(y)dy = 1. \tag{13.1}$$

In this way, the double-hurdle model used in the first stage of taking the decision to incur the expenditure and, subsequently, the stage of incurring the expenditure is defined as:

$$1 - p(y = 0)$$

$$1 - \Phi_1 \Phi_2 \tag{13.2}$$

$$2 - f_+(y)$$

$$\frac{1}{\sigma} \Phi\left(\frac{y - \beta_2^{\mathrm{T}} x_2}{\sigma}\right) \Phi_1 \tag{13.3}$$

where Φ_1 corresponds to the standard normal distribution function of the latent variable defined in the first stage:

$$\Phi_1 = \Phi(\beta_1^T x_1) \tag{13.4}$$

while Φ_2 corresponds to the second stage, in which the latent variable is defined as:

$$y_2^* = \beta_2^T x_2 + \varepsilon_2$$

$$\Phi_2 = \Phi\left(\frac{\beta_2^T x_2}{\sigma}\right) \tag{13.5}$$

Φ being the standard normal distribution function.

For further details about the mathematical formulation of the model used, see the paper by Carlevaro, Croissanty, and Hoareau (2012) and, specifically, in the context of tourism, the work by Brida et al. (2013b).

R computer software was used for the statistical analysis, with the mhurdle package, which is specifically for double-hurdle models (Carlevaro et al., 2012). The statistical testing was performed at a significance level of 5%.

13.4 Results and Discussion

The results obtained are grouped into two large blocks. In the first (Sect. 13.4.1), there is a descriptive analysis of the four groups of variables included in the questionnaire (socio-demographic variables, variables related to the characteristics of the trip, variables related to the characteristics of the destination and the psychological variables of the tourist), as well as other aspects related to the budget for the trip and the expenditure incurred. To perform this analysis, the tables with data obtained through SPSS 21.0 have not been included in order to avoid the repetition of information and, above all, to abbreviate this article.

The second block, which includes all of the other subsections of this Sect. 13.4, shows the results of the double-hurdle model for expenditure on accommodation to analyze the factors influencing it.

13.4.1 Descriptive Analysis

Using descriptive statistical tools, by means of the SPSS 21.0 statistical software, an initial analysis was performed in which the categorical variables were described, using frequencies and percentages. The quantitative variables gathered were summarized through the mean, standard deviation, median, maximum and minimum, and the confidence interval of 95% for the mean value is given.

The distribution of interviewees was practically even, with 50% of men and women. Of the interviewees, 50% were between 45 and 65 years of age, the majority with university education and income falling in the medium-high band (49.9% had an income of between €1,200 and €2,100, although 23.2% declared a disposable income of less than €655). With respect to the country of residence, the interviewees were mainly resident in Spain (88.2%), and a similar percentage were of Spanish nationality.

With respect to the employment situation, most were employed (65.8%), followed by students (18.8%). The largest groups by professional category among the employed were liberal professionals (23.2%) and public employees with university qualifications (23.7%). Only 4.2% of interviewees made the visit accompanied by persons residing in Úbeda or Baeza. Of the interviewees, 56.4% spent the night in Úbeda, while 43.6% did so in Baeza. Lastly, it can be seen that the predominant value among interviewees was a comfortable life (61.3%), followed by a stressful life (19.5%) and an exciting life (12.4%).

A description of the responses to the variables related to the characteristics of the trip is given below. Practically all of the tourists would recommend the city in which they were surveyed as a tourism destination. The most common type of trip was a visit by a couple with or without children, at around 31% each, followed by a trip with friends (29.3%). It can be seen that the majority of interviewees were new to the destination cities (60.4% had never visited them), that most did not visit other places (62%) and that 87.5% answered affirmatively with respect to the possibility of returning to Úbeda or Baeza.

As regards the organization of the trip, almost all visits were organized privately, with half of the interviewees staying in three-star hotels (followed by two- or one-star hotels) and making little use of the Internet for transport, vehicle rental or tickets for cultural attractions, in contrast to the use made for accommodation, where 90.8% of interviewees made the purchase online. Almost 50% of the interviewees used the Internet to search for restaurants. The same occurs with places to visit, with 54.9% of interviewees declaring that they had used the Internet to seek information about attractions. It is also notable that, among almost all of the interviewees, there were no problems regarding payments, that is, when they paid for the services and products acquired in the destination, they were able to pay in cash, with a credit card or even with gift vouchers.

With respect to the means by which interviewees heard of the destination, a higher proportion of them learned of it through friends or relatives, personal experience or through the knowledge that it was a World Heritage Sites (34.5%, 19.6% and 23.8%, respectively), while, at the other extreme, the least relevant sources of information were press publicity (0.2%) and offers and catalogues (0%). Likewise, regarding the resources by which the tourists learned about the city, there is a tendency to low use of search engines and social media, with the values of 26.5% and 18.9%, respectively. With respect to the means of transport used, private cars predominated (89.3%).

With respect to the quantitative variables, it can be seen that the mean duration of visits was around 2–3 days, by 4–5 persons spending 2 or 3 nights in the destinations. The existence of such variability is explained by the heterogeneity of the interviewees since, despite the mean values falling within said intervals, there were minimums and maximums of 1 and 20 (in the case of days/nights) and of 1 and 50 (in the case of the number of persons).

Thirdly, descriptive results are given of the variables related to the characteristics of the destination. All of the interviewees declared that they had found what they expected on the visit, and so it can be concluded that the visit satisfied their expectations. With respect to the activities in the destinations, the short daytrip (99.9%), guided routes (88.9%), going out for *tapas* (96.2%) and, to a lesser extent, going for a drink (46.7%), were the main activities undertaken by the interviewees, contrasting with buying books (1.1%), visiting museums (2.8%), buying artisan products (3.8%) or cultural routes (9.7%).

There follows a description of the responses to the questions related to the psychological variables of the tourists and the motives for the trip. The most significant data shows that 53.1% of interviewees considered themselves to have an open mentality, together with 29.7% who had a jovial personality. Other qualities, such as serenity, responsibility and courtesy, scored lower. With respect to the motive for the trip, leisure and holidays (96.4%) predominated, followed, at a great distance, by visits to relatives and friends (2.5%), with the rest of the categories being of little relevance. In response to the question regarding satisfaction with the trip, the highest percentages of interviewees declared very positive or positive satisfaction (67.3% and 30.8%, respectively).

With respect to the quantitative variables, the responses of interviewees to a number of aspects related to the destinations analyzed must be considered. Scores close to 10 express greater satisfaction with these aspects. Accommodation, cultural activities, value for money, leisure and enjoyment, landscapes, restaurants, tranquility and public transport receive a mean score greater than 8, and are, therefore, the characteristics which are most highly valued by the interviewees. In contrast, signage/tourist information and traffic/roads generated the greatest dissatisfaction among visitors.

With respect to the economic aspect of the trip, among the most relevant data we can highlight that the mean budget per person per day of the tourists is €129.43, although the value that is most repeated in the survey (the median) is a budget of €110. Most of the tourists visiting Úbeda and Baeza (99.2%) did not make any payments related to the trip in their place of residence and, furthermore, none of them bought package tours.

Finally, with respect to expenditure by the tourists, it should be noted that the main item of expenditure was accommodation, on which the interviewees had a mean daily spend of €50.47, followed by the purchase of food (€48.81), vehicle rental (€35.95), meals (€30.94) and transport in the destination (€29.45). In all events, it should be noted that 85.75% of interviewees did not make any purchases of food, and so this is really a token item of expenditure, in comparison with meals, on which 98.35% of interviewees incurred expenditure. Only €14.58 was spent on organized visits and excursions. It is particularly striking that 93.93% of the interviewees did not incur any expenditure on gifts, souvenirs, etc., while 61.71% did not spend on leisure (museums, exhibitions, sporting activities, etc.).

13.4.2 Expenditure on Accommodation

Table 13.3 shows the results of the estimates for the parameters of the variables associated with accommodation expenditure. It can be observed that the probability of expenditure on accommodation is lower in the 19–29 age group, which is the group which spends least on accommodation, which coincides with all of the bibliography analyzed in the previous section, except Brida, Pulina, Riaño, and Zapata (2013c). The unemployed are less likely to spend on accommodation, although their expenditure is the same amount as the employed. However, the retired/homemakers spend a significantly greater amount on accommodation than the employed, which contradicts the results of Brida et al. (2013b). Visitors with post-secondary or university education are more likely to spend on accommodation, as are tourists in the liberal professions, who also have a higher mean spend then managers and other professionals.

Tourists with an income of between €901 and €1,200 are less likely to spend on accommodation than tourists with a lower income, and the higher their income, the higher their expenditure (Marrocu, Paci, & Zara, 2015). The probability of foreign visitors spending on accommodation is lower than among Spanish visitors, and the latter spend more, according to Brida, Disegna, and Scuderi (2013a). Tourists whose values are liberty/emotion and those who are stressed are more likely to spend on accommodation than tourists whose values are comfort/safety, although the latter have higher expenditure. The probability of spending on accommodation was higher among tourists staying in Baeza than in Úbeda, although those staying in Úbeda spent more.

The number of days spent planning the stay was associated with lower expenditure on accommodation, despite Marrocu et al. (2015) finding the reverse. It was also observed that those who spent most and showed greater probability of spending were tourists visiting with friends, followed by couples without children and, with a lower spend on accommodation, those who were travelling alone, despite Andrade (2016) finding that family with children spent more than friends or tourist were traveling alone. The probability of spending when the tourist had not previously visited the city was significantly greater than when they had visited previously on one or more occasions (Brida et al., 2013a), as occurred with those persons who would not return to the destination in the future, although, in this case, these findings contradict part of the literature analyzed (Brida et al., 2013a).

Table 13.3 Results of the double-hurdle model adjusted to expenditure on accommodation

Expenditure on accommodation model	Stage 1			Stage 2		
	Estimate	S.E.	P-value	Estimate	S.E.	P-value
Age 19–29 versus ≤18	−0.874	0.243	<0.001	−6.104	2.403	0.011
Age ≥30 versus ≤18	−0.347	0.308	0.261	3.926	2.905	0.177
Education: Occupational versus up to secondary	0.981	0.261	<0.001			
Education: University versus up to secondary	0.442	0.231	0.056			
Employment: Unemployed versus employed	−1.171	0.283	<0.001	4.082	3.413	0.232
Employment: Retired/homemaker versus employed	0.290	0.200	0.147	4.637	1.195	<0.001
Employment: Student versus employed	−0.649	0.421	0.123	2.970	3.106	0.339
Category: Management versus liberal professions	−0.498	0.160	0.002	−4.607	1.319	<0.001
Category: Public service and workers versus liberal professions	0.095	0.142	0.502	−3.410	0.971	<0.001
Income: 901–1200 versus ≤900	−0.810	0.350	0.021	−0.840	2.021	0.678
Income: 1201–1800 versus ≤900	−0.410	0.335	0.221	2.084	1.817	0.251
Income: >1800 versus ≤900	−0.134	0.344	0.696	3.693	1.826	0.043
Country: Foreign versus Spain	−0.568	0.131	<0.001	6.414	1.295	<0.001
Values: Exciting life/liberty versus comfortable life/security/pleasure/wisdom/equality	0.343	0.150	0.022	−3.238	1.059	0.002
Values: Stressful life versus comfortable life/security/pleasure/wisdom/equality	0.477	0.148	0.001	−1.741	0.972	0.073
Place of stay: Baeza versus Úbeda	0.208	0.105	0.047	−7.559	0.763	<0.001
R²	0.150					
No of days				−0.893	0.254	<0.001
Type of Trip: Family with children versus couples without children	0.690	0.366	0.060	−3.107	0.933	0.001
Type of Trip: Friends versus couples without children	3.267	0.803	<0.001	3.015	0.984	0.002
Type of Trip: Alone/other versus couples without children	2.061	2.392	0.389	−9.843	2.101	<0.001

(continued)

Table 13.3 (continued)

Expenditure on accommodation model	Stage 1			Stage 2		
	Estimate	S.E.	P-value	Estimate	S.E.	P-value
Visits: 1 or 2 versus none	−1.075	0.429	0.012			
Visits: 3 or more versus none	−0.775	0.334	0.020			
Accommodation: Rural houses/apartments and rented houses/owned property versus hotels/apartments	−3.781	0.652	<0.001			
Hotels/apartments 1–2* or more versus hotels/apartments 3* or more				−1.781	0.801	0.026
Accommodation: Rural houses/apartments and rented houses/owned property versus hotels/apartments 3* or more				−10.344	1.715	<0.001
Visits to more places: Yes versus No	2.032	0.576	<0.001	−4.932	1.181	<0.001
Return in the future: Yes versus No	−4.153	0.847	<0.001			
No use of the Internet versus use of the internet for accommodation	−2.247	0.500	<0.001	3.727	0.805	<0.001
No use of the Internet versus use of the internet for places to visit				−2.398	0.768	0.002
No use of the internet versus use of the internet for restaurants	1.719	0.524	0.001	−10.346	1.527	<0.001
Use of search engines: Yes versus No				−10.097	1.529	<0.001
Use of social media: Yes versus No				−5.501	1.856	0.003
Use of institutional portals: Yes versus No				−8.884	1.504	<0.001
Use of Google maps: Yes versus No				−11.669	1.665	<0.001
Use of other resources: Yes versus No				25.167	2.267	<0.001
Knowledge of destination through travel agent recommendation: Yes versus No				2.903	1.018	0.004
Knowledge of destination from personal experience: Yes versus No				3.173	1.306	0.015
Knowledge of destination through own initiative: Yes versus No				8.729	1.941	<0.001
Knowledge of destination—other: Yes versus No				11.387	4.827	0.018
Means of transport—car: Yes versus No						

(continued)

Table 13.3 (continued)

Expenditure on accommodation model	Stage 1			Stage 2		
	Estimate	S.E.	P-value	Estimate	S.E.	P-value
Means of transport—bus: Yes versus No				−11.955	3.598	0.001
Means of transport—train: Yes versus No				29.110	5.531	<0.001
Means of transport—plane: Yes versus No				6.817	1.560	<0.001
R^2	0.436					
Residents Úbeda/Baeza: Yes versus No	−1.640	0.157	<0.001			
Cultural activities—guided routes: Yes versus No	0.816	0.126	<0.001			
Cultural activities—shopping in the area: Yes versus No	−1.027	0.200	<0.001	10.072	2.388	<0.001
Cultural activities—going for drinks: Yes versus No	0.355	0.111	0.001	4.545	0.804	<0.001
Cultural activities—going for *tapas*: Yes versus No	−1.509	0.292	<0.001	−12.135	2.500	<0.001
Cultural activities—other: Yes versus No	0.801	0.190	<0.001	6.126	1.054	<0.001
R^2	0.124					
Personality—open-minded: Yes versus No	−0.389	0.109	<0.001	−3.088	1.026	0.003
Personality—jovial: Yes versus No	−1.068	0.198	<0.001	−3.739	1.152	0.001
Personality —affectionate: Yes versus No	−0.128	0.029	<0.001	−9.339	2.666	<0.001
Satisfaction with tourism signage	−0.182	0.062	0.003			
Satisfaction with landscapes	0.153	0.050	0.002	−1.385	0.429	0.001
Satisfaction with internet access				1.225	0.399	0.002
Satisfaction with roads and communications				0.771	0.257	0.003
Satisfaction with cleanliness				2.142	0.421	<0.001
Satisfaction with health services				2.392	0.439	<0.001
Satisfaction with tourist information				−1.627	0.237	<0.001
R^2	0.115					

Sources Own elaboration

The tourists with a lower probability of spending on accommodation were those who stayed are in rural houses/rented accommodation/owned property. Furthermore, the amount spent on accommodation was significantly lower when 1–2 star hotels (Marrocu et al., 2015 and Amir et al., 2015) or rural houses/rented accommodation/owned property were chosen than when staying in hotels of three stars or more.

The probability of spending on accommodation was significantly lower when the tourist did not seek accommodation on the Internet and did not seek places to visit. However, those who stayed and who had not used the Internet to seek places to visit spent significantly more on accommodation than those who did use it. Furthermore, Internet searches for restaurants and places to visit were directly associated with the higher or lower cost of accommodation, respectively. With respect to knowledge of the destination and its association with expenditure on accommodation, no relationship was found between the variables and expenditure on accommodation, although it was observed that those with prior knowledge of the destination spent significantly more. Tourists who travelled by coach spent less on accommodation than those who used other means of transport.

In the case of tourists accompanied by residents (Brida et al., 2013) of Úbeda/Baeza, the probability of spending on accommodation was significantly lower. Persons who followed guided routes, went out for drinks and engaged in cultural activities showed a higher probability of spending on accommodation, while persons who shopped in the area or went out for *tapas* were less likely to spend on accommodation.

Persons with an open-minded personality spent less on accommodation than the rest. Jovial and affectionate persons were the least likely to incur this expenditure.

Those who expressed greatest satisfaction with tourism signage and landscapes were least likely to spend on accommodation and, if they did, they spent less. Those with the highest probability and the highest spending on accommodation were those persons who were most satisfied with Internet access, roads and communications, cleanliness and health services. Greater satisfaction with tourist information implies lower expenditure on accommodation.

13.5   Conclusion and Implications

Firstly, it should be noted that the objectives proposed at the beginning of this research have been achieved. The variables that influence expenditure by tourists in the cities studied have effectively been identified, even detecting some factors hitherto not identified in the literature.

The socio-demographic variables of the sample analyzed in this study show that tourists who visit Úbeda and Baeza are persons of between 45 and 65 years of age, with a university education, Spanish nationality, who are not accompanied by residents of these destinations, who are employed and who consider that they have a comfortable life.

All of the interviewees would recommend Úbeda and Baeza as destinations to visit and would return. The trip is organized privately by the tourists, using the Internet, especially to reserve or purchase accommodation, and using a private car to reach the destinations. Furthermore, the majority of tourists who visit these destinations travel in groups of 4 or 5 persons, for a mean stay of 2–3 days.

Most of the interviewees were not accompanied by residents of the area and stated that they found what they expected in the place visited. In general, they make short daytrips, follow guided routes and go out for *tapas*. Most of them consider themselves to be open-minded, and they visit these destinations for holiday or leisure reasons, declaring a very high degree of satisfaction with the visit.

The results obtained after the application of the analytical model have allowed us to determine that there is a relationship between expenditure on accommodation and the age, educational level, nationality, duration of stay, category of accommodation, places visited during the trip, loyalty to the destiny, type of tourist and the accompanying person, participation in activities in the destination, reasons for the trip and satisfaction obtained by the visitors from the trip. The relationship is as indicated by previous authors who have addressed this question. Therefore, the hypothesis that gave rise to this research has been verified.

Furthermore, this study has made it possible to discover new variables that influence the expenditure on accommodation of tourists in World Heritage Cities. Specifically, it has been demonstrated that, depending on the values and personality of the tourist, they will have a specific pattern of behavior with respect to expenditure on accommodation in World Heritage Cities. Moreover, it has been shown that whether the tourists stay in Úbeda or in Baeza will influence both the probability of spending on accommodation, which is greater in the case of those accommodated in Baeza, and also the amount of expenditure on accommodation finally incurred, which is higher when the tourist is accommodated in Úbeda. The fact that the tourist is accompanied by residents in the destinations under study also has an influence, since they tend to spend less on accommodation. The intention to return to the destination in the future and the repetition of the visit are variables that also impact on spending on accommodation in the cities analyzed.

A more in-depth study has also been made of the influence on expenditure on accommodation of the type of activities undertaken in the destination. The analysis has also looked more profoundly into the influence of tourist satisfaction on tourism expenditure on accommodation in these cities, since the authors analyzed did not study this variable.

The analysis of the "use of Internet" variable shows the impact that the Internet has on tourism expenditure on accommodation in these cities, and that the impact depends on the use made. In order to reach a grounded conclusion on this aspect, a more detailed analysis has been made, distinguishing between the different uses that can be made of the Internet and which have a different influence on the expenditure on accommodation of tourists. Furthermore, it has been determined that prior knowledge of the destination and how that information was obtained by tourists directly affects spending on accommodation in the cities analyzed, as does the fact that the tourist has made prior bookings.

The research has a number of limitations that must be recognized and which must be overcome in future studies. Firstly, the survey was performed in specific months of the year (June, July, August and September 2016), and so the final result may be biased. The special relevance of seasonality in the tourism sector—which can even change the preferences of tourists, depending on the moment at which they visit the destination, requires that the survey be taken over a longer period. In all events, it should be noted that the period when the survey was taken was the high season.

Secondly, with respect to the model used, and as has already been stated, it was not possible to adjust a single multivariate model with the data available in the four blocks of information studied due to problems of overestimation of parameters and of co-linearity between variables in different blocks, as well as asymptotic problems in the adjustment of the model as a consequence of the high number of parameters simultaneously estimated. In this regard, it is necessary to continue testing with other types of models that will allow these limitations to be overcome and to estimate the variables that influence the total expenditure made by tourists visiting these cities.

Despite these limitations, the novel aspect contained in this study with respect to existing literature is the fact that it has identified the variables that condition expenditure on accommodation by tourists who visit the cities studied.

This information is enormously useful to policymakers, destination managers and companies, since it informs decision-making with respect to the measures to be taken in order to attract and retain tourists with a higher mean daily spend. In this way, the stakeholders can focus their marketing efforts, develop products, activities and services that will increase tourist interest in visiting these destinations, improve the quality of the services and resources which are of more interest to the visitor in order to increase their satisfaction, etc.

Finally, given the volume of information provided by this study, there are questions pending which it has not been possible to address and which we intend to analyze in future research. Specifically, it would be interesting to segment the tourists on the basis of the expenditure incurred on the different items considered. This segmentation would furthermore allow us to characterize each one of the segments identified, determine the composition of the expenditure, the level of satisfaction of each segment with respect to the destinations visited, etc.

References

Amir, S., Osman, M., Bachok, S., & Ibrahim, M. (2015). Understanding domestic and international tourists' expenditure pattern in Melaka, Malaysia: Result of CHAID analysis. *Procedia Social and Behavioral Sciences, 172*, 390–397.

Andrade, T. G. (2016). Perfil del turista que visita la ciudad de Cuenca, influido por su reconocimiento como ciudad patrimonio de la humanidad. http://dspace.ucuenca.edu.ec/handle/123456789/26148.

Blundell, R., & Meghir, C. (1987). Bivariate alternatives to the tobit model. *Journal of Econometrics, 34*, 179–200.

Brida, J. G., Disegna, M., & Scuderi, R. (2013a). Visitor to two types of museums: do expenditure patterns differ? *Tourism Economics, 19*(5), 1027–1047.

Brida, J. G., Monterubbianes, P. D., & Zapata-Aguirre, S. (2013b). Análisis de los factores que infuencian el gasto de los turistas: el caso de los visitantes de museos de Medellin. *Revista de Economia del Rosario, 16*(1), 149–170.

Brida, J. G., Pulina, M., Riaño, E., & Zapata, S. (2013c). Cruise passengers in a homeport: A market analysis. *Tourism Geographies, 16*(1), 68–87.

Cárdenas-García, P. J., Pulido-Fernández, J. I., & Mudarra-Fernández, A. B. (2014). Direct economic impact of tourism on World Heritage Cities: An approach to measurement in emerging destinations. *Czech Journal of Tourism, 3*(2), 91–106.

Carlevaro, F., Croissant, Y., & Hoareau, S. (2012). Multiple hurdle tobit models in R: The mhurdle Package. ftp://mirror3.mirror.garr.it/mirrors/CRAN/web/packages/mhurdle/vignettes/mhurdle.pdf.

Cragg, J. G. (1971). Some statistical models for limited dependent variables with applications for the demand for durable goods. *Econometrica, 39*(5), 829–844.

Deaton, A., & Irish, M. (1984). A statistical model for zero expenditures in household budgets. *Journal of Public Economics, 23,* 59–80.

Disegna, M., Scuderi, R., & Brida, J. G. (2012). Visitors of two types of museums: Do expenditure patterns differ? *Tourism Economics, 19*(5), 1027–1047. https://doi.org/10.5367/te.2013.0295.

Esteban, A., Mondejar, J. A., & Cordente, M. (2009). Segmentación de turistas en una Ciudad Patrimonio de la Humanidad. Turismo cultural en ciudades Patrimonio de la Humanidad: 107–128. Coord. by Juan Antonio Mondéjar Jiménez, Miguel Angel Gómez Borja, 2009. ISBN 978-84-8427-586-2, 11–52.

Lara, F., & López-Guzmán, T. (2004). El turismo como motor de desarrollo económico en ciudades patrimonio de la humanidad. *Pasos, 2*(2), 243–256.

Marrocu, E., Paci, R., & Zara, A. (2015). Micro-economic determinants of tourist expenditure: A quantile regression approach. *Tourism Management, 50,* 13–30.

McFadden, D. (1974). The measurement of urban travel demand. *Journal of Public Economics, 3,* 303–328.

Molina, A., Martín-Consuegra, D., Esteban, A., & Díaz, E. (2007). Segmentación de la demanda turisticas: Un analisis aplicado a un destino de turismo cultural. *Revista de Análisis Turístico, 4*(2), 36–48.

Pulido-Fernández, J. I., Cárdenas-García, P. J., & Carrillo-Hidalgo, I. (2016). Trip cultural activities and tourism expenditure in emerging urban-cultural destinations. *International Journal of Tourism Research, 18*(4), 286–296.

Serra, J., Borges, M. R., & Marujo, M. N. (2016). Expenditure pattern analysis of cultural tourists at World Heritage Sites: Empirical evidence based on CHAID analysis. In ATLAS Annual Conference 2016 Tourism, Lifestyles and Locations Canterbury, United Kingdom, September 14–16, 2016, Book of extended abstracts. ISBN 978-90-75775-91-4.

Siebinga, A. S. (2013). *Multicolored or black and white. The effect of World Heritage listing on curacao tourism.* Roterdam: Erasmus Universiteit Rotterdam.

Tobin, J. (1958). Estimation of relationships for limited dependent variables. *Econometrica, 26*(1), 24–36.

Troitiño, M. A. (1998). Turismo y desarrollo sostenible en las ciudades historicas con patrimonio arquitectónico-monumental. *Estudios Turísticos, 137,* 5–53.

Vuong, Q. H. (1989). Likelihood ratio tests for model selection and non-nested hypothesis. *Econometrica, 57*(2), 307–333.

Webster, J., & Watson, R. T. (2002). Analyzing the past to prepare for the future: Writing a literature review. *MIS Quarterly, 26*(2), 13–23. http://uicphdmis.pbworks.com/w/file/fetch/54311383/Writing%20a%20Literature%20Review.pdf.

Chapter 14
Analysis of the Spatial Distribution Pattern of Tourist Activity: An Application to the Volume of Travellers in Extremadura

Cristina Rodríguez-Rangel and Marcelino Sánchez-Rivero

14.1 Introduction

Spatial econometrics emerged as a branch of general econometrics due to the need for developing a set of techniques that would allow the adequate treatment of data affected by the so-called spatial effects: spatial autocorrelation or dependence and spatial heterogeneity. The proliferation of georeferenced databases motivates a greater need for knowing what is happening with those data in their spatial distribution, and especially whether this distribution involves any structure that should be known in order to better understand the relationships that occur between the variables in space. Anselin (2001) defines it as "a section of econometrics dedicated to the treatment of spatial interaction (spatial dependence) and spatial structure (spatial heterogeneity) in cross-section and panel data regression models". As can be deduced from Anselin's definition, there are two main effects that motivate the appearance of a subfield within traditional econometrics: spatial heterogeneity and spatial dependence or autocorrelation.

Spatial heterogeneity or lack of structural stability arose as a consequence of using different spatial units to explain a single phenomenon, and it can be solved with today's techniques for the treatment of time series (Moreno & Vayá, 2004). Indeed, as the authors indicate, the effect of heterogeneity, although it is related to the unequal distribution of a variable in space, does not require the development of new techniques to be treated, since this can be achieved with techniques that have already been proposed by traditional econometrics.

C. Rodríguez-Rangel (✉) · M. Sánchez-Rivero
Faculty of Economics and Business Studies, University of Extremadura,
Avda Elvas, s/n, 06006 Badajoz, Spain
e-mail: mcrisrod@unex.es

M. Sánchez-Rivero
e-mail: sanriver@unex.es

© Springer Nature Switzerland AG 2019
A. Artal-Tur et al. (eds.), *Trends in Tourist Behavior*,
Tourism, Hospitality & Event Management,
https://doi.org/10.1007/978-3-030-11160-1_14

Thereby, the present work is focused on analysing the second spatial effect, i.e. spatial dependence or autocorrelation. The emergence of spatial econometrics is motivated by the fact that the multidirectionality of this effect cannot be treated with the traditional econometric techniques. Spatial dependence or autocorrelation is defined as the phenomenon that takes place when there is a relationship between what happens in a specific point in space and what occurs in other points of such space (Anselin, 1988).

Considering this definition, it can be inferred that the presence of spatial effects is expected, mainly, in those variables that measure aspects of economic activities that are especially linked to their development in a specific space. In regional economics, this effect has been studied in different variables, such as production, unemployment, available income, etc. Tourism stands out as an activity that is strongly related to the geographic space in which it is developed (Sánchez, 2008). Therefore, it is surprising to find very few studies in the literature to analyse the distribution patterns of tourist variables in space.

The aim of the present work is to study the distribution patterns of a variable that is usually associated with tourism, i.e. "the number of travellers", to determine whether it is randomly distributed in space or, on the contrary, there is spatial autocorrelation or dependence. This will ultimately show that the modelling of any phenomenon related to tourism will require the use of the techniques developed by spatial econometrics for the treatment of data affected by the spatial effects.

To this end, the present work is distributed in the following manner: after this first introduction section that describes the objective of this investigation, the next section presents a review of the existing literature, highlighting the main contributions up to the present day in the field of spatial econometrics, especially in the techniques proposed for the exploratory analysis of spatial data. Then, another section describes the methodology used to achieve the objectives of the study. After the methodology, the main results obtained from the analysis conducted are presented and, lastly, a final section includes the main conclusions and implications.

14.2 Literature Review

The analysis of spatial data has gained great interest in the last few decades, especially in those fields of regional economics that are strongly related to their development in a specific geographic space (Button & Kulkarni, 2001; Chasco & Vicéns, 2000; López, Palacios, & Ruiz, 2001; Moreno & Vayá, 2000, 2004).

Tourism stands out among these activities for being clearly affected by its location; therefore, it is obviously one of the fields in which studies are being conducted on the use of techniques proposed by spatial econometrics (Barros & Matias, 2007; Ma, Hong, & Zhang, 2015; Pavlyuk, 2010, 2013; Sanchez, 2008; Sánchez, Sánchez, & Rengifo, 2013, 2018; Zhou, Maumbe, Deng, & Selin, 2015).

The first works carried out in this regard can be attributed to Student, who in the year 1914 conducted the first studies in this topic, with the aim of understanding how spatial effects can influence the validity of statistical methods.

Kmenta (1971) stated that the hypothesis of the independence of observations in cross-section data was the most questionable one, especially in specific cases. It was in the field of geography where researchers began to wonder about the lack of reliability of this hypothesis of traditional statistics. Thus, Cliff and Ord (1973, 1981) published their pioneer studies about the lack of independence that usually occurs between the observations of cross-section units.

An important milestone in the future evolution of these new techniques is their compilation under the specific name of "spatial econometrics", which was proposed by Paelinck and Klaasen (1979).

The first studies conducted in this field were focused on the proposal of techniques to detect the presence of spatial autocorrelation between the observations of a sample. In this line, the formal indices proposed by Moran (1948) and Geary (1954) constitute the first tools to allow diagnosing the presence, or absence, of spatial autocorrelation between the observations of a variable.

Despite these first efforts, the great development of spatial econometrics did not take place until the 1980s, with the works of Anselin (1980, 1988), Arbia (1989), Bloommestein (1983) and Cliff and Ord (1981), which are considered to be the basic studies that lay the foundation for the methodology of spatial econometric analysis.

These works constitute the basic pillars on which spatial econometrics develops; in fact, as Chasco (2003) pointed out, the book "Spatial Econometrics: Methods and Models", by Anselin (1988), has been considered as the reference proceedings book for studies conducted in this topic since the 1990s.

Later, other studies have been published in journals of regional economics that posed specific contributions for the advancement of this subfield of econometrics, such as the series of articles by Anselin and Florax (1995), and Anselin and Rey (1997).

Anselin and Florax (1995) considered that a convergence was taking place between different factors that were promoting an increasing interest for spatial econometrics, such as: a greater interest for the role of space and spatial interaction in social networks, the availability of large georeferenced economic databases and the development of an efficient and inexpensive technology that allows the application of these techniques, through computerised geographic information systems, to carry out the analysis of spatial data.

Despite this trend, it cannot be considered that nowadays spatial econometrics had managed to become a reference in applied analysis; this fact is confirmed by its low presence in proceedings books of econometrics, which barely mention these techniques. As Moreno and Vayá (2000) indicate, the number of specific publications in the present time is still very low in this topic, especially in the Spanish scope.

Chasco (2003) studied the aspects that are hindering the dissemination of these techniques among the research community, concluding that the convergence of factors such as the priority to develop prediction techniques, the scarcity of microterritorial statistical information and the absence of useful and inexpensive software, were contributing to the poor acceptance of spatial econometric techniques among researchers.

Now that some of these limitations are being overcome, on the one hand, a large variety of specific software, GIS (geographic information systems), can be found in the marked, which include the use of spatial statistic techniques. Among the most commonly used, it is worth highlighting: SpaceStat, developed by Luc Anselin (1992, 1995a), ArcGIS and S+SpatialStats, among others.

On the other hand, the possibilities offered by new technologies to obtain geo-referenced data, such as those of applications that allow geolocalization in smart-phones, "geotagging" in social networks, and GPS technology, among others, help researchers to analyse the movements of tourists in their destinations (Shoval and Ahas, 2016), obtaining, also, data with a high level of reliability and precision.

All this leads to think of a favourable evolution of spatial econometric techniques, now that some of the barriers that initially hindered their development are being overcome.

On the other hand, the present study does not suggest that the techniques proposed by spatial econometrics should now be used in every case. However, given their suitability and validity when a variable is affected by some of the so-called spatial effects, first of all, it should be analysed whether this is happening, and, secondly, when the existence of this effect in the analysed variable is confirmed, this should be treated with the methods proposed to that end. In this sense, the analysis of a variable's spatial autocorrelation becomes a fundamental part of a first exploratory phase of any analysis. It is considered that there is autocorrelation when a relationship is confirmed between what takes place in a specific point of a given space and what occurs in other points of that space (Anselin, 1988).

For the diagnosis of autocorrelation, a series of formal indicators have been pro-posed, which allow confirming the presence, or absence, of this spatial effect in a variable. Among the most commonly used, it is worth highlighting the indices pro-posed by Moran, with the global I test (1948), the Geary's c test (1954) and the G(d) test of Getis and Ord (1992).

When analysing the spatial autocorrelation of a variable with any of these pro-posed indices, three different scenarios can take place. The first scenario is the lack of spatial autocorrelation, that is, those cases in which the variable analysed is dis-tributed in space following a random pattern. The second scenario is the detection of a positive spatial autocorrelation pattern. In this scenario, the presence of a specific phenomenon in a region leads to its expansion to other nearby regions (Moreno and Vayá, 2004). In the specific case of tourism, the presence of this type of autocor-relation poses the presence of similar values of the tourist variable between nearby destinations, which means that there is a "contagion" effect (Sánchez, 2008). This would be the case of tourist attractions, or the lack of these, that cause the attraction of tourists in nearby locations. The last possible scenario is the presence of negative spatial autocorrelation, when the presence of a phenomenon in a region prevents or hinders its appearance in neighbour regions (Moreno and Vayá, 2004). In the field of tourism, this is known as the "absorption" effect (Sánchez, 2008).

As was previously stated, the exploratory phase of any analysis will require verifying whether the study variable is, or is not, affected by spatial autocorrelation, in order to determine the most suitable techniques to treat it. The aim of the present work is to analyse the distribution pattern of the variable "number of travellers" in Extremadura. To this end, the next section describes the methodology used to reach this objective.

14.3 Methodology

The methodology used in the present work lies in exploratory spatial data analysis (ESDA), which emerged as a specific part of exploratory data analysis (EDA) with the aim of focusing on the specific treatment of spatial data.

Therefore, it is defined as the set of techniques that allow describing spatial distributions, identifying atypical localizations (spatial outliers), discovering schemes of spatial association (spatial cluster) and suggesting spatial structures, as well as other forms of spatial heterogeneity (Anselin, 1999). As can be understood, ESDA is characterised by combining statistical analysis with a graphical-geographic-cartographic approach. Thereby, the development of specific modules within GISs has posed a great advancement for these techniques. Within this set of more general techniques that is ESDA, the present work is focused on analysing the phenomenon of spatial dependence or autocorrelation. To this end, the ArcGIS software was used, which, under a geostatistical perspective, allows conducting the analysis of spatial dependence or autocorrelation employing the most commonly used formal indices.

The study variable was the number of travellers that visited Extremadura in June 2015, with the data provided by the Tourism Observatory of Extremadura, using a sample of 270 establishments, of which 131 were hotels and the rest were non-hotel accommodations. The study of spatial autocorrelation or dependence of the mentioned variable in the territory of Extremadura was analysed from a double perspective: global and local. The contrast of spatial dependence in the global perspective was used to identify spatial tendencies or structures in a specific geographic space. To achieve this, the indicators proposed by Moran (1948) and Getis and Ord (1992) were employed. These indicators were the first formulations proposed in the literature as statistical measurements of the effect of spatial autocorrelation. Moreover, they are characterised by their capacity to summarise a general scheme of dependence in a single indicator (Moreno & Vayá, 2000). Both contrasts pose an objective statistical criterion that allows confirming or rejecting the presence of spatial tendencies or structures in the distribution of a variable. In both tests, the null hypothesis to be contrasted was the absence of spatial dependence, that is, the randomness of the variable's distribution in the selected territory.

Moran's I test (1948) is given by the following formula:

$$I = \frac{N}{S_0} \frac{\sum_{ij}^{N} w_{ij}(y_i - \bar{y})(y_j - \bar{y})}{\sum_{i=1}^{N}(y_i - \bar{y})} \quad i \neq j. \tag{14.1}$$

where;

w_{ij} is the element of the matrix of spatial weights that correspond to the pair (i, j);
s_0 is the sum of the spatial weights $\sum_i \sum_j w_{ij}$;
$\bar{y}$ mean or expected value of the variable;
N   number of observations.

Upon row standardisation of the matrix of spatial weights $S_0 = N$, index I adopts the following expression:

$$I = \frac{\sum_i \sum_j w_{ij}(y_i - \bar{y})(y_j - \bar{y})}{\sum_{i=1}^{N}(y_i - \bar{y})}. \tag{14.2}$$

According to Cliff and Ord (1981), when the sample size is large enough, it is distributed as a normal standard N(0, 1). The inferential process uses the standardised values (z) of each of them, obtained by the quotient of the difference between the initial value and the theoretical mean divided by the standard deviation, as shown in the following formula:

$$z = \frac{I - E[I]}{SD[I]}. \tag{14.3}$$

The interpretation of the values obtained in the test was carried out in the following manner: non-significant values of the I test led to accept the null hypothesis of the variable's random distribution in the study space. On the other hand, significantly positive values of the variable (above 1.96 at 5% significance level) indicated the presence of positive spatial autocorrelation, that is, they indicated that it was possible to identify values of the variable, high or low, spatially grouped in space to a greater extent than expected if they were following a random pattern. Significantly negative values of the variable (below -1.96 at 5% significance level) indicated the existence of negative spatial autocorrelation, that is, the detection of a non-grouping pattern of similar values (high or low) of the variable, more obvious than expected in a random spatial pattern.

To complete the global analysis of the variable's distribution, the set of indicators proposed by Getis and Ord (1992) were used, which stand out for employing a different criterion to measure spatial autocorrelation, based on the indices of distance and spatial concentration.

The calculation of this index requires the definition of a critical distance (d); from such distance, an influence radius is established, from which it is determined which units are neighbours, based on whether or not they are within the influence radius determined by the critical distance.

Its expression is as follows:

$$G(d) = \frac{\sum_{i=0}^{n} \sum_{j=0}^{n} w_{ij}(d) y_i y_j}{\sum_{i=0}^{N} \sum_{j=0}^{N} y_i y_j} \quad for \ i \neq j \qquad (14.4)$$

where two pairs of spatial units i and j are neighbours if they are within a given distance d, with w_{ij} being 1 when this is the case, or 0 in the opposite case.

The statistical significance is verified through the standardised index z, which is distributed asymptotically according to a normal $N(0, 1)$. The interpretation of this test for those cases that showed statistical significance was the following: a positive (or negative) z value, above 1.96 in absolute value, indicated a tendency of similar high (or low) values to concentrate. Once the distribution pattern of the variable "travellers in the region", the analysis was completed with the study of local spatial autocorrelation. One of the main limitations of these global autocorrelation tests is that they are unable to detect local spatial structures, i.e. hotspots or coldspots that can or cannot expand to the global pattern structure (Anselin, 1993, 1995b; Getis and Ord, 1992; Moreno and Vayá, 2000; Openshaw, 1993; Tiefeldsdorf and Boots, 1997; Vayá and Suriñach, 1996).

To overcome this limitation, the local spatial autocorrelation tests were developed. The aim of these tests is to detect specially high or low values (hotspots or coldspots) of a variable with respect to its mean values. They are characterised by being calculated for each of the spatial units to be analysed, thus they allow detecting which of these units concentrate higher or lower values than expected in a homogenous distribution. In the study of local spatial autocorrelation, two different scenarios can take place, in contrast with global spatial autocorrelation, as stated by Vayá and Suriñach (1996). In the first scenario, a distribution pattern of concentration or dispersion of values is not detected in a specific space at the global level, while there are small clusters in which high (or low) values of the variable are concentrated. In the second scenario, in the presence of a global distribution pattern, some spatial units contribute to a greater extent to that global indicator. Thereby, the analysis of autocorrelation at the local level is a good complement for the study of global distribution.

Local Indicators of Spatial Association (LISA) proposed by Anselin (1995a, 1995b) and the set of G_i indices of Getis and Ord (1992) and Ord and Getis (1995), are the most commonly used indicators for the study of spatial autocorrelation at the local level. Anselin (1995b) proposed a set of local indicators of spatial association whose purpose is, on the one hand, to determine significant local spatial groups, i.e. clusters, and, on the other hand, to detect spatial instability, understood as the presence of atypical values. Among the indicators proposed by this author, it is worth highlighting Moran's local I_i index, which is expressed as follows:

$$I_i = \frac{z_i}{\sum_i z_i^2 / N} \sum_{j \in j_i} w_{ij} z_j \qquad (14.5)$$

where z_i is the normalised value of spatial unit i, and j_i is the set of neighbour spatial units near i. Under the hypothesis of random distribution, the expectancy of the index is:

$$E_A(I_i) = -\frac{w_i}{N-1} \qquad (14.6)$$

where: w_i is the sum of all the elements of the row of unit i.

The hypothesis that standardised I_i is distributed as a normal $N(0, 1)$ was assumed. The interpretation of the standardised index was performed in the following manner: a positively high z-score value (above 1.96 at 5% significance level) indicated the presence of clusters of high, or low, values of the variable. On the other hand, a significantly negative value (below -1.96 at 5% significance level) indicated the existence of spatial outliers. Getis and Ord (1992) proposed their set of G_i indicators for the analysis of local spatial autocorrelation.

First of all, they proposed the G_i index, which has the following formula:

$$G_i(d) = \frac{\sum_{j=1}^{N} w_{ij}(d)Y_j}{\sum_{j=1}^{N} Y_j} \quad j \neq i \qquad (14.7)$$

where Y is the variable of interest (not normalised) and W_{ij} (d) are the elements of the contiguity matrix W for an established d distance. Then, the authors proposed an alternative to their index, which includes the observation for which the index is calculated, that is, the previous $j \neq i$ restriction is removed. This new index is expressed as follows:

$$G_i^*(d) = \frac{\sum_{j=1}^{N} W_{ij}(d)Y_j}{\sum_{j=1}^{N} Y_j} \qquad (14.8)$$

Both indices have two important restrictions. First of all, they can only be used with positive natural variables, and, second of all, they require symmetric contiguity matrices that are not standardised by rows. In order to overcome both limitations, Ord and Getis (1995) respecified their indices with the following expressions:

$$New\ G_i(d) = \frac{\sum_{j=1}^{N} W_{ij}Y_j - W_i\bar{y}(i)}{S(i)\{[((N-1)S_{1i}) - W_i^2]/(N-2)\}^{1/2}} j \neq i \qquad (14.9)$$

$$New\ G_i^*(d) = \frac{\sum_{j=1}^{N} W_{ij}Y_j - W_i^*\bar{y}}{\{[(NS_{1i}^*) - W_i^{*2}]/(N-1)\}^{1/2}} \qquad (14.10)$$

where; $S(i)^2 = \frac{1}{N-1}\sum_j (Y_j - \bar{y}(i))^2$; $\bar{y}(i) = \frac{1}{N-1}\sum_j Y_j$; $S_{1i} = \sum W_{ij}^2\ para\ j \neq i$; $S_{1i}^* = \sum_j W_{ij}^2$.

As can be observed, these indices were obtained from the standardisation of the previous ones. Once such standardisation was performed, the results obtained were interpreted in the following manner: a significantly positive (or negative) value indicated the presence of clusters of high (or low) values.

It is important to point out the differences in the interpretation of the obtained results between the two contrasts explained. While the set of G_i indices detect positive spatial autocorrelation, understood as the presence of groups of high values, and negative spatial autocorrelation, as groups of low values, Moran's I_i index allows identifying also spatial outliers. In this case, the diagnosis of positive spatial autocorrelation is understood as the presence of groups of similar values, either high or low, and negative spatial autocorrelation involves the existence of dissimilar values grouped in space. Therefore, as was the case for global indices, the combined calculation of both indices contributes to complete and enrich the study of local spatial autocorrelation. Once the different contrasts to be used in the present study have been analysed, the next section presents the main results obtained from the analysis of spatial autocorrelation, at a local and global level, of the variable "number of travellers that visited Extremadura".

14.4 Results

The present study was based on a sample of 270 establishments in the region of Extremadura (Spain), which provided their data of travellers who used their facilities in July 2015. The exploratory analysis of the distribution pattern of the variable "number of travellers" in Extremadura was conducted, firstly, from a general perspective, including the total of travellers that visited the region regardless of the type of accommodation used. In a second phase, this first analysis was completed with the study of the distribution of travellers based on the type of accommodation used, considering two large groups: hotels and non-hotel accommodations. The reason why it was decided to conduct this separation was the difference in the accommodation capacity of each of the establishment types to be analysed, which could influence the results depending on the variable of interest used.

For the thorough analysis of the distribution pattern of the variable in the whole territory, the most commonly used global contrasts of spatial autocorrelation were employed: Moran's I and Getis and Ord G(d). To carry out the analysis, the ArcGIS 10.3 software was used. This software works from a geostatistical perspective and in its Spatial Statistics Tools module it allows analysing spatial autocorrelation with the most commonly used formal indices. To conduct the analysis from a global perspective, it was decided to specify the neighbourhood relationship according to the criterion of reverse distance, using euclidean distance as a method and proceeding to the row standardisation of the matrix of spatial weights. Moreover, in both contrasts, the null hypothesis to verify is the random spatial distribution of the variable in the whole territory. The following table shows the results obtained from the global Moran's I test and Getis and Ord's general G using the ArcGIS software for the analysis of travellers in Extremadura.

Table 14.1 Results of global Moran's *I* test and Getis and Ord's *G* in the total number of travellers in Extremadura

Global Moran's I		General G summary	
Moran's index	0.180913	Observed general G	0.006051
Expected index	−0.003717	Expected general G	0.003717
Variance	0.001806	Variance	0.000000
z-score	4.344949	z-score	4.131847
p-value	0.000014	p-value	0.000036

Source Own elaboration using ArcGIS 10.3

As can be seen in the obtained results in the Table 14.1, the null hypothesis of random distribution of the variable in the whole study region is rejected with 1% significance level. Considering also Moran's index and z-score, it can be concluded that the distribution of travellers in the entire territory shows a concentration of similar values of that variable. In other words, the values of the variable "travellers" tend to concentrate in high or low values in the study region. To confirm the data obtained, and also to amplify their information, the next step was to carry out the contrast proposed by Getis and Ord with their general G(d) to analyse the distribution pattern of the number of travellers in the whole of the territory studied.

As was the case with Moran's test, the p-value obtained indicated that the hypothesis that the travellers are randomly distributed in the territory of Extremadura had to be rejected, with 1% significance level. From the analysis of the G value and z-score, it was also concluded that the variable tends to concentrate in space in high values. Therefore, in view of the obtained results, it can be concluded that the travellers that visit Extremadura are not randomly distributed in the territory, that the differences found are statistically significant and that the variable tends to concentrate in high values in this region. In order to enrich the results obtained from this analysis, it was decided to separate the data into two large groups. On the one hand, hotels, for which a subsample of 131 establishments was created, and, on the other hand, non-hotel accommodations, whose subsample consisted of a total of 139 establishments.

The reason for this division was the inherent differences between the two types of establishment, which are mainly due to their different guest capacity. Therefore, the next step was to conduct the same analysis for each of the mentioned establishment types into which the sample was divided. Firstly, for hotels, the following results were obtained.

The results obtained in Moran's I test, Table 14.2, show that, in the case of travellers who stay in hotels, the null hypothesis of random spatial distribution of the variable must be rejected, with 1% significance level. Furthermore, the z-score shows a positive value, which indicates that the values of the variable tend to follow a concentration pattern of similar values in space. Likewise, the Getis and Ord's test confirmed the obtained results. As can be observed, the p-value suggests the need to reject the null hypothesis of random distribution of the number of travellers in

Table 14.2 Global Moran's I test and Getis and Ord's general G (d) for travellers in hotels

Global Moran's I		G general summary	
Moran's index	0.133746	Observed general G	0.009735
Expected index	−0.007692	Expected general G	0.007692
Variance	0.002885	Variance	0.000001
z-score	2.633144	z-score	2.493937
p-value	0.008460	p-value	0.012634

Source Own elaboration using ArcGIS 10.3

Table 14.3 Global Moran's I test and Getis and Ord's general G (d) for travellers in non-hotel establishments

Global Moran's I		General G summary	
Moran's index	0.022905	Observed general G	0.008571
Expected index	−0.07246	Expected general G	0.007246
Variance	0.002568	Variance	0.000008
z-score	0.594973	z-score	0.479609
p-value	0.551861	p-value	0.631506

Source Own elaboration using ArcGIS 10.3

the whole territory, with 5% significance level. Moreover, the interpretation of the z-score indicates that travellers in hotels tend to concentrate spatially in high values.

In order to confirm whether the distribution pattern detected up to this point according to the spatial autocorrelation tests was the same for the two establishment types into which the sample was subdivided, the present analysis of global distribution was completed with the study of the variable "number of travellers that stayed in non-hotel accommodation establishments".

In view of the results obtained, Table 14.3, in the contrasts conducted, in both cases, the null hypothesis of random distribution of the variable cannot be rejected. Therefore, it is not discarded that travellers who stay in non-hotel establishments are randomly distributed in the analysed territory. Considering the different results obtained, it can be asserted that the concentrated distribution pattern of travellers in the region is motivated by the behaviour of the travellers who choose hotels as the accommodation option. As has been described in the previous section, the study of autocorrelation at the local level helps explaining the results obtained in the analysis at the global level, allowing to determine whether the concentration or dispersion pattern is governed by some specific spatial units, or detecting the concentration of units affected by spatial autocorrelation that were not identified in the global study.

Thereby, in order to complete this analysis, the next step was to conduct the study at the local level, using the local Moran's I_i, and the New G_i^* to carry out the Getis and Ord's analysis of hotspots and coldspots. First, Fig. 14.1 shows the results of

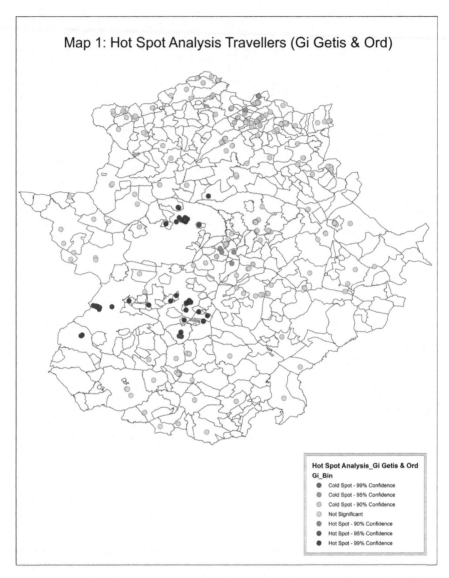

Fig. 14.1 Map hot spot analysis travellers (G_i Getis & Ord). *Source* Own elaboration using ArcGIS 10.3 (Color figure online)

the local Getis and Ord's test, indicating the hotspots and coldspots of high and low values of the number of travellers in the different points of the territory for all the establishments of the sample. In all the cases analysed, the fixed distance band criterion was used to establish the neighbourhood relationship, using the euclidean distance as a reference.

As can be seen in the map, there are some hotspots and coldspots at the local level in specific areas of the territory. Thus, there are hotspots between the two main cities: Merida and Badajoz. Their influence area reaches the closest towns, where the existence of hotspots is detected, with 99% confidence level, in which the concentration of travellers is higher than expected in a random distribution pattern. The same case was diagnosed in the third main city of the region, Caceres, where the existence of hotspots of the variable was detected, whose influence reaches the closest towns.

On the other hand, there were also units in which the variable analysed showed significantly low values. Thus, the existence of a series of coldspots was detected in the centre of Extremadura, in the area of Abertura, Almoharin and Montanchez towns. More surprising was the case of the north of the province of Caceres, which despite the strong tourist tradition rooted in the study areas, it showed the presence of coldspots of values of the variable when the number of travellers was jointly analysed, i.e. without separating the two types of establishment.

The next step was to break down the number of travellers according to the two large groups of accommodation options, hotels and non-hotel establishments, to verify whether the obtained results remained the same or whether this division would unravel new evidence about the local distribution pattern. To this end, the analysis conducted in each of the two types of establishment was replicated. Figure 14.2 shows the results obtained from the Getis and Ord's analysis of hotspots and coldspots when considering as the variable of interest the number of travellers who stayed in hotels in Extremadura.

Figure 14.2 shows how the location of hotspots and coldspots changes the distribution when only considering the travellers who stay in hotels, thus it becomes obvious that the type of establishment affects the distribution of the variable. The analysis identified the presence of spatial units in which the variable was concentrated in high values, mostly around three of the main cities of the region, Caceres, Merida and Badajoz. As can be observed, the presence of high values is detected with different significance levels, which also occurred in the combined analysis. Furthermore, the map shows that in the area of La Serena (in blue) there are cold points of values of the variable.

The main differences in the analysis of the distribution of the variable "travellers in hotels", with respect to the previous combined analysis of both accommodation options, is the larger number of hotspots in the main cities and the disappearance of coldspots in the northern area of the region. In order to delve further into the obtained results, the next step was to analyse the distribution of the travellers who stayed in non-hotel establishments, whose results are shown in Fig. 14.3.

Finally, when analysing the hotspots and coldspots in the distribution of the variable considering only the travellers who stayed in non-hotel establishments, the results reveal the inherent differences between the two types of accommodation analysed. Thus, in the distribution of travellers in non-hotel establishments there are hotspots in the north of the region, which are close to the coldspots identified in the combined analysis of the entire sample. These differences may be due to the large

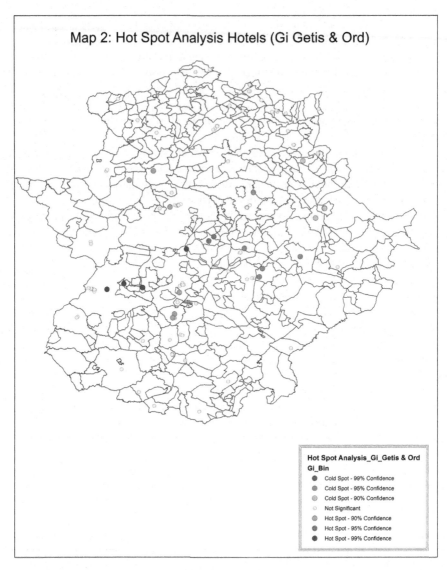

Fig. 14.2 Map hot spot analysis hotels (G_i Getis & Ord). *Source* Own elaboration using ArcGIS 10.3 (Color figure online)

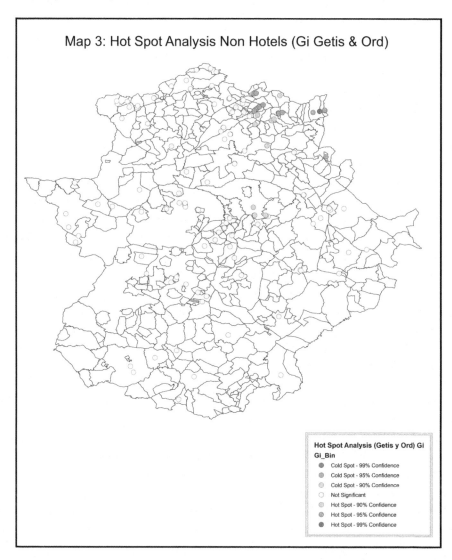

Fig. 14.3 Hot spot analysis non hotels (G_i Getis & Ord). *Source* Own elaboration using ArcGIS 10.3 (Color figure online)

number of non-hotel establishments in this area, which constitute the main type of accommodation offered.

The results obtained in Getis and Ord's new G_i^* test are complemented with the local Moran's I_i autocorrelation test, which allowed to identify spatial outliers and clusters of high and low values. To this end, the analysis of local spatial autocorrelation was conducted using Moran's I_i index for the total number of travellers who visited the region. This was achieved by specifying the neighbourhood relation-

Fig. 14.4 Moran's local I travellers. *Source* Own elaboration using ArcGIS 10.3 (Color figure online)

ship with the same criteria that were used for the global correlation, that is, reverse distance, with the method of euclidean distance and the row standardisation of the matrix. The obtained results are shown in Fig. 14.4.

The map shows the existence of several clusters of high values in three of the main cities of the region, Badajoz, Caceres and Merida, which also occurred in the diagnosis performed with Getis and Ord's G_i^* index. On the other hand, the analysis also detected spatial outliers of low-high values, in the vicinity of Merida. Once again, the analysis was conducted dividing the sample into the two accommodation types chosen by the travellers, in order to determine whether the separate analysis could add more information to the obtained results.

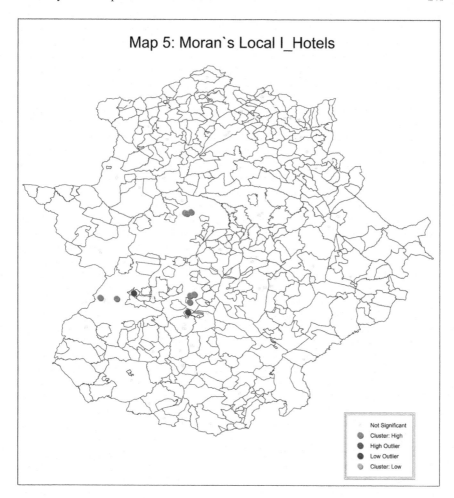

Fig. 14.5 Moran's local I in hotels. *Source* Own elaboration using ArcGIS 10.3 (Color figure online)

First, following the same order, the analysis of the distribution of travellers who stayed in hotels was conducted, whose results are shown in Fig. 14.5.

The map shows the similarities of the obtained results with respect to those identified in the analysis conducted with the travellers considering both accommodation options. The analysis confirmed the existence of clusters of high values in three of the main cities of the region, as well as the presence of outliers of low values surrounded by high values in towns near the cities of Badajoz and Merida.

To conclude the present analysis of spatial autocorrelation at the local level, the local Moran's I test was conducted for the travellers who stayed in non-hotel establishments. The results are shown in Fig. 14.6.

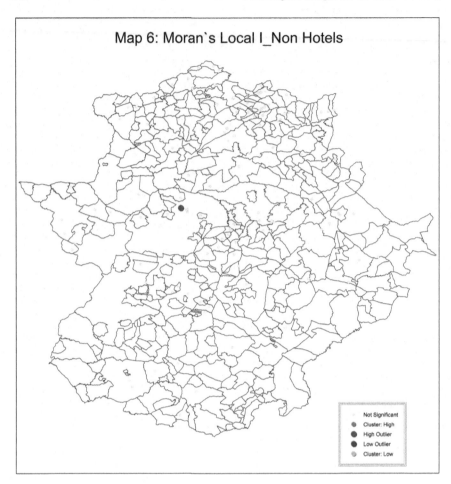

Fig. 14.6 Moran's local I in non hotels. *Source* Own elaboration using ArcGIS 10.3 (Color figure online)

Lastly, the map shows the results obtained in the local Moran's I_i autocorrelation test, with only one spatial outlier of high values surrounded by low values in the city of Caceres.

14.5   Conclusion and Implications

The evolution of GIS technologies, along with the greater availability of georeferenced data, makes it possible for the spatial analysis of data to have a greater dissemination in different fields of social science. Thus, the previous analysis of the distribution of the variables, especially those strongly related to their development in a specific geographic territory, is essential. Tourism stands out among them for being strongly related to the area in which it is developed.

The results of the spatial autocorrelation study conducted for the variable "number of travellers", both for the combination of the two types of accommodation chosen by them and separately, showed that this variable does not have a random distribution, neither in the entire territory analysed (global spatial autocorrelation), nor in the individualised study of the different spatial units (local spatial autocorrelation). Thereby, the next step was to obtain more detailed information on how the variable was distributed in the region.

First, the results of the tests conducted for the study of the distribution pattern of the variable in the entire territory analysed showed that this distribution tends to concentrate in high values in space. Separating the sample by the type of accommodation chosen allowed detecting that this pattern is governed by the distribution of travellers who stayed in hotels, since in the case of those who stayed in non-hotel accommodations the hypothesis of random distribution of the variable cannot be rejected.

Secondly, the study of autocorrelation at the local level revealed that the non-uniform distribution of the variable in space could be due to the contribution of the values reached in three of the main cities of the region, Badajoz, Caceres and Merida, over the rest of the values. The high values reached in these specific points could be the ones contributing strongly to the fact that the global pattern is not uniform in the whole of the territory.

On the other hand, from the results obtained in this analysis, it can also be concluded that, although at the global level the hypothesis of random distribution of the variable "travellers in non-hotel establishments" was not rejected, it shows hotspots in the region. Specifically, it was observed that in the north of Extremadura, in the area of La Vera and El Valle de Ambroz, the variable shows higher values than expected in a random distribution of this variable.

In conclusion, and regardless of the particular values obtained, it is concluded that the study variable "number of travellers" does not follow a random pattern. In other words, each of the spatial units is spatially interdependent. This means that once the presence of a spatial effect is detected in the exploratory phase, such as spatial autocorrelation, it must be taken into account that further modelling, in which such variable is included, as well as any confirmatory analysis, will require considering the techniques proposed by spatial statistics for the treatment of this effect.

For further research, the authors consider that it would be interesting to use a wider time frame. It must be taken into account that the spatial relationships detected took place with the values of the variable in a specific month (July), thus it cannot be asserted that these are constant in time. A panel data analysis, including all the other months of the year, would greatly enrich the analysis conducted. Likewise, it would significantly benefit the analysis to repeat it with other variables that are typically associated with tourism, such as the degree of occupation, overnight stay, average stay, etc. The analysis of the spatial distribution of these variables that help describing the evolution of an activity could also help to understand how they are related.

References

Anselin, L. (1980). *Estimation methods for spatial autoregressive structures*. Regional science dissertation and monograph Series, Ithaca, NY.

Anselin, L. (1988). *Spatial econometrics: Methods and models*. The Netherlands: Kluwer Academic Publisher.

Anselin, L. (1992). *SpaceStat tutorial. A workbook for using SpaceStat in the analysis of spatial data* (Technical Reports S-92-1). Santa Barbara: University of California; National Center for Geographic Information and Analysis.

Anselin, L. (1993). *The Moran scatterplot as an ESDA tool to assess local instability in spatial association*. GISDATA Specialist Meeting on GIS and Spatial Analysis, Amsterdam, The Netherlands.

Anselin, L. (1995a). *SpaceStat version 1.80: Users' guide*. Regional Research Institute West Virginia University: Morgantown.

Anselin, L. (1995b). Local indicators of spatial association (LISA). *Geographical Analysis, 27*(2), 93–115.

Anselin, L. (1999). The future of spatial analysis in the social sciences. *Geographic Information Sciences, 5*(2), 67–76.

Anselin, L. (2001). Spatial econometrics. In Baltagi (Ed.), *A companion to theoretical econometrics* (pp. 310–330). Oxford: Basil Blackwell.

Anselin, L., & Florax, R. (1995). New directions in spatial econometrics: Introduction. In L. Anselin & R. J. G. M. Florax (Eds.), *New directions in spatial econometrics* (pp. 3–18). Springer.

Anselin, L., & Rey, S. (1997). Introduction to the special issue on spatial econometrics. *International Regional Science Review, 20*, 1–8.

Arbia, G. (1989). *Spatial data configuration in statistical analysis of regional economics and related problems*. Dordrecht: Kluwer.

Barros, C. P., & Matías, A. (2007). Efficiency in a chain of small hotels with a stochastic production frontier model. In A. Matías, P. Nijkamp, & P. Neto (Eds.), *Advances in modern tourism research: Economic perspectives* (pp. 107–129). Heidelberg: Physica-Verlag.

Bloommestein, H. (1983). Specification and estimation of spatial econometric models: A discussion of alternative strategies for spatial economic modelling. *Regional Science and Urban Economics, 13*, 130–251.

Button, K., & Kulkarni, R. (2001). *Spatial and distance statistics of the trucking and warehousing industries using GIS tools*. 41th Congress of the European Association of Regional Science (ERSA) Zagreb.

Chasco, M. C. (2003). *Econometría espacial aplicada a la predicción-extrapolación de datos microterritoriales*. Madrid: Consejería de Economías e Innovación Tecnológica de la Comunidad de Madrid.

Chasco, C., & Vicens, J. (2000). *EU-membership impacts in the Spanish province income convergence: A spatial autocorrelation perspective*. Oviedo: Anales de Economía aplicada XIV Reunión de ASEPELT.

Cliff, A., & Ord, J. (1973). *Spatial autocorrelation*. London: Pion.

Cliff, A., & Ord, J. (1981). *Spatial processes, models and applications*. London: Pion.

Geary, R. (1954). The contiguity ratio and statistical mapping. *The Incorporated Statistician, 5*, 115–145.

Getis, A., & Ord, J. (1992). The analysis of spatial association by use of distance statistics. *Geographical Analysis, 24*, 189–206.

Kmenta, J. (1971). *Elements of econometrics*. New York: MacMillan.

López, F. A., Palacios, M. A., & Ruiz, M. (2001). Modelos explicativos del desempleo en términos de localización: una aplicación a las provincias españolas. *Anales de Economía Aplicada*, XV Reunión de ASEPELT. Santiago de Compostela.

Ma, T., Hong, T., & Zhang, H. (2015). Tourism spatial spillover effects and urban economic growth. *Journal of Business Research, 68,* 74–80.

Moran, P. (1948). The interpretation of statistical maps. *Journal of the Royal Statistical Society, 10,* 243–251.

Moreno, R., & Vayá, E. (2000). *Técnicas econométricas para el tratamiento de datos espaciales: la econometría espacial* 44. Universitat de Barcelona.

Moreno, R., & Vayá, E. (2004). Econometría Espacial: nuevas técnicas para el análisis regional. Una aplicación a las regiones europeas. *Investigaciones regionales 1,* 83–106.

Openshaw, S. (1993). Some suggestions concerning the development of artificial intelligence tools for spatial modelling and analysis in GIS. In M. M. Fisher & P. Nijkamp (Eds.), *Geographic information system, spatial modelling and policy evaluation* (pp. 17–33). Berlin: Springer Verlag.

Ord, J. K., & Getis, A. (1995). Local spatial autocorrelation statistics: Distributional issues and an application. *Geographical Analysis, 27*(4), 286–306.

Paelinck, J. H. P., & Klaasen, L. H. (1979). *Spatial econometrics*. Saxon House.

Pavlyuk, D. (2010). Multi-tier spatial stochastic frontier model for competition and cooperation of European airports. *Transport and Telecommunication, 11*(3), 57–66.

Pavlyuk, D. (2013). Distinguishing between spatial heterogeneity and inefficiency: Spatial stochastic frontier analysis of European airports. *Transport and Tecommunication, 14*(1), 29–38.

Sánchez, M. (2008). Análisis Espacial de Datos y Turismo: Nuevas Técnicas para el Análisis Turístico. Una aplicación al caso extremeño. *Revistas empresariales. Segunda Época, 2,* 48–66.

Sánchez, J. M., Sánchez, M., & Rengifo, J. I. (2013). La evaluación del potencial para el desarrollo de turismo rural. Aplicación metodológica sobre la provincia de Cáceres. *Geofocus, 13*(1), 1–20.

Sánchez, J. M., Sánchez, M., & Rengifo, J. I. (2018). Patrones de distribución de la oferta turística mediante técnicas geoestadísticas en Extremadura (2004–2014). *Boletín de la Asociación de Geógrafos Españoles, 76,* 276–302.

Shoval, N., & Ahas, R. (2016). The use of tracking technologies in tourism research: The first decade. *Tourism Geographies, 18*(5), 587–606.

Student. (1914). The elimination of spurious correlation due to position in time or space. *Biometrika, 10,* 179–180.

Tiefelsdorf, M., & Boots, B. (1997). A note on the extremities of local Moran's I_i and their impact on global Moran's I. *Geographical Analysis, 29*(3), 249–257.

Vayá, E., & Suriñach, J. (1996). Contrastes de autocorrelación espacial: una aplicación al ámbito de las provincias españolas. X Reunión ASEPELT, Albacete (Castilla la Mancha).

Zhou, Y., Maumbe, K., Deng, J., & Selin, S. (2015). Resource-based destination competitiveness evaluation using a hybrid analytic hierarchy process (AHP): The case study of West Virginia. *Tourism Management Perspectives, 15,* 70–80.